Why the West Is Best

PRAISE FOR *WHY THE WEST IS BEST*

In his new book, Ibn Warraq continues his courageous and brilliantly written evaluation of contemporary societies. He provides an eloquent, fervent, and much-needed advocacy of Western principles and values, which he considers superior to those in any other societies, and challenges Western intellectuals who are unprepared or unwilling to defend those values.

—Michael Curtis, Distinguished Professor
Emeritus of Political Science, Rutgers University

A brilliant, uncompromising, and exceedingly powerful defense of the West's civilizational heritage by one of the bravest and most original public intellectuals writing today.

—Efraim Karsh, Director, Middle East Forum

WHY THE WEST IS BEST

A Muslim Apostate's Defense of Liberal Democracy

Ibn Warraq

ENCOUNTER BOOKS • NEW YORK • LONDON

First American edition published in 2011 by Encounter Books,
an activity of Encounter for Culture and Education, Inc.,
a nonprofit, tax exempt corporation.
Encounter Books website address: www.encounterbooks.com

Manufactured in the United States and printed on
acid-free paper. The paper used in this publication meets
the minimum requirements of ANSI/NISO Z39.48 1992
(R 1997) (*Permanence of Paper*).

FIRST AMERICAN EDITION

LIBRARY OF CONGRESS CATALOGING-IN-PUBLICATION DATA
Ibn Warraq.
Why the West is best: a Muslim apostate's defense of
liberal democracy/by Ibn Warraq.
p. cm.
Includes bibliographical references and index.
ISBN-13: 978-1-59403-576-0 (hardcover: alk. paper)
ISBN-10: 1-59403-576-8 (hardcover: alk. paper) 1. East and West.
2. Values—Western countries. 3. Civilization, Western—Philosophy. I. Title.
CB251.I18 2011
909'.09821—dc23
2011025537

10 9 8 7 6 5 4 3 2 1

for Deborah

ACANTHUS (Greek: ακανθος, derived from *ake*, "point, thorn") is a genus of about thirty species of flowering plants of the Acanthaceae family, found in temperate and tropical climates of the Mediterranean basin and Asia. It has been used as a decorative motif throughout the history of Western art: on Corinthian capitals of ancient Greek and Roman columns, in the ornate decorations of Byzantine architecture, on Romanesque buildings, in sculpted wood and stone of the Middle Ages, in the borders and ornamented initials of illuminated manuscripts, on sumptuous fabrics, in baroque and rococo styles, in Nordic woodcarving and painting, on Italian ceramics, in the designs of William Morris. The acanthus has graced almost every form of visual art across millennia, from the Mediterranean to Scandinavia. Given this ubiquity and the centrality of our classical heritage, the acanthus is a fitting symbol of Western civilization. "Acanthus" wallpaper, designed by William Morris, 1875. (The Stapleton Collection/Art Resource, NY)

Limbourg brothers (fl. 1399–1416), detail from the *Très Riches Heures du Duc de Berry*. (Réunion des Musées Nationaux/Art Resource, NY)

Acanthus-trimmed capitals on the cathedral in Syracuse, Italy, by Andrea Palma, completed in 1753. (Photo © Giovanni Dall'Orto, WikiCommons)

CONTENTS

PREFACE

A story about Mahatma Gandhi has been circulating for years. After being given a tour of Great Britain, he was asked in Parliament what he thought of British civilization. Gandhi's answer: that it might be a good idea. The story is hard to trace to its source and may be apocryphal. Even so, that reply—revealing little wit and even less wisdom—aptly sums up Gandhi's ingratitude, hypocrisy, arrogance, and incomprehension.

Gandhi's philosophy of nonviolence was effective with the British precisely because they were not inclined to use excessive force against unarmed civilians. Instead, they behaved in a civilized manner, and they left. Would Gandhi's tactics have worked with the Nazis? Moreover, the British departure from India was followed by violence, as Muslims slaughtered Hindus and vice versa. Nirad Chaudhuri, an Indian intellectual, always blamed Gandhi. "To me all these demands of Mahatma Gandhi [on the British government] seemed not only extreme, but even crude and irrational," Chaudhuri wrote. "It appeared to me that his entire ideology was driven by a resolve to abandon civilized life and revert to a primitive existence."[1]

What of your own Indian civilization, Mr. Gandhi? The British banned one manifestation of it, the custom of suttee, where a widowed Hindu woman was forced to immolate herself on her husband's funeral pyre. The Portuguese and later the French and the Dutch also banned the practice in their own Indian colonies. Another shameful expression of Indian civilization, the iniquitous caste system, remains in force even today, depriving millions of their human rights, even after sixty-five years of de jure prohibition.

What of your own racism, Mr. Gandhi? In a well-documented critique, G. B. Singh points out that during the Zulu Wars in South Africa, the Mahatma was urging Indians to show patriotism by killing blacks. "Gandhi is overly eager to see his Indians in a war against blacks," Singh writes. "After all, he tells them rather frankly, they too are colonists over blacks and therefore, standing shoulder to shoulder with fellow white colonists is a natural progression."[2]

And to what can we attribute the stark failures of India today? In 2007, the World Bank reported that 80 percent of India's 1.1 billion people survived on less than two dollars a day—which meant that more than one-third of the world's poor lived in India.[3] Two years later, the World Health Organization estimated that "about 49 per cent of the world's underweight children, 34 per cent of the world's stunted children and 46 per cent of the world's wasted children" lived in India, despite the impressive progress in the overall economy.[4] The Global Hunger Index found "that 'serious' rates of hunger persisted across Indian states that had posted enviable rates of economic growth in recent years, including Maharashtra and Gujarat."[5] India currently has the largest illiterate population of any nation on earth. Racism and drug addiction are widespread and growing.[6] One could even suggest that Indian civilization might be a good idea.

Gandhi's contemptuous dismissal of the British is refuted by the facts on both sides—of colonizer and colonized. On pulling up stakes, Britain left India with an elected parliamentary government that survives to this day, a sure indication that democracy was planted deeply in the political mind of India. The constitution formulated by Indians includes a bill of rights derived from the U.S. Constitution, even using some identical phrasing—an indirect British legacy. The British bequest included the rule of law. In fact, the entire legal system they had introduced over the years was left unaltered. It was constructed by Lord Macaulay, whose genius "gives life to modern India as we know it," according to the Indian historian K. M. Pannikar.[7] India also inherited a British-style administrative machine, the incorruptible Indian Civil Service, to carry on the business of government in a vast country of disparate religions and languages.

The British left India with well-trained doctors, teachers, engineers, and craftsmen, and an infrastructure of railways, roads, bridges, and irrigation systems, along with distinguished Victorian architecture. The English language enables an Indian from the south whose native tongue is Tamil to communicate with someone from Delhi who speaks Hindi or Punjabi. A mastery of English is allowing India to take her place in the world economy today. There were also spiritual gifts: British and other European scholars gave back to India her own history and culture. With their insatiable intellectual curiosity, the British wrote about every aspect of life, literature, philosophy, religion, language, art and architecture in India. Their scholarship is still revered and taught to every Indian schoolchild. British civilization was, indeed, not only a great idea but a great blessing.

Much of what has been most valuable to the nations emerging from colonialism was bequeathed to them by the British and other European powers. Yet many Western academics, along with some Third World intellectuals, claim that the West has taken more from the world than it has contributed, and that its material success has come at the expense of others. Western leaders have been bullied into constantly apologizing for the West's sins. It is considered "Eurocentric" or racist to assert that the West is superior to other cultures; instead, we are encouraged to repeat that Western civilization is culturally, intellectually, and spiritually defective. But we know this is nonsense.

This essay argues that Western civilization is good for the world. I will sketch out a moral ideal by drawing a particular set of values from the history of the West—values that are both explicit and implicit in Western liberal democracies, and enshrined in that magnificent document, the Constitution of the United States of America. We can trace these ideals back as far as the Bible and Greek antiquity. A fascist or a communist might also trace his own principles back through time to ancient Greece, perhaps to Sparta rather than Athens. My advocacy of a different branch of our Western heritage is neither arbitrary nor subjective, however. The political and social configurations of the West in the second decade of the twenty-first century indicate that we have reached a certain measure of agreement on the principles that resulted in the stability and prosperity we have enjoyed since the end of the Second World War.

Among the most important of these principles are liberty and individual dignity. But our freedoms are often taken for granted; we seem to forget that we need to guard them lest they disappear without our noticing until it is too late. We may not realize how serious are the threats to our fundamental values, both from foreign enemies and from multicultural appeasement at home. As Andrew Jackson said, "Eternal vigilance by the people is the price of liberty."[8] In this book, I suggest ways to be vigilant and offer some tools for defending Western civilization from the threats it faces.

* * *

Some readers may be puzzled to see a whole chapter devoted to New York City in a book about defining and defending Western civilization. In New York, I show the principles of the United States Constitution being applied in a real, vibrant place. I give the term "Western civilization" a physical context in the very concrete of the city. The details of New York's streets and structures create a believable, breathing image of Western civilization, just as Dickens created believable, breathing characters. See this building, I say—it's an example of beautiful architecture, one of the glories of New York, and as integral to Western civilization as the works of Shakespeare. See that building—it's the New York Public Library. Inside the Beaux Arts masterpiece is an institution that embodies key aspects of Western civilization: philanthropy, education, the love of knowledge, the preservation of all the best that has been written and published. Each time you admire the façade of the New York Public Library, you are paying homage to Western civilization. Each time you consult a book in the magnificent Main Reading Room, you are participating in the maintenance of Western civilization. By working and living in New York, you are breathing Western civilization, continuously reminded of its benefits and its values.

Describing a New York street that became known as Tin Pan Alley and the area known as Broadway led me into the Great American Songbook, created by composers and lyricists who were born and lived and worked in that great city. Discussions of Western civilization are too often confined to works of high art that reflect a relatively narrow element of public taste and experience. I maintain that Western popular culture at its best is worthy of respect and should be cherished as much as the operas of Wagner. The work of composers like George Gershwin, born and bred in New York, embodies Western ideals over and above the aesthetic principles of the music itself. I could have written at length about various artists associated with the metropolis—Fred Astaire, P. G. Wodehouse, George Kaufman, the Marx Brothers (born in the Yorkville section of the Upper East Side)—and their contributions to Western popular culture, with creations that are witty, graceful, inspired, and at times touched with genius.

Do you ever ask yourself, as you listen to Frank Sinatra singing "The Lady Is a Tramp," what made it possible? What principles or institutions should we thank for it? This book is, in part, an effort to provide an answer.

* * *

I should like to thank, as ever, Fred Siegel for his wise counsel and his encouragement of this endeavor; Irfan Khawaja and Austin Dacey, whose critical spirit saved me from many errors; Hugh Fitzgerald, who picked up on many grammatical solecisms and improved my style no end; and Phyllis Chesler, for her friendship, kindness, and advice. None of them can be held accountable for the opinions expressed here.

ॐॐ

PROLOGUE

THE SUPERIORITY OF WESTERN VALUES IN EIGHT MINUTES

I n a public debate with Tariq Ramadan in London on October 9, 2007, I was given eight minutes to argue for the superiority of Western values. This was my defense of the West:

The great ideas of the West—rationalism, self-criticism, the disinterested search for truth, the separation of church and state, the rule of law, equality before the law, freedom of conscience and expression, human rights, liberal democracy—together constitute quite an achievement, surely, for any civilization. This set of principles remains the best and perhaps the only means for all people, no matter what race or creed, to live in freedom and reach their full potential.[1] Western values—the basis of the West's self-evident economic, social, political, scientific, and cultural success—are clearly superior to any other set of values devised by mankind. When Western values have been adopted by other societies, such as Japan or South Korea, their citizens have reaped benefits.

Life, liberty, and the pursuit of happiness: this triptych succinctly defines the attractiveness and superiority of Western civilization. In the West we are free to think what we want, to read what we want, to practice our religion, to live as we choose. Liberty is codified in human rights, a magnificent Western creation but also, I believe, a universal good. Human rights transcend local or ethnocentric values, conferring equal dignity and value on all humanity regardless of sex, ethnicity, sexual preference, or religion. At the same time, it is in the West that human rights are most respected.

It is the West that has liberated women, racial minorities, religious minorities, and gays and lesbians, recognizing and defending their rights. The notions of freedom and human rights were present at the dawn of Western civilization, as ideals at least, but have gradually come to fruition through supreme acts of self-criticism. Because of its exceptional capacity for self-criticism, the West took the initiative in abolishing slavery; the calls for abolition did not resonate even in black Africa, where rival African tribes took black prisoners to be sold as slaves in the West.

Today, many non-Western cultures follow customs and practices that are clear violations of the Universal Declaration of Human Rights (1948). In many countries, especially Islamic ones, you are not free to read what you want. Under sharia, or Islamic law, women are not free to marry whom they wish, and their rights of inheritance are circumscribed. Sharia, derived from the Koran and the practice and sayings of Muhammad, prescribes barbaric punishments such as stoning to death for adultery. It calls for homosexuals and apostates to be executed. In Saudi Arabia, among other countries, Muslims

10

are not free to convert to Christianity, and Christians are not free to practice their faith. The Koran is not a rights-respecting document.

Under Islam, life is a closed book. Everything has been decided for you: the dictates of sharia and the whims of Allah set strict limits on the possible agenda of your life. In the West, we have the choice to pursue our desires and ambitions. We are free as individuals to set the goals and determine the contents of our own lives, and to decide what meaning to give to our lives. As Roger Scruton remarks, "the glory of the West is that life is an open book."[2] The West has given us the liberal miracle of individual rights and responsibility and merit. Rather than the chains of inherited status, Western society offers unparalleled social mobility. The West, Alan Kors writes, "is a society of ever richer, more varied, more productive, more self-defined, and more satisfying lives."[3]

Instead of the mind-numbing certainties and dictates of Islam, Western civilization offers what Bertrand Russell called liberating doubt.[4] Even the process of politics in the West involves trial and error, open discussion, criticism, and self-correction.[5] The quest for knowledge no matter where it leads, a desire inherited from the Greeks, has produced an institution that is rarely equaled outside the West: the university. And the outside world recognizes the superiority of Western universities. Easterners come to the West to learn not only about the sciences developed in the last five hundred years, but also about their own cultures, about Eastern civilizations and languages. They come to Oxford and Cambridge, to Harvard and Yale, to Heidelberg and the Sorbonne to acquire their doctorates because these degrees confer prestige unrivalled by similar credentials from Third World countries.

Western universities, research institutes, and libraries are created to be independent institutions where the pursuit of truth is conducted in a spirit of disinterested inquiry, free from political pressures. The basic difference between the West and the Rest might be summed up as a difference in epistemological principles. Behind the success of modern Western societies, with their science and technology and their open institutions, lies a distinct way of looking at the world, interpreting it, and rectifying problems: by lifting them out of the religious sphere and treating them empirically, finding solutions in rational procedures. The whole edifice of modern science is one of Western man's greatest gifts to the world.[6] The West is responsible for almost every major scientific discovery of the last five hundred years, from heliocentrism and the telescope, to electricity, to computers.

The West has given the world the symphony and the novel. A culture that engendered the spiritual creations of Mozart and Beethoven, Wagner and Schubert, of Raphael and Michelangelo, Leonardo da Vinci and Rembrandt does not need lessons in spirituality from societies whose vision of heaven resembles a cosmic brothel stocked with virgins for men's pleasure.

The West gave us the Red Cross, Doctors Without Borders, Human Rights Watch, Amnesty International, and many other manifestations of the humanitarian impulse. It is the West that provides the bulk of the aid to beleaguered Darfur, while Islamic countries are conspicuous by their absence.

The West does not need lectures on the superior virtue of societies where women are kept in subjection, endure genital mutilation, are married off against their will at the age of nine, have acid thrown in their faces or are stoned to death for alleged adultery, or where human rights are denied to those regarded as belonging to lower castes.[7] The West does not need sanctimonious homilies from societies that cannot provide clean drinking water or sewage systems for their populations, that cannot educate their citizens but leave 40 to 50 percent of them illiterate, that make no provision for the handicapped, that have no sense of the common good or civic responsibility, that are riddled with corruption.

No Western politician would be able to get away with the kind of racist remarks that are tolerated in the Third World, such as the anti-Semitic diatribes of the Malaysian leader Mahathir Mohamad. Instead, there would be calls for resignation, both from Third World leaders and from Western media and intellectuals. Double standards? Yes, but also a tacit acknowledgment that we expect higher ethical standards from the West.

The Ayatollah Khomeini once famously said there are no jokes in Islam. The West is able to look at its own foibles and laugh, even make fun of its own fundamental principles. There is no Islamic equivalent to *Monty Python's Life of Brian*. Can we look forward to seeing *The Life of Mo* anytime in the future?

The rest of the world recognizes the virtues of the West in concrete ways. As Arthur Schlesinger remarked, "when Chinese students cried and died for democracy in Tiananmen Square, they brought with them not representations of Confucius or Buddha but a model of the Statue of Liberty."[8] Millions of people risk their lives trying to get to the West—not to Saudi Arabia or Iran or Pakistan. They flee from theocratic or other totalitarian regimes to find tolerance and freedom in the West, where life is an open book.

❧

CHAPTER ONE

NEW YORK, NEW YORK; OR, LIFE, LIBERTY, AND THE PURSUIT OF HAPPINESS

The beauty of the idea of the pursuit of happiness. Familiar
words, easy to take for granted; easy to misconstrue.
—V. S. NAIPAUL, "OUR UNIVERSAL CIVILIZATION," 1990

I had originally thought of using the city of New York as a meta-phor or even a synecdoche for the West, but it is unfair to ask even such a great city to assume that burden of responsibility; and besides, New York, like life, is its own excuse. Nonetheless, no other city in the West—or indeed, in the world—so well exemplifies the inexhaustible possibilities of a modern metropolis, where the inventive and enterprising put into practice the many freedoms guaranteed under the U.S. Constitution. The implausible, well-nigh-miraculous functioning anarchy that we know as New York is adorned with every excellence of Western art. It is a city of manifold suggestions, which ministers to every ambition, engenders a thousand talents, nurtures ingenuity and experimentation. Henry James, going up the East River, found the wide waters of New York exhilarating.[1] But it was left to P. G. Wodehouse's Bertie Wooster to discover the *what* and *why* of New York:

> *The odd part of it was that after the first shock of seeing all this frightful energy the thing didn't seem so strange. I've spoken to fellows since who have been to New York, and they tell me they found it just the same. Apparently there's something in the air, either the ozone or the phosphates or something, which makes you sit up and take notice. A kind of zip, as it were. A sort of bally freedom, if you know what I mean, that gets in your blood and bucks you up, and makes you feel that "God's in His Heaven: All's right with the world," and you don't care if you've got odd socks on.*[2]

A sort of bally freedom, yes indeed.

Many New Yorkers take all they are offered for granted. Some even complain about the inadequacies of the subway system, or the schools, or the parks, or the lack of facilities for the disabled. But they do so because New York itself has already created expectations that are high and growing higher, and because people have the constitutional right to complain, to petition their government, or to vote out the incompetent politicians. While cities such as Cairo or Delhi or Mumbai have yet to solve such elemental problems as overflowing sewage in their garbage-filled streets and are unable to provide clean water for millions, New York disposes of over 25,000 tons of garbage a day and provides drinking water to a population of 8.36 million by drawing over 1.2 billion gallons daily from reservoirs, some of which are a hundred miles from the city.

Living just down the street from a subway station, I am inconvenienced by ongoing construction work, but I realize that the city is taking its responsibilities seriously and performing the ever necessary task of renovating the infrastructure, at a cost of several billion dollars a year. In addition to government expenditure to improve the lives of citizens, billions are invested by private concerns to renew the city's energy and telecommunication infrastructure. And what a service New York City provides for its inhabitants! Every day, approximately seven million people use the subway, which boasts 722 miles of railway track, while more than four million use the bus system. The Metropolitan Transportation Authority, which oversees the public transit system, practices moral responsibility in the effort it makes to meet the needs of the disabled, such as by fitting buses with special lifts for wheelchair users. The MTA's website offers information in over thirty languages, mirroring the ethnic mix of New York.

There are more than a million students in New York's public elementary, middle, and high schools, and another 200,000 in the city's public university. The city's public hospitals cope with over a million emergencies each year. One of the glories of New York City is its system of parks, covering nearly 27,000 acres, over 13 percent of the city's land area.[3] Far from being an environmental disaster, New York is, in some ways, a model of ecological responsibility. With 82 percent of Manhattanites using public transportation or going to work on foot or bicycle, the consumption of fossil fuels is far less in New York than in many other big cities.[4]

The multifarious interests of free men and women are mirrored in the extraordinary number of activities available for the enthusiast, the curious, the intellectually and culturally alert. Even a cursory look at the hundred or so pages of the weekly magazine *Time Out New York*—which tries to list or review every single cultural or intellectual event in the city—leaves one breathless at the myriad possibilities for cultural nourishment: from classical music and opera to popular open-air concerts; from off-Broadway plays to Shakespeare in the Park; from an exhibition of the paintings of James Ensor to the glories of the permanent collections at the Frick and the Metropolitan Museum of Art; from book signings at Barnes & Noble to the Center for Book Arts; from the Natural History Museum to the New York Historical Society.

New York is a testament to the robustness of Western culture and to its welcoming catholicity, giving equal attention, respect, and opportunities to works and artists from an astonishing number of both Western and non-Western countries. Korean and Chinese violinists, East European and Gypsy melodies, Afro-Peruvian jazz, paintings from Tibet and Nepal, plays from Japan, Iran, Budapest, Argentina, South Africa, and the Congo—all are embraced and become part of the cultural landscape, perhaps to be imitated at some later date. Every ethnic community has the space to celebrate and promote its particular experience, and also to teach the rest of us, broadening our horizons and knowledge: from the Latino musical *In the Heights* by Lin-Manuel Miranda and Quiara Alegria Hudes, to the Indian-themed play *D'Arranged Marriage* by Tarun Mohanbhai and Rajeev Varma. Art galleries and museums offer a wide-ranging aesthetic fare: Gustave Caillebotte, Sun K. Kwak, and "Light of the Sufis: The Mystical Arts of Islam" were all on view at the Brooklyn Museum at the same time; the Asia Society presented "Asian Journeys: Collecting Art in Post-war America" and "Seven Intellectuals in a Bamboo Forest"; the Rubin Museum featured the eighteenth-century Tibetan artist Situ Panchen and a photo exhibit on the "Nagas: Hidden Hill People of India"; and so on.

෨
TIN PAN ALLEY AND THE GREAT AMERICAN SONGBOOK

Rose Gershwin, mother of the composer George, dined at Lindy's on Broadway nearly every night after her husband's death in 1932.[5] Whether or not she met the motley crew of smalltime hoodlums who also ate there—such as Izzy Cheesecake, Franky Ferocious, Milk Ear Willie, Nicely Nicely, Dave the Dude—it is pleasing to think of Rose sitting in the restaurant made famous by Damon Runyon as Mindy's, a symbol of popular song meeting New York theater, Tin Pan Alley intersecting Broadway, and yielding sophisticated musical comedies. Leo "Lindy" Lindermann opened his deli and restaurant at 1626 Broadway in 1921, between 49th and 50th streets. A branch opened at 1655 Broadway in 1929. Lindy's appears in the Frank Loesser musical *Guys and Dolls* (1950), which is based on Runyon's writings and peopled with characters of dubious morality and even more dubious albeit colorful syntax.

Tin Pan Alley was a real place in New York City, West 28th Street between Fifth and Sixth avenues, where a plaque on the sidewalk tells us that this was "where the business of the American popular song flourished during the first decades of the 20th Century." Tin Pan Alley was also the publishing business that hired composers and lyricists to create popular songs, with success depending on how many copies of sheet music were sold. *Pace* the plaque, Tin Pan Alley moved uptown between 1903 and 1908, toward West 42nd Street; from 1911 to 1919, most of the publishers settled the West Forties. In 1931, when the Brill Building was completed at Broadway and 49th Street, not far from Lindy's, the popular-music publishing industry acquired a permanent home.[6]

The story of Tin Pan Alley and Broadway is the story of New York, of popular song, of musical comedy, of American popular culture at its best. Many of the creators of the Great American Songbook were either born in New York or grew up there; were inspired by the city, tried to evoke it, or paid handsome tribute to it. Jerome Kern (1885–1945) was born in Sutton Place, the city's brewery district, but grew up on East 56th Street. Irving Berlin (1888–1989) was born in Russia, but from the age of five he lived on the Lower East Side, Cherry Street, and the Bowery; later he worked in Chinatown and Union Square. As he became more and more successful, Berlin changed addresses several times, living on Riverside Drive, West 46th Street, and West 72nd Street, before settling at 17 Beekman Place, in a residential enclave close to the East River extending from 49th to 51st Street. It was not far from where Kern was born. Berlin is responsible for the Music Box Theater, an architectural landmark at 236 West 45th Street, between Broadway and Eighth Avenue, built in 1920 in a style that evokes English Georgian. George Gershwin (1898–1937) was born in Brooklyn but spent nearly all of his childhood and adolescence in Manhattan, attending schools in Harlem and the Lower East Side, and then the High School of Commerce on 155 West 65th Street. Richard Rodgers (1902–1979) was born in Queens, attended Columbia University, and lived all his life in New York City. His lyricist Lorenz Hart (1895–1943) was born in Harlem. Oscar Hammerstein II (1895–1960) was born in New York and also attended Columbia.

As the musicologist Charles Hamm explained, the golden age of American popular song was very much a creation of New York:

Even more than had been the case during the formative years of Tin Pan Alley, the field was dominated by composers and lyricists born and trained in New York, writing songs for publishers who not only had their offices in New York but were themselves the products of the city. . . . There was little effective cultural input

20

from the rest of America into New York in these days, and to the extent that Tin Pan Alley songs reflected American culture in a broader sense, they did so because the rest of the country was willing to accept a uniquely urban, New York product. . . . The songs of Kern, Gershwin, Porter and their contemporaries were urban, sophisticated, and stylish, and they were intended for people who could be described by one or more of these adjectives—or aspired to be.[7]

Irving Berlin, a Jew whose family had fled persecution in Russia, assimilated quickly and became eternally grateful to America for granting his family refuge and freedom. "His patriotism was a genuine belief, one of the few he ever held outside the values of Tin Pan Alley," his biographer tells us.[8] Berlin found the United States to be an extraordinarily free society, tolerant of Jews and of immigrants in general. He never forgot how the freedom and the copyright laws of this great country had allowed him to get rich. His mother used to say "God bless America," a phrase he turned into an anthem of gratitude. The money he earned from that song was donated entirely to charity. Berlin's patriotism was also in evidence when he mounted a morale-boosting revue on Broadway, *This Is the Army,* after Roosevelt declared war on Japan, and gave the proceeds to Army Emergency Relief.

As Walter Cronkite noted at the time of Berlin's one hundredth birthday celebrations, Berlin had expressed in song the thoughts and feelings, rhythms and sounds of Americans. "Irving Berlin helped write the story of this country by capturing the best of who we are and the dreams that shape our lives," said Cronkite, adding that in the 1,500-plus songs Berlin had written "we find our history, our holidays, our homes and our hearts."[9] Jerome Kern praised Berlin's verse for its humor, pace, and originality, accompanied by lovely melodies, where the average United States citizen was perfectly epitomized.

Kern famously declared that "Irving Berlin has no place in American music. HE IS AMERICAN MUSIC."[10]

Berlin learned early on that familiar tunes expressing simple sentiments appealed the most to New York audiences.[11] His own composition "Blue Skies," for example, was an expression of happiness but with an underlying fragility.[12] In the Twenties, he wrote a number of mournful ballads that captured the melancholy and loneliness of the times.[13] But in the Thirties he created robust satire, including the revue *As Thousands Cheer* (1933), with book by Moss Hart. By turns witty and poignant, the revue scrutinized newspapers, politics, finance, high society, and the arts—all the foolishness and absurdity in every sector—with a sharp, ironical eye. Each scene was introduced with a sensationalistic newspaper headline. For instance, "UNKNOWN NEGRO LYNCHED BY FRENZIED MOB" was followed by the song "Supper Time," the lament of a wife telling her children they will never see their father again.[14] In the original production it was sung by Ethel Waters (1900–1977), who was given equal billing with the white performers. In *Call Me Madam* (1950), Berlin parodied foreign aid, the use of sex as a tool of diplomacy, and the corruptive influence of money in politics.[15]

Berlin's songs, and those of the other great composer-lyricists such as George and Ira Gershwin, helped to unify American society and also to create an American identity. Their melodies became "part of the ineffable glue of society," as Laurence Bergreen put it. "They were something Americans had in common, like the weather, the Depression, the bittersweet memories of a romance or vanished youth."[16]

While growing up in New York, George Gershwin absorbed a wide range of popular music from the city's various ethnic communities, including traditional American songs, English, Scottish and Irish melodies, Negro spirituals and jazz, Russian-Jewish folk tunes and cantorial songs from the synagogues, even the occasional Asian air.[17] "Wherever I went I heard a concourse of sounds," Gershwin wrote.

22

Many of them were not audible to my companions, for I was hearing them in memory. Strains from the latest concert, the cracked tones of a hurdy gurdy, the wail of a street singer to the obbligato of a broken violin, past or present music, I was hearing within me. Old music and new music, forgotten melodies and the craze of the moment, bits of opera, Russian folk songs, Spanish ballads, chanson's [sic], rag-time ditties, combined in a mighty chorus in my inner ear. And through and over it all I heard, faint at first, loud at last, the soul of this great America of ours.[18]

In his openness to all this music, Gershwin was "true to his melting pot ideal of which he often spoke," as Howard Pollack noted in his superb biography of the composer.[19]

I had hoped to avoid using that much-abused term "melting pot," but it would have been perverse to do so given Gershwin's own use of the expression, and given the striking resemblances between Gershwin and the main character of Israel Zangwill's play *The Melting Pot* (1908), which brought the term into common usage. Like Gershwin, the character of David Quixano is from a Russian-Jewish family, with no formal musical education, yet he aspires to write an "American symphony" that draws inspiration from "the seething of the Crucible," and specifically from the New York experience. "When I am *writing* my American symphony, it seems like thunder crashing through a forest full of bird songs," says Quixano. He enthuses over the appearance of the new American who "will be the fusion of all races, perhaps the coming superman. Ah, what a glorious Finale for my symphony."

Quixano points to the city of New York from a roof garden where his "American Symphony" has just been premiered, and he remarks,

There she lies, the great Melting Pot—listen! Can't you hear the roaring and the bubbling? There gapes her mouth—the harbor

> *where a thousand mammoth feeders come from the ends of the world to pour in their human freight. Ah, what a stirring and a seething! Celt and Latin, Slav and Teuton, Greek and Syrian,— black and yellow—*

Similarly, Gershwin recalled how it was hearing a "kaleidoscope of America, our vast melting pot," that had inspired him to compose his *Rhapsody in Blue* (1924). He was going to Boston on the train, "with its steely rhythms, its rattle-ty-bang that is often so stimulating to a composer," he wrote.

> *And there I suddenly heard—even saw on paper—the complete construction of the rhapsody, from the beginning to end. No new themes came to me, but I worked on the thematic material already in my mind, and tried to conceive the composition as a whole. I heard it as a sort of musical kaleidoscope of America, our vast melting pot, of our unduplicated national pep, of our blues, our metropolitan madness.*[20]

There is evidence that Gershwin may also have planned a large collection of preludes to be called *The Melting Pot*.[21]

Today, the very notion of a melting pot is no longer considered admirable in the West, where an ideological multiculturalism has destroyed what were surely not ignoble ideals, even if they were often crudely expressed. David Quixano in *The Melting Pot* hints at principles of forgiveness and reconciliation, when the "blood hatreds and rivalries," the "feuds and vendettas" are finally forgotten, as people look forward and together forge common goals rather than rest isolated in ghettoes, nursing grievances with resentful persistence. The hope was that, as Irving Howe once put it, "the weight of American freedom" would break down socially divisive "fixed rituals" and lead to the creation of a secular republic. *E pluribus unum*—Out of many, one.

Rhapsody in Blue is both New York and America, evoking the blues along with "the hurdy-gurdies of the Lower East Side, the calliopes of Coney Island, the player pianos of Harlem, the chugging of trains leaving Grand Central Station, the noisy construction of midtown skyscrapers, and so forth," all within the classical tradition of the piano concerto. It mirrors what Ann Douglas called "Mongrel Manhattan."[22] William Saroyan explained how the composition reflects both New York and America generally:

> *The* Rhapsody in Blue *is an American in New York City; at the same time it is an American in any city of the United States. It is also an American in a small town, on a farm, at work in factory, in a mine or a mill, a forest or a field, working on the railroad or on the building of a highway. It is an American remembering and making plans for the future: dreaming. It is earnest, not sophisticated. There is great loneliness and love in it. Those who were young when they first heard the* Rhapsody in Blue *are still deeply moved by it, and those who are now young believe the* Rhapsody *speaks both to and for them as no other music in the world does.*[23]

Saroyan's interpretation is confirmed by Gershwin himself. The *Rhapsody* could "mean almost anything to anybody," he wrote. "But it is all New York, all America. It is a picnic party in Brooklyn or a dark-skinned girl singing and shouting her blues in a Harlem cabaret. I try to depict a scene, a New York crowd. And it's vulgar. It's full of vulgarisms. That's what gives it weight. I never tried to prettify it as most composers do."[24]

Gershwin's charm, grace, and inventiveness were evident in the songs he wrote for his musical comedies, a form that is aesthetically demanding, with its interweaving of dance and song, orchestra and chorus, scenery and costumes. Despite the inherent limitations of their form, musical comedies took on serious topics. They demand respect for exemplifying one of the defining characteristics of Western art and civilization: cultural self-criticism.

Gershwin's *La-La-Lucille* (1919) addressed important subjects such as "money, marriage, and a woman's place in society, a heightened concern as the nation approached passage of the Nineteenth Amendment giving women the vote."[25] *East Is West* explores two points of view on the subject of race: that of the hero's father, who argues for a "racial determination as relentless as the laws of the Universe," and the opposite sentiments of the hero's Chinese friend, who defends the view that "In the infinite . . . whence all things come, there is no East, there is no West. West is East, and East is West." The unsatisfactory resolution to many of these comedies should not overshadow the fact that they dared to raise controversial issues in the least hectoring, most pleasing manner possible.

The Twenties proved to be the heyday of plays and comedies about mixed marriages: *Abie's Irish Rose* (1922), with its Jewish boy courting and marrying a Catholic girl; Gershwin's *Tell Me More* (1925), also featuring a Jewish-gentile romance; Tierney-McCarthy's *Rio Rita* (1927), with an American hero and a Mexican heroine. Also in 1927 there were Sigmund Romberg's *Cherry Blossoms*, with a Japanese-American theme; Kern's *Show Boat*, taking on black-white relations; and Kern's *Lucky*, about "a poor Ceylonese pearl diver betrothed to a rich American and suffering prejudice which is eventually overcome."[26] Many of the composers and lyricists were Jewish, and it is surely not farfetched to assume that they were pleading for tolerance.[27]

The wits of New York daringly mocked religious fundamentalism, as in Ira Gershwin's lyrics to "It Ain't Necessarily So" from *Porgy and Bess*. When Buddy DeSylva got together with Ira Gershwin on another George Gershwin song, "I'll Build a Stairway to Paradise," they took aim at preachers who opposed dancing, asserting that "the steps of gladness" could lead one to heaven.[28] Gershwin provided the music for the silent movie *The Sunshine Trail*, a satire on the Pollyanna theme.[29] Ira Gershwin and DeSylva wrote the lyrics to "Mr. and Mrs. Sipkin," which punctured class pretensions with witticisms such as: "My line of conversation / Delights an eager nation / For it is styled / On Oscar Wilde / And Mr. Bernard Shaw." Gershwin's musical *Tip Toes* lampoons the nouveau riche. *Strike Up the Band,* with lyrics by Ira Gershwin and book by Morrie Ryskind (based on George Kaufman's original book), is political satire with bite. The song "Tell the Doc," with lyrics by Ira, from Gershwin's *Funny Face* is probably the earliest satire on psychoanalysis.

George Kaufman and Morrie Ryskind surpassed themselves when they sketched out a parody of an American presidential election in which the two principal parties compete to produce the best national anthem, only to find that their offerings are nearly the same.[30] They approached the Gershwins, and soon they were all working on *Of Thee I Sing,* which attacked the hypocrisy and chicanery of political life in the United States, against the background of the Great Depression. Kaufman and Ryskind added a romantic element so the whole also functioned as a romantic comedy, hinting, as Pollack suggested, "that the pretensions and absurdities of our personal lives and those of the body politic reflect one another and that political reform requires examination of our social and cultural mores and vice versa."[31]

Of Thee I Sing opened on December 26, 1931, at Irving Berlin's Music Box Theater. It was immediately recognized as a significant event in the annals of the American stage. One reviewer wrote that it spotlighted the "mush, gush and slush, lungs, lunacy and larceny, punk, junk and bunk, bluff, bull and blah, hokum, hooey and hooliganism with which we are fed every day and in the midst of which we live and move and have our being—such as it is! . . . And we Americans in the audience roar, chortle, wheeze, shout, howl and whistle our approval at every shot that is taken at the whole political game in this country from the rise of curtain until its fall."[32] Another reviewer suggested that the audience's rage was released through the laughter.[33] The musical won the Pulitzer Prize in 1932 for its "biting and true satire on American politics and the public attitude towards them."[34]

Porgy and Bess (1935) was Gershwin's last major work of consequence. It was based on Edwin DuBose Heyward's novel *Porgy* (1925), which was unusual for its extensive use of African American dialect. It was generally considered even by African Americans to be a sympathetic and vivid depiction of a black community. The novel was successfully transferred to the stage on Broadway, with a historically important black cast of sixty-six.

Gershwin drew upon his knowledge of African American oratory and music, and his opera alludes to the black popular music of W. C. Handy and Cab Calloway, black folk music, street cries, and Negro spirituals. But Gershwin thought of the opera as American rather than black, with "an American flavor in the melodies." He added, "I believe that American music should be based on American material."[35] The first production was described as a wondrous collaboration of a Jewish composer and lyricist, an Armenian director, a Russian set designer, a white southern librettist, and a black cast, resulting in "the most American opera that has yet been seen or heard."[36]

In *Porgy and Bess,* Gershwin created something humane and sensitive, depicting both the dignity and the despair of an oppressed group. Although (perhaps inevitably) it was attacked as "racist," the opera's first defenders were the black cast members. William Warfield, an African American who performed in *Porgy and Bess* in 1952, wrote that the opera was "a celebration of our culture, and not an exploitation of it. The work didn't snigger at African-Americans. It ennobled the characters it depicted." Warfield called it "a story of triumph, not degradation, despite our very real problems," and one that transcended race to achieve universality.[37]

Among lyricists from New York, one particular favorite is Lorenz Hart (1895–1943), who wrote a veritable hymn to the city,

"Manhattan." Along with P. G. Wodehouse, Hart was responsible for the use of vernacular lyrics, which had a liberating influence on later writers. His collaboration with Richard Rodgers was a clash between "sentimental melody and unsentimental lyrics," as Rodgers himself put it. Hart was famous for his witty polysyllabic and internal rhymes, triple rhymes and false rhymes, and thoroughly conversational rhymes. Like Ira Gershwin, he was adept at using syllabic fragmentation to achieve his rhymes, as in "Manhattan":

And tell me what street
compares with Mott Street
in July?
Sweet pushcarts gently gli-
ding by.

More examples of Hart's playful words and his "caustic rhymes" concealing deep emotions can be found in Philip Furia's indispensable study, *The Poets of Tin Pan Alley.*[38]

American popular music is a manifestation of Western civilization, created largely in New York. Precisely because of its wide appeal and wit, it is not always given sufficient credit for its seriousness, sophistication, and above all, artfulness. The songs from the golden age of musical theater, heard apart from the froth and frivolity of the musical comedies in which they are embedded, give expression to the people's yearnings, their often unobtainable ideals, their pathos and tenderness. These songs lend dignity to the lives and struggles of ordinary people.

Popular culture as conveyed in these musical comedies is an affirmation of life, brimming with energy and vitality, aesthetically sophisticated but with the broadest appeal. As Lorenz Hart once wrote to Ira Gershwin, "songs can be both popular and intelligent."[39] Since these songs are moving expressions of basic human feelings, they are able to cross all the boundaries of race, class, and religion. The music asks you, everyone, to join in. It is inviting and inclusive, a social adhesive that forms a common culture and a collective memory.

The genius of the Great American Songbook lies in the way everyday words are used in memorable ways to sing of the regrets and sorrows, and also the hope and optimism of the common heart on its journey through modern life. The narrator of Damon Runyon's "The Snatching of Bookie Bob" says that after the stock-market crash, "many citizens of this town are compelled to do the best they can. There is very little scratch anywhere and along Broadway many citizens are wearing last year's clothes and have practically nothing to bet on the races or anything else, and it is a condition that will touch anybody's heart." Dorothy Fields' "I Can't Give You Anything But Love," written in 1927, helped many a young couple get through the Depression years, as did her 1930 song "On the Sunny Side of the Street."[40] Muddling through as best one can is what Billie Holliday sings about in "Getting Some Fun Out of Life." Some of this music still evokes emotions that for many of us are the closest we shall get to a glimpse of the transcendental in this secular age. We must cherish it as a worthy part of Western civilization.

ℭℵℭ

LAUGHING AT OURSELVES

Time Out New York has a section of five or six pages devoted to "Comedy," beginning with interviews of comedy writers such as Harold Ramis, Dan Mazer, and Paul Feig. Then comes a listing of comedy clubs: the Broadway Comedy Club, Carolines on Broadway, Comedy Cellar, Comedy Corner, Comic Strip Live East, Comix, Dangerfield's, Eastville Comedy Club, Gotham Comedy Club, and many others. There are pages listing the acts of certain stand-up comedians: Andy Borowitz at the 92nd Street Y, Danny Leary at the

Duplex, Jena Friedman at the Pyramid Club, and so on. Comedy is alive and well in New York—a sure sign of a healthy society.

Humor is an indispensable ingredient of any culture. It can be seen as a form of self-criticism, which is a defining virtue of the West. It is also a social safety valve, allowing us to laugh at each other's foibles and failures, to laugh off our differences in an act of conciliation and live in relative harmony. The ethnic joke, if not invented in New York, was certainly given new life there as Jews, Irishmen, Poles, and Italians, all competing for space in a teeming metropolis, developed self-deprecating humor, the necessary lubricant for a complex social organism. Jews are particularly gifted in self-mockery, and the rabbinical tradition is full of jokes pointing to the irony of God's chosen people having to fight harder than most others in order to survive.[41]

Any civilization that cannot laugh at itself is in a state of decline, and it is dangerous.[42] The Ayatollah Khomeini once declared that "there are no jokes in Islam." Without the tempering of humor, Muslims are ever ready to take offense. In fact, they seem to have invented a new right: the right not to be offended. Even the European Union seems determined not to permit any humorous remarks about Islam, promulgating laws designed to silence criticism and censor those indispensable social critics, the comedians, when it comes to the subject of Islam.

⟳

A SOCIAL LUBRICANT

In a corner of Grand Central Terminal, that imposing Beaux Arts structure completed in 1913, sits an elegant public bar and cocktail lounge called the Campbell Apartment. It was once the office (never an apartment) of the financier John W. Campbell, who leased the space from one of the Vanderbilts, original owners of the New York Central Railroad. Campbell commissioned the architect Augustus

N. Allen to transform the space into a thirteenth-century Florentine palazzo. Allen installed a hand-painted plaster of Paris ceiling, leaded windows, and a mahogany balcony with a quatrefoil design. After years of neglect, the whole interior was restored in 1999.

The Campbell Apartment is a most civilized setting for enjoying cocktails, many of them invented, or claimed to have been invented, in Manhattan. The eponymous Manhattan (whiskey, sweet vermouth, and bitters) was possibly created as early as the 1860s. The Bloody Mary (based on vodka and tomato juice) was first served around 1939 by some accounts. Wine is also served, but alas, not always of a quality to satisfy connoisseurs.

The civilized pleasure of alcohol is connected with the social customs and rituals that define our society. Wine in moderate amounts also "inspires and encourages," argues Leon Kass. Wine "provides partial relief from the hardships of life and the need to sweat for our bread. It gladdens the heart, loosens the tongue, and enlivens the soul. Under its influence we forget our troubles, lose our inhibitions, speak our minds: *In vino veritas.* A psychic midwife, wine delivers us of hidden insights and affections. It can even transport us toward realms apart—in love, in song, in ecstasy, in 'madness.'" Kass ascribes a deep human significance to wine as an instrument to improve intellectual and moral life, to elevate us "beyond necessity and calculating rationality."[43]

The philosopher Roger Scruton identifies alcohol as a lubricant of the Western dynamo. "You see this clearly in America," he writes, "where cocktail parties immediately break the ice between strangers and set every large gathering in motion, stimulating a collective desire for rapid agreement among people who a moment before did not know each other from Adam."[44] Scruton contrasts this Western tradition with Islamic customs of the hookah, the coffee house, and the bathhouse. (He might have included the Yemeni tradition of chewing qat, a leafy narcotic.) The latter forms of association, he says, "are also forms of withdrawal, a standing back

32

from the business of government in a posture of peaceful resignation. Drink has the opposite effect: It brings strangers together in a state of controlled aggression, able and willing to engage in any business that should arise from the current conversation."[45]

While alcohol has an openly acknowledged place in American social life, the Islamic world officially, strictly bans it—yet harbors secret alcohol consumption by the powerful. Hanif Kureishi, a British writer with a father from Pakistan, went to several parties in Karachi. At one of these, attended by people of power—landowners, businessmen, diplomats, politicians—Kureishi found them "drinking heavily. Every liberal in England knows you can be lashed for drinking in Pakistan. But as far as I could tell, none of this English-speaking international bourgeoisie would be lashed for anything. They all had their favourite trusted bootleggers." Kureishi added, "I once walked into a host's bathroom to see the bath full of floating whisky bottles being soaked to remove the labels, a servant sitting on a stool serenely poking at them with a stick."[46]

Charles Glass recounted a similar story of hypocrisy from Saudi Arabia: "Possession of alcohol was illegal, but I was offered wine and, in the houses of royal princes, cabinet ministers and ambassadors, whisky (the favored drink was Johnny Walker Black Label). I learned that a prince with whom I had shared a whisky in the evening would in the morning sentence a man to prison for drinking."[47]

෨෧
MARBLE AND STONE

The silent stones as much as the noisy democratic bustle of New York City speak of its values. New York's architecture is witness to the West's aspirations and creativity. It pays constant homage to the West's classical heritage, a heritage linked to the motivating principles of the United States Constitution. The inspiration behind the Greek Revival, for example, was both political and aesthetic, its elegant forms calling to mind the origins of Western democracy in ancient Greece. Although the architectural movement predates the Greek War of Independence against the Ottoman Turks (1821–1829), it gained further impetus from that event, which reminded Americans of their own fight for independence. The Federal Hall National Memorial (originally the U.S. Custom House) at 28 Wall Street, built between 1833 and 1842, is a Doric-columned marble temple, in essence a simplified Parthenon.[48] Other Greek Revival buildings in New York include LaGrange Terrace in Lafayette Place and Sailor's Snug Harbor on Staten Island.

The City Beautiful movement of the 1890s and 1900s advocated monumental grandeur in cities as a way of promoting moral and civic virtue among urban populations, and thus a harmonious social order. One product of this initiative was the Manhattan Appellate Courthouse (1900). The architect, James Brown Lord, was entrusted with the unprecedented sum of $700,000, a large part of which was to be devoted to decoration, including sculpture and murals.

The felicitous outcome is a three-story marble palace drawing inspiration from the Beaux Arts school, with its attention to detail and ornament. On the 25th Street façade we find a dignified, triangular-pedimented portico over a screen of six two-story Corinthian columns. The Madison Avenue façade is equally imposing, with four Corinthian columns supporting a flat cornice. The interior is considered one of the most sumptuous in New York. The main hall boasts an ornate coffered ceiling, Siena marble walls divided by Corinthian pilasters, paneling, gilding, stained glass, and painted friezes depicting legal themes.[49]

Sixteen sculptors were responsible for the thirty figures on the building's exterior. The roof balustrade is graced by statues of historical figures associated with lawgiving: Zoroaster, Alfred the Great, Lycurgus, Solon, Louis IX, Manu, Justinian, Confucius, Moses—reflecting New York's generous recognition of other cultures and the universality of law. Along with these, one finds sculptures embodying more abstract notions: Peace flanked by Strength and Abundance; Justice flanked by Power and Study; and four caryatids representing the seasons, implying the temporal continuity of law.

Originally, ten lawgivers were honored, the tenth being Muhammad. The eight-foot marble figure by Charles Albert Lopez was described by the *New York Times* as being "broad-shouldered, with thick, powerful hands. Under his turban, his brows are prominent and frowning. A long, heavy beard flows over his robe. In his left hand, he holds a book, symbolizing the new religion he founded, and in his right, a scimitar, connoting the Moslem conquest."

At the time of a general renovation in the early 1950s, the Muhammad statue came to the notice of the Egyptian, Indonesian, and Pakistani ambassadors to the United Nations, who immediately demanded that the U.S. Department of State use its influence to have the figure removed, despite the obvious fact that the intent of the architect was to honor Muhammad as comparable to such great lawgivers as Confucius and Solon. The State Department complied, sending two functionaries to persuade the city's public works commissioner, Frederick H. Zurmuhlen, to give in to the ambassadors' demands. The appellate court also received letters from Muslims asking that the statue be taken down. All seven justices recommended to Zurmuhlen that he remove it. Eventually, the Muhammad statue was carted off to a warehouse in New Jersey; its ultimate fate is unknown. Zurmuhlen then shifted around some of the remaining statues to fill in the vacant spot.[50] This episode was a foreshadowing of things to come, as Chapter Six relates. It also illustrates the contrast between Islam's sense of its own exclusive authority on the one hand, and the West's openness and inclusiveness in honoring a Muslim lawgiver on a Western court of law.

New York architecture is as receptive to outside ideas as its theaters and art galleries. At 33 Union Square West there is the decidedly Veneto-Islamic caprice of John Edelmann's 1893 Decker Building, with its tiled roof, domed minaret, ogees, arches, filigree, and arabesques.[51] At No. 7 Tenth Street in Manhattan there is an exotic, intricately carved teakwood bay window copied from the domestic architecture of Gujarat, in India. This window adorns a building commissioned by Lockwood de Forest, an American Orientalist who had traveled and worked in India, founding workshops in Ahmadabad to revive the native art of woodcarving.[52]

WHAT A MAGAZINE STAND REVEALS

Americans are often accused of insularity, but a stroll through the Barnes & Noble bookstore in Union Square should dispel that notion. Entering the charming red brick, terra cotta, and white stone building (1881) designed by William Schickel and browsing through the stacks of tomes by the entrance, representing the current best-sellers, we are immediately struck by the number of books on non-Western cultures, whether fiction or nonfiction, many by authors of Asian origin, such as Amitav Ghosh, Aravind Adiga, Rohinton Mistry, Jhumpa Lahiri, Orhan Pamuk, Ma Jian, and Bei Dao. Khaled Hosseini's *The Kite Runner* sold more than four million copies in the United States.

Two years ago, while working as a research fellow at the Center for Inquiry in Amherst, New York, I was responsible for looking after a colleague from Iraq, Dr. W. Ali,[53] who was traveling outside his country for the first time at the age of forty-five. He stayed with us for three months and expressed himself freely on many issues, making observations and comparisons of an anthropological, sociological, and political nature. He was evidently fascinated by everything he saw, much moved by his experiences, and on occasion frankly overwhelmed. On almost every subject, he revealed an open and refreshing admiration for various aspects of American life. I took him several times to the local Barnes & Noble. Once, I left him in the shop to browse and returned half an hour later to find him photographing the magazine stands. Dr. Ali explained that he had phoned a close friend in Baghdad and described to him the number and variety of magazines available. His friend was skeptical, refusing to accept that there were so many titles; hence Dr. Ali's effort to record it all photographically.

We made a very rough estimate, and came to the conclusion that there must have been over a thousand magazines on the stands, covering almost every human endeavor, every interest, every hobby and activity of modern Western men and women. The owner of a shop on 14th Street near Union Square in Manhattan informed me that he had seven thousand magazines on display, while the American Society of Magazine Editors (ASME) listed 22,652 titles published in 2007, two thousand of which had a sizable circulation.

Such possibilities for enriching one's life, unmolested by government interference, came as a shocking revelation to Dr. Ali, who by his own description had lived a constricted life, with leisure activities limited to discussing the latest conspiracy theory while drinking coffee on the streets of Baghdad. It was a sudden realization that not only had a large part of his life perhaps been wasted, but his country had failed to create the necessary conditions—the political and social structures, the principles and values—for such diverse activities to flourish.

The word "magazine" might evoke an image of garish vulgarity, but the genre also includes subjects that I would unhesitatingly call spiritual as well as aesthetic and intellectual. The ASME listed 186 magazines devoted to art and sculpture, 120 to architecture, 24 to archaeology and paleontology, 14 to astronomy, 88 to chemistry, 28 to physics, 18 to botany, 93 to literary reviews, 65 to literature and linguistics, 135 to history, 14 to philosophy, 196 to poetry and creative writing, and 762 to religion and theology. Some of these publications are not-for-profit ventures, underwritten by university presses or independent institutions of higher education, and are designed to serve the academic community. Many of them simply reflect intellectual curiosity, an interest in knowledge for its own sake.

Friedrich Hayek pointed out that totalitarian states and ideologies have always condemned the pursuit of knowledge or any other cultural interest for its own sake.[54] A seemingly ordinary display of magazines in a bookstore reveals a host of values that distinguish liberal democracy from other types of regime or society.[55] These values, as V. S. Naipaul said, are far too often taken for granted.

℘✄
MEDICINE CHEST OF THE SOUL

(Photo © David Dea, 2011. Used under license from Shutterstock.com.)

There is said to have been an inscription over the door of the library at Thebes, in ancient Egypt, reading, "Libraries: Medicine Chest of the Soul." Libraries are not only a refuge for the individual soul, where one can "beguile" one's sorrows, as Shakespeare's Titus Andronicus put it, but a requisite for a healthy society, a precondition for culture and civilization.[56] Our attitudes toward our libraries—the memory of humankind—reflect our values, our faith in knowledge, our concern for future generations.

The doorway to the Main Reading Room of the New York Public Library is an aedicule in wood, composed of quarter-engaged fluted Doric columns with egg-and-dart capitals, which support a rounded pediment inscribed thus: "A good Booke is the pretious life-blood of a master spirit, imbalm'd and treasur'd up on purpose to a life beyond life." It comes from a passionate plea for freedom of expression in Milton's *Areopagitica* (1644), a passage that is worth quoting in full:

> *For Books are not absolutely dead things, but doe contain a potencie of life in them to be as active as that soule was whose progeny they are; nay they do preserve as in a violl the purest efficacie and extraction of that living intellect that bred them. I know they are as lively, and as vigorously productive, as those fabulous Dragons teeth; and being sown up and down, may chance to spring up armed men. And yet on the other hand unlesse warinesse be us'd, as good almost kill a Man as kill a good Book; who kills a Man kills a reasonable creature, Gods Image; but hee who destroyes a good Booke, kills reason it selfe, kills the Image of God, as it were in the eye. Many a man lives a burden to the Earth; but a good Booke is the pretious life-blood of a master spirit, imbalm'd and treasur'd up on purpose to a life beyond life.*

The "Library Bill of Rights" that was first adopted in 1939 by the American Library Association, with its stand against censorship, gave official expression to the principle of intellectual freedom that was present at the inception of the New York Public Library in 1911.

One of the great libraries of the world, the New York Public Library (NYPL) houses an enormous set of scholarly research collections over a vast intellectual and cultural range, from the parochial to the universal. Its history reflects much of what is best in the Western tradition. The NYPL owes its existence to civic-minded wealthy New Yorkers—such as John Jacob Astor, James Lenox, and the former governor of New York, Samuel J. Tilden—who saw libraries as "emblems of civilized society and civic culture."[57] They were spurred into action when New York's rivals were constructing monumental central libraries: Boston in 1895, Chicago in 1897, and Washington D.C. with the Library of Congress, also in 1897. Through trusts and foundations, these citizens established "a private, nonprofit corporation, operating a reference library and governed by a self-perpetuating Board of Trustees," writes Phyllis Dain. "The board—whose most active members belonged to a new public-spirited, well-educated, culturally oriented elite—wanted to create a grand institution on a par with the Bibliothèque Nationale de France and the British Museum Library, and one open fully and freely to the public."[58]

A site was needed, so the trustees began a public-private partnership, asking the city to provide the site and to construct and maintain a building, while they pledged to run a library and reading room, and operate a free circulating branch with books for home use.[59] A grant from Andrew Carnegie in 1901 provided the buildings for dozens of branch libraries in the city's neighborhoods. One of the richest men in the United States in his lifetime, Carnegie believed that the surplus of great fortunes should be disbursed for public benefit. By 1917 he had given away $180 million, $56 million of which was designated to build over 2,500 public libraries throughout the English-speaking world. The story of the NYPL's funding illustrates one aspect of Adam Smith's "invisible hand": capitalism creates not only wealth (material capital) but also public trust (moral capital). The invisible hand stimulates three kinds of public good: first, everyone is made better off by market exchanges, all else being equal; second, the wealthy benefit the community and the nation by their philanthropy; finally, the moral capital of society is enlarged by the environment of trust, fidelity, and integrity that both encourages and flows from commerce.[60]

The NYPL was conceived as an educational institution, to help prepare citizens for their civic responsibilities in a democracy and facilitate the assimilation of new immigrants. The inscription in the central building proclaims: "The City of New York has erected this building to be maintained as a free library for the use of the people. On the diffusion of education among the people rest the preservation and perpetuation of our free institutions." The first director, Dr. John Shaw Billings, was a man of wide learning and catholic taste who realized that the library must fulfill multiple functions, both utilitarian and scholarly. It would be a repository of documents necessary for modern life, and also a collection of books and manuscripts to serve the needs of disinterested research and scholarship. By 1913, the library had a collection of more than a million volumes.

Incidentally, the first book loaned out by the library on the day it opened to the public, May 24, 1911, was a Russian-language study of Nietzsche and Tolstoy, borrowed by a Russian émigré. One observer in Russia later described the operations of the library this way:

I have before me the report of the New York Public Library for 1911. That year . . . there were 246,950 readers using the reading-room and they took out 911,891 books. . . . The New York Public Library has forty-two branches and will soon have a forty-third. . . . The aim that is constantly pursued is to have a branch of the Public Library within three-quarters of a verst, i.e., within ten minutes' walk of the house of every inhabitant, the branch library being the centre of all kinds of institutions and establishments for public education. . . . The New York Public Library has opened a special, central, reading-room for children, and similar institutions are gradually being opened at all branches. The librarians do everything for the children's convenience and answer their questions. . . . Such is the way things are done in New York. And in Russia?[61]

Thus spake V. I. Lenin in 1913. Sadly, this is not the kind of library that the Leninist revolution brought to Russia, as the description by one recent scholar makes clear:

> *The basic rules of Soviet librarianship opened with the point on educating the Soviet public in the Marxist-Leninist spirit as libraries' main goal. The bosses strictly limited and selected information, especially social, political, economic and humanitarian. Ideologists divided it into good and bad, of vital and inferior importance. Priority was given to scientific and technological information, such as heavy industry, which dominated the Soviet economy. As the result, secret services, the army and attached industries were about the only spheres with powerful and reliable information infrastructures when the regime collapsed in Russia. With negligible exceptions, libraries had never been clearly told to provide free, quick and easy access to domestic, let alone world information resources.*[62]

In contrast, the NYPL was an independent institution, able to range far and wide in a liberal spirit. Its research collection was assiduously put together by dedicated librarians who were committed to "the modern, open-ended, limitless, objective, scientific search for knowledge."[63] Striving for universality, they tried to acquire "everything," and the result was "a grand array of documentary and intellectual resources for an extraordinary variety of scholarly work."[64] This universality is illustrated by the startling fact that the research wing houses items in more than 1,400 languages. The Slavic and Baltic Division, for example, collects material in twelve Slavonic languages along with Latvian and Lithuanian, and receives more than 750 periodicals and 120 newspapers each year. The Oriental Division houses materials in more than a hundred languages. "If the devil himself wrote a book, we'd want it in the Library," quipped the NYPL's second director, Edwin H. Anderson. Material was to be selected on the principle of "intellectual hospitality," he explained.

"None of us here would think of allowing his own personal opinions to influence the selection of books. . . . Practically everything is grist that comes to our mill."[65]

The library was not designed to indoctrinate citizens in the local equivalent of "the Marxist-Leninist spirit," but rather to encourage the life of the mind—an independent mind free to choose where to roam and explore the riches of Western culture or any other. Far from wishing to commit "cultural genocide," the NYPL encouraged immigrants to take an interest in their own culture of origin. According to Esther Johnston, who headed the branch libraries in early years, the idea of a melting pot or Americanization "always had something that was a little chauvinistic about it, and that was one reason we wanted books in foreign languages; we wanted exhibits so that children could see the culture from which they had sprung and [we] didn't think that forced interest in American life was very wholesome." The library aimed to provide "good reading matter," hoping that "the ones who read it would a little sooner find themselves understanding the country."[66]

In the center of the entrance floor there is a moving inscription that justifies all the hopes the original founders entertained for this august institution:

> *Inscribed here are the words of an immigrant whose life was transformed by the library and whose estate now enriches it. In Memory Martin Radtke, 1883–1973. "I had little opportunity for formal education as a young man in Lithuania, and I am deeply indebted to the New York Public Library for the opportunity to educate myself. In appreciation, I have given the library my estate with the wish that it be used so that others can have the same opportunity made available to me."*

The New York Public Library's home is a masterpiece of architecture in the Beaux Arts style. It was built out of white marble found in Vermont, which was easy to carve and would acquire a pearly gray quality over time.[67] The structure calls to mind the words of Friedrich Schiller: "Man has lost his dignity, but Art has saved it, and preserved it for him in expressive marbles."[68] The architects, John Merven Carrère and Thomas Hastings, were graduates of L'École Nationale Supérieure des Beaux-Arts in Paris, where they studied the great buildings and monuments of antiquity and learned the five classical orders. From this discipline came a deep understanding of proportion and scale and the role of ornament as an integral part of design, along with a feeling for the accumulated classical heritage that began in Athens and Rome.[69] Hastings explained that the exterior of the library was designed "so as to express in facade the interior arrangement of the building."[70] In designing rooms, halls, alcoves, and stairs, the architects were mindful of the interdependence of every part, of proportion, scale, balance, and symmetry. Their concept of proportion could not be divorced from the details that went into it, so they gave scrupulous attention to workmanship in everything from the carved ceilings and intricate bronze chandeliers, to the doors and the marble floors. These details impart grace and coherence, humanity and beauty to the whole.[71] The NYPL is a grand and beautiful civic monument, as well as an eminently practical one.

ೲ

CURRY HILL SPICE AND RICE

New York City is "literally a composite of tens of thousands of tiny neighbourhood units," wrote E. B. White. Despite their cosmopolitanism, or perhaps because of it, New Yorkers have a need for local attachments, a place where they feel totally at home when they return from their global jaunts. They are like the Cosmopolite in the O. Henry short story, who "wouldn't stand for no knockin'" his own place of origin, Mattawamkeag, Maine.[72]

Just south of Murray Hill and north of Gramercy, a district officially called Rose Hill has more than a touch of India, especially around 28th Street, where one finds a bustling mini bazaar of dazzling, diaphanous silks and sarees from Varanasi, rugs from Kashmir, sweets and spices and other delicacies from all over the Indian subcontinent.[73] The bazaar and a number of south Indian restaurants—Saravanaas, Pongal, Madras Mahal, Chennai Garden, Tiffin Wallah, among others—justify this neighborhood's unofficial name of "Curry Hill."

Of particular interest for us is 123 Lexington Avenue, where on September 20, 1881, Chester Arthur was sworn in as president of the United States, having been thrust into the position by the assassination of James Garfield.[74] The site is now a many-splendored store of foodstuffs—spices, rice, pulses, oils, sauces, chutneys, preserves, canned drinks. Stainless steel thalis and other kitchen utensils, Madhur Jaffery's Indian cookbooks, Najmieh Batmanglij's *From Persia to Napa: Wine at the Persian Table,* posters, dandruff remedies, henna for weddings, and much more add to the mix. As Richard Brookhiser wrote, "123 Lexington is an epitome of today's city, complete with a view of the Empire State Building."[75] Israeli sunflowers (salted or unsalted) sit in large plastic containers next to dried Egyptian watermelon. Along with California peaches, pears and plums, there are Australian glacé pineapple and "Alo Bokhara Persian sweet and sour prunes." Thai crystalized ginger is much cheaper than the Australian variety. There is undoubtedly a subtle difference between Israeli and Lebanese or Turkish halva, not to mention Macedonian halva with cocoa. Israeli whole wheat couscous, Lebanese Moghrabeyah couscous, kosher Moroccan fine duram semolina and the Tunisian variety attest to a healthy competition. Could the way to peace be through Mediterranean commerce, as in the days when Venetians were the dominant traders in the region?

And did you ever realize there were so many kinds of rice? There is idli rice, "used in making soft and tasty idli's [*sic*]"; Sri Lankan red rice; Riz Rouge de Camargue, a rather coarse variety from southern France; black Japonica, which is a combination of Asian black short-grain rice and medium-grain mahogany rice; Riso Venere, an Italian Chinese hybrid; Bhutanese red rice, which when cooked is "pale, pink, soft, and tender, and slightly clingy, easy to eat with chopsticks"; Indonesian volcano rice; Madagascar pink rice, grown in the Lac Alatra region of the island; Thai jasmine rice; Indian long-grain basmati rice from Dehra Dun; saffron rice; bamboo rice; Chinese black rice, also known as "Forbidden rice," since it was once the "exclusive grain of the emperors and known as blood enchriching [*sic*] and longevity rice. It is a med. grain rice with white kernals [*sic*] inside the black bran, very tender when cooked, has nutty taste." Then there are the varieties of salt: Flor de Sal from Portugal, Hiwa Kai from Hawaii, Trapani from Sicily, Aguni from Japan, Peruvian pink, Cyprus Black Lava, Bolivian from Salar de Uyuni. And it really is time you tried something other than English breakfast tea: how about Indian masala chai, Moroccan mint, Lebanese Aphrodisiac, Afghan green tea for the returning soldiers, Argentina's yerba mate, Nilgiri, Oolong, Ti Kuan Yin, Gulabi, Assam, Fujian green, Turkish black, or classic Darjeeling, to name just a few possibilities. I shall take you away from our store, Kalustyan's, having no doubt dazzled if not bewildered you.

New York is a powerful example of the possibilities of life in a free city in the free world; every single aspect of it, every single activity and art reenacted there speaks volumes about its values. Behind the success of New York lie a host of institutions—legal, economic, political, cultural—that have evolved over hundreds of years and that distinguish the West from the rest of the world. New York is, as Whitman said, a "city of superb democracy," and we shall leave the last word on New York to him:

The general subjective view of New York and Brooklyn—(will not the time hasten when the two shall be municipally united in one, and named Manhattan?)—what I may call the human interior and exterior of these great seething oceanic populations, as I get it in this visit, is to me best of all. After an absence of many years, (I went away at the outbreak of the secession war, and have never been back to stay since,) again I resume with curiosity the crowds, the streets I knew so well, Broadway, the ferries, the west side of the city, democratic Bowery—human appearances and manners as seen in all these, and along the wharves, and in the perpetual travel of the horse-cars, or the crowded excursion steamers, or in Wall and Nassau streets by day—in the places of amusement at night—bubbling and whirling and moving like its own environment of waters—endless humanity in all phases—Brooklyn also—taken in for the last three weeks. No need to specify minutely—enough to say that (making all allowances for the shadows and side-streaks of a million-headed-city) the brief total of the impressions, the human qualities, of these vast cities, is to me comforting, even heroic, beyond statement. Alertness, generally fine physique, clear eyes that look straight at you, a singular combination of reticence and self-possession, with good nature and friendliness—a prevailing range of according manners, taste and intellect, surely beyond any else-where upon earth—and a palpable outcropping of that personal comradeship I look forward to as the subtlest, strongest future hold of this many-item'd Union—are not only constantly visible here in these mighty channels of men, but they form the rule and average. To-day, I should say—defiant of cynics and pessimists, and with a full knowledge of all their exceptions—an appreciative and percep-tive study of the current humanity of New York gives the directest proof yet of successful Democracy, and of the solution of that para-dox, the eligibility of the free and fully developed individual with the paramount aggregate. In old age, lame and sick, pondering for years on many a doubt and danger for this republic of ours—fully aware of all that can be said on the other side—I find in this visit to New York, and the daily contact and rapport with its myriad people, on the scale of the oceans and tides, the best, most effective medicine my soul has yet partaken—the grandest physical habitat and surroundings of land and water the globe affords—namely, Manhattan island and Brooklyn, which the future shall join in one city—city of superb democracy, amid superb surroundings.[76]

CHAPTER TWO

WHY DID THE WEST BECOME SUCCESSFUL?

New York stands as a concrete definition of Western civilization in its energy and creativity, its air of unlimited possibility. In the preface I asked, what made it all possible? Why do so many people come from all over the world to New York, or to many other thriving Western cities, to find a better life? What has made the West successful while so many countries in other parts of the world fail to provide adequate food and shelter for their citizens, or to guarantee security or protect human rights?

Many scholars have emphasized geography as an explanation for different rates of cultural development and for disparate levels of economic well-being in the modern world. In particular, they point out that the advanced industrial nations are located in the temperate zones, while the great majority of poor countries lie in the tropics, which are said to have most of the disadvantages. Clearly geography plays some part in explaining the economic success of certain countries over others. But as Deirdre McCloskey points out, geography does not account for why England had an industrial revolution in the eighteenth century whereas the Chinese people of the temperate zone did not.[1] Lawrence E. Harrison points to the more recent economic success of Singapore and Hong Kong, both in the tropics, and Taiwan, which lies halfway in the tropical zone. He also notes the prosperity of the Chinese minorities in tropical Thailand, Indonesia, Malaysia, and the Philippines, as well as the Japanese minorities in tropical Peru and Brazil.[2] Geography alone cannot explain why Haiti, once the richest colony in the Caribbean, is today mired in poverty and misery, while Barbados, a former slave colony, is now prosperous.[3]

A corollary of the geography argument is one that highlights the "germs" in Jared Diamond's title, *Guns, Germs, and Steel: The Fate of Human Societies*. Scholars have noted the prevalence of disease in the tropical ecozones, where so many poor countries are located. But McCloskey replies that "northwestern Europe initiated the modern world when still debilitated by cholera and smallpox and tuberculosis and especially by the malaria so devastating to modern Africa," called "ague" at the time. This latter disease was at its peak in the nineteenth century, while Europe was industrializing.[4]

Another variant of the geographical theory is a focus on natural resources. But as white South Africans, for example, came to understand, "merely having a stock of gold and diamonds in the ground does not make for a modern economy," especially if a substantial part of the population, or "human capital," is kept uneducated. On the other hand, some countries with few natural resources— Denmark, Hong Kong, Japan—have managed to develop modern industrial economies.[5] Natural endowment is far less consequential than the ability to use it productively, and that ability is an outcome of culture.

"If we learn anything from the history of economic development, it is that culture makes all the difference," argues David Landes. By way of illustration, he mentions the relative success of various expatriate minorities in comparison with the dominant population: "the Chinese in East and Southeast Asia, Indians in East Africa, Lebanese in West Africa." He also points to the Jews and Calvinists as successful cultural minorities in much of Europe.[6] In other words, "Max Weber was right on," Landes adds, referring to the thesis that Weber made famous in *The Protestant Ethic and the Spirit of Capitalism* (first published in 1904). The economic and technological success of the West began with culture, and with principles embodied in its characteristic institutions.

The origins of the modern West are often seen in the Enlightenment of the seventeenth and eighteenth centuries, but the roots of the Enlightenment can be found in habits of mind cultivated in Athens, Rome, and Jerusalem, and in the institutions that grew from them. The Greeks gave us the city and the notion of citizenship, the ideals of democracy and liberty, rationalism and science, philosophy and history. The Romans systematized the law, defined private property, and emphasized individual responsibility. Judeo-Christianity added a sense of conscience and charity, tempering justice with forgiveness, and the concept of linear rather than cyclical time, which allowed for the possibility of progress. The Middle Ages brought a deeper synthesis of Athens and Rome with Jerusalem, laying the foundations for the scientific revolution, the industrial revolution, the Enlightenment, and pluralistic liberal democracy.

No civilization is pure, just as there are no pure races. As a character in Nabokov's *Lolita* says, we are all a salad of racial genes, and this is even more true of civilizations: each is a salad of cultural genes. Foreign elements are absorbed and transmuted in an ongoing exchange of goods and ideas. What we view as ancient tradition, deeply rooted in a national past, often turns out to be a recent import.

The history of the West encompasses various ethnic groups that willingly adopted values rooted in other cultures and regions. The ancient Greeks were open to new ideas from the outside, and were strongly influenced by the older civilizations of the Near East and Egypt.[7] Greek philosophy may also have incorporated aspects of the Vedic culture from India.[8] Subsequently, the Romans accepted Hellenization; the Gauls, Latinization; pagan Europeans, Christianization. Then, Christian Europe refreshed its inheritance again by "adopt[ing] Roman law and Greek science, combining them into a narrative of its own, establishing them as the source of its cultural norms, collective imagination, and shared identity," as Philippe Nemo put it. "Each of these communities adopted retrospectively a spiritual affiliation with the source, which reflected neither its biological nor its ethnic origins."[9] Thus, many Europeans today feel closer to Socrates, Cicero, Moses and Jesus than to the Celts or Gauls.

❦

GREEK REASON

The agora, or public square, represents a new way of doing politics in ancient Greece. It was a place where citizens gathered to participate directly in the political life of a city-state, or polis. The very notion of a citizen was a Greek achievement. Citizens were equals before the law, and equal in dignity by virtue of their rational faculties, irrespective of ethnic origin. In the agora they heard different points of view and submitted their ideas to examination by fellow citizens. Out of this practice came the art of discourse, or rhetoric, and rational argumentation, the science of dialectic.[10]

The discussion of public affairs in the agora represents a secularization of the state, a separation of politics from religion that would run through Western history. In the tragedies of Aeschylus and Sophocles we can see how the tension between sacred and temporal spheres was working itself out in Greek antiquity. The *Oresteia* of Aeschylus examines a conflict between the primordial gods of vengeance on the one hand, and the social order that is maintained through manmade laws and negotiations on the other. In the end, "justice replaces vengeance," as Roger Scruton explains. "It is through politics, not religion, that peace is secured. Vengeance is mine, saith the Lord; but justice, says the city, is mine."[11]

This theme was taken up by Sophocles in *Antigone,* where the public law of the state runs up against private family love and an essentially religious duty to a brother. Polynices, at war with his native city, has fallen before the gates of Thebes. The city's king, Creon, proclaims a law that anyone who gives the honor of burial to this enemy of the city is to be killed. Polynices' sister Antigone cannot accept this command in the public interest; her loyalty or *pathos* (passion, affection) is to the family. In piety and love, she fulfills the holy duty of burial for her brother, appealing to the law of the gods—but these are the underworld gods of Hades, of feeling and kinship, not the daylight gods of public life.[12] Creon's concern is the safety and good order of the polis, which require that private loyalties yield to the city's needs and its laws.[13] The laws that govern cities are the fruit of man's reason and his ingenuity in conquering nature.[14]

For the Greeks, law is public and impersonal, detached from any person's whim. "The rule of law is preferable to that of any individual," said Aristotle. Each citizen takes responsibility for his actions under the impartial rule of law. But while the law of cities is impersonal, it is also a human creation that can be criticized and reformed. Manmade law is part of the conventional order, *nomos,* as opposed to the natural order, *physis,* which has its own kind of law.

The distinction between *nomos* and *physis* lies beneath the Greek invention of science, the aim to find natural rather than supernatural explanations for observable phenomena, formulated in general and necessary laws of nature. Greek science is also the fruit of a driving curiosity and a sense of man as a distinctively rational being. "Man differs from other [creatures] in that he alone understands," wrote Alcmaeon of Croton, who lived in the fifth or sixth century BCE.[15] The ability to acquire knowledge of the world and appreciate our surroundings is something that gives value to human life. Anaxagoras said that the primary reason to enjoy his existence was "For the sake of viewing the heavens and the whole order of the universe." The Greeks, as Bruce Thornton notes, saw learning as central to the very essence of humanity.[16] "All men by nature desire to know," said Aristotle. The desire and capacity to learn about the world sets humans apart: other animals "live by appearances and memories," whereas "the human race lives also by art and reasonings."[17] E. R. Dodds made the case that the Greeks were more attuned to the nonrational elements of human experience than had commonly been assumed,[18] but nevertheless they bequeathed to us a tradition of critical reason that runs throughout Western history as a stream that occasionally goes underground but always reappears.

While they viewed curiosity and reason as characteristically human, the Greeks surpassed other contemporary civilizations in applying these qualities to the study of nature. In comparison with their Near Eastern neighbors, they developed a more abstract way of analyzing their observations and more general theories for understanding the world. The result was an astonishing array of discoveries in mathematics, astronomy, physics, medicine, physiology, zoology, and biology—a rich legacy on which Western civilization has drawn through the centuries. Curiosity and openness also yielded the wide-ranging history of the Persian Wars by Herodotus, and the beginning of a more scientific approach to recording history with Thucydides.

Pursuing knowledge and arts for their own sake was central to the Greek ideal of *paideia,* meaning excellence or perfection, the fulfillment of human potential. The Greeks established a system of independent educational institutions: primary schools, where reading, writing, and arithmetic were taught; secondary schools, which gave instruction in grammar and literature along with a course in critical thinking; and institutions of higher learning in philosophy, rhetoric, and medicine. A well-rounded education was regarded as ennobling and served as essential preparation for active citizenship and liberty.[19]

ROMAN LAW

Though the Greeks invented the rule of law, it was left to Roman magistrates and jurists to devise an intricate system of private law, which became the basis for modern civil codes. The Roman judiciary established a flexible legal framework that combined tested formulas with ongoing innovation. Their cosmopolitan empire led the Romans to broaden their ideas of law and to formulate the notion of a natural law common to all. Roman law gave a definition to private property, creating a formal way "to separate very precisely what is yours from what is mine: to each by right."[20] Private spheres were clearly delineated from public space, encouraging a new sense of the person as an individual with his own character and inner life and a unique destiny.

By recognizing the private sphere, Roman law laid the basis for Western humanism, argues Philippe Nemo. "There would be no humanism without private law, no humanism without the protection of property by law. Rome promoted a concept of law that freed humanity from 'social holism.' The West duly recorded this advance, alongside the Greek contribution of civics. In contrast, the East ignored them both."[21] In a humanistic culture, the autonomy of the person takes precedence over group identity, and no individual may be sacrificed for some collective utopian goal, as F. A. Hayek observed.

❦
JERUSALEM: THE ETHICS OF THE BIBLE

After their experience of bondage in Egypt, the Hebrews always remained hostile to autocracy. They also showed a sense of property rights that rulers must not infringe, as Davd Landes points out:

> When the priest Korach leads a revolt against Moses in the desert, Moses defends himself against charges of usurpation by saying, "I have not taken one ass from them, nor have I wronged any one of them" (Numbers 16:15). Similarly, when the Israelites, now established in the Land, call for a king, the prophet Samuel grants them their wish but warns them of consequences: a king, he tells them, will not be like him. "Whose ox have I taken, or whose ass have I taken?" (I Samuel 12:3).[22]

The Bible provided medieval Christians with arguments against the pretensions of kings and in support of private property. The church could maintain that the Lord was the ultimate owner of everything, and therefore earthly rulers were not free to do as they pleased.

The biblical prophets dared to rebuke the powerful and to exalt the humble. This egalitarian notion became a major force in shaping the West after the Bible was translated into the vernacular by various heretical sects, such as the Waldensians in the twelfth century, followed by the Lollards and then the Lutherans and the Calvinists.[23] Biblical passages that dignify manual labor, such as where God tells Noah to build an ark, were echoed in Martin Luther's doctrines on the worthiness of work. The Bible teaches the subordination of nature to man, in contrast to animistic beliefs that bestow divine properties on trees and forest streams. It also empowers humanity by promoting a linear rather than cyclical sense of time, thus allowing both progress and regress.[24] It is the possibility of change over time

56

that gives substance to the ethical obligation of alleviating human suffering. Thus, linear time underpins moral responsibility.

The Judeo-Christian ethic introduced compassion and forgiveness, along with a refusal to accept hardship and evil as the norm.[25] Jesus' Sermon on the Mount (Matthew 5–7) exhorts each person to take responsibility for human suffering even if he is not the cause. Christian love demands that we go the extra mile for our neighbor and fight evil on behalf of all people. Our humanity is inseparable from our responsibility for others.[26]

During the early Middle Ages, the pessimistic theology of Saint Augustine seemed to suppress activism by casting doubt on the possibility of changing the world for the better. In the late eleventh century, however, Saint Anselm of Bec revolutionized the value of human action in the world with his doctrine of atonement (as expounded in *Cur deus homo?*), in which all works are accounted in the final reckoning. Even the doctrine of purgatory encouraged good works by those who might otherwise have thought it was too late to matter. All human action in the world has significance, and good works will always find favor in the eyes of God.[27] Around the same time, Western art began to depict Jesus in a way that emphasized his suffering and humanity, and thereby underlined the worth of human action.[28]

☾✕☽

CHURCH AND STATE: THE LEGAL REVOLUTION

A distinction between sacred and secular powers was in evidence when Hebrew prophets presumed to challenge kings, and when Jesus said, "Render therefore to Caesar the things that are Caesar's; and unto God the things that are God's" (Matthew 22:21). Caesar had his proper role, not in the economy of salvation but in the orderly administration of life on earth.[29] Saint Augustine offered a subtle analysis of the relationship between spiritual and temporal powers in *The City of God,* where he described the whole of human history as being marked by tension between two invisible societies, a heavenly city of God and an earthly city of the world. These are mirrored in the visible institutions of church and state, each with its own proper responsibilities: the ecclesiastical order concerns itself with salvation, while the civil order is charged with the governance of temporal affairs.

Pope Gelasius I (r. 492–496) formulated a "doctrine of the two powers" in a famous letter to the Byzantine emperor Anastasius I, among other works. Gelasius explained that the last to have been both priest and king was Christ himself, who separated the functions of ecclesiastical and royal authorities ever after, making each sovereign in its own sphere. Christian monarchs needed assistance from priests to gain eternal life, while priests depended on the secular power to administer temporal affairs. The clergy owed obedience to the king or emperor, who in turn was obliged to submit to the clergy and especially the pope in religious matters. The two powers had equal standing and each one set limits on the other.[30]

An early successor to Gelasius, Pope Gregory I (r. 590–604), wrote a *Pastoral Rule* in which he required the clergy to practice civil obedience to the secular authorities.[31] By the later eleventh century, his namesake Pope Gregory VII (r. 1073–1085) considered it imperative to rein in the influence that lay powers were exercising over the clergy. In his *Dictatus papae* he declared the pope to be supreme over secular powers, but his efforts to implement his clerical reforms led to a dramatic and ultimately humiliating conflict with the Holy Roman emperor, Henry IV.

Gregory VII meanwhile had revived the study of Roman law in order to bolster his case against the emperor and to create a more systematic church or canon law. One result was the founding of the first European university at Bologna, where the law code of Justinian I, the *Corpus juris civilis,* was taught along with the liberal arts. The interlinear commentary by Irnerius (c. 1050–after 1125) laid the foundation for a systematic and comprehensive European law.[32] A new system of canon law, the *Corpus juris canonici,* grew out of a compilation known as the *Decretum* of Gratian, an Italian legal scholar. The *Decretum* (1140) set forth the principle that custom must be measured by reasonableness and according to natural law, and it must be uniformly applied.[33] The revival of Roman law encouraged the use of God-given rational faculties to weigh the validity of custom and traditional authorities. It also called for people to settle their disputes through law, an essential basis for an orderly constitutional state.[34]

Another far-reaching consequence of this legal revival was the principle of treating collective actors as a single entity or corporate body. People in medieval societies would sometimes join together to form groups for religious, educational, economic, or social purposes. Canon law recognized these groups as legal entities, or legal personalities, with specific rights of assembly, ownership, and representation.[35] These collectives, including guilds and other professional associations, also passed laws to govern their own members, resulting in new systems of law, such as urban law and merchant law.[36] Toby Huff explains the revolutionary implications of this concept:

> *The emergence of corporate actors was unquestionably revolutionary in that the legal theory which made them possible created a variety of new forms and powers of association that were in fact unique to the West, since they were wholly absent in Islamic as well as Chinese law. Furthermore, the legal theory of corporations brings in its train constitutional principles establishing such political ideas as constitutional government, consent in political decision making, the right of political and legal representation, the powers of adjudication and jurisdiction, and even the power of autonomous legislation.[37]*

The effect on intellectual and cultural developments was profound. As Hastings Rashdall put it, "Ideals pass into great historic forces by embodying themselves in institutions. The power of embodying its ideals in institutions was the peculiar genius of the medieval mind."[38] One of these institutions was the university, founded as a corporate body with the power to enact and enforce its own internal statutes.[39] While many European universities grew out of cathedral schools, others were originally lay institutions, such as the University of Bologna. These "scholarly guilds" took form without explicit authorization by either religious or secular authorities. "They were spontaneous products of that instinct of association which swept like a great wave over the towns of Europe in the course of the eleventh and twelfth centuries," writes Huff.[40]

The legal notion of corporate bodies with institutional rights was absent from Islamic law. Thus, the Islamic religious colleges or madrasas were pious endowments governed by religious law. The universities of Europe, on the other hand, were legally autonomous bodies with the right to govern themselves, to make contracts, to own property, and so on.[41] Because Western universities were independent institutions, they could engage in relatively unfettered research into a multitude of subjects and cultivate a rational approach to studying the world.

⨕⨕
THE ENLIGHTENED MIDDLE AGES

A. C. Crombie began his classic survey of medieval and early modern science by observing that "the most striking result of recent scholarship" in the history of science was "the essential continuity of the Western scientific tradition from Greek times to the 17th century and, therefore, to our own day."[42] This continuity runs through early medieval scholars such as Isidore of Seville (c. 560–636), who diligently preserved fragments of classical learning that would otherwise have been lost.[43] Isidore studied at the cathedral school of Seville, quickly mastering Greek and Hebrew as well as Latin. Eventually he rose through the church hierarchy to become bishop of Seville. Under his leadership, the Fourth Council of Seville (633) issued a decree commanding all bishops to establish seminaries in their cathedral cities patterned after the school at Seville, which prescribed the study of Greek and Hebrew along with the seven liberal arts, divided into the *trivium* (grammar, rhetoric, dialectic) and the *quadrivium* (arithmetic, geometry, astronomy, music), and encouraged the study of law and medicine as well.

Isidore was probably the first Christian to compile a summa or compendium of universal knowledge, both ancient and modern, drawing from earlier scholars such as Boethius, Lactantius, Pliny, and Suetonius. Isidore's *Etymologiae* covered subjects including medicine, libraries, law, God, the church, languages, etymology, the physical world, agriculture, beasts and birds. It was used throughout the Middle Ages in many educational institutions and often reprinted, even into the fifteenth century. Isidore's other works include the *Chronicon,* a universal chronicle, and the *Synonyma,* a dialogue between Man and Reason.

The reign of Charlemagne brought an intellectual revival that continued through the ninth century. Carolingian schools were not notably original in thought, but many were effective centers of education, and they served generations of scholars by producing editions and copies of the classics, both Christian and pagan.[44] The most important Carolingian scholar was Alcuin, educated at the cathedral school in York and later invited to join Charlemagne's court as an adviser. Alcuin wrote on subjects ranging from grammar and biblical exegesis to arithmetic and astronomy. He also collected rare books, which formed the nucleus of the library at York Cathedral. His enthusiasm for learning made Alcuin an effective teacher. "In the morning, at the height of my powers, I sowed the seed in Britain," he wrote; "now in the evening when my blood is growing cold I am still sowing in France, hoping both will grow, by the grace of God, giving some the honey of the holy scriptures, making others drunk on the old wine of ancient learning."[45] Another prominent figure in the Carolingian renaissance was Theodulf of Orléans, a refugee from the Islamic invasion of Spain who became involved in the cultural circle at the imperial court before Charlemagne appointed him bishop of Orléans. Theodulf's greatest contribution to learning was his scholarly edition of the Vulgate Bible, drawing on manuscripts from Spain, Italy, and Gaul, and even the original Hebrew.[46]

When the Arab conquests shattered the ancient Mediterranean unity, Europe was cut off from its classical heritage, and the medieval era began, in Henri Pirenne's famous thesis.[47] By the ninth century, however, independent Italian cities such as Venice, Naples, Bari, and Amalfi were trading with the Arabs of Sicily and the eastern Mediterranean, followed soon by Pisa and Genoa. Eventually, fruitful contact between Europeans and the Islamic world, in effect, gave back to the West its own Greek heritage. Medievalists and historians of science have talked about how the West "received" Greek and Arabic learning, or how this science "passed" to the West. But Western scholars were not passive in the process. With their curiosity and intellectual openness, they came to admire the Islamic culture they saw in Spain, "sometimes extravagantly," as Richard Southern said.[48] Beginning in the tenth century, Western Europeans actively sought out Greco-Arabic works from Spain, southern Italy, and Sicily, as well as translators and teachers of Arabic. The Norman rulers of Sicily in the twelfth century fostered a climate of tolerance in which Latin, Greek, and Muslim subjects lived together in comparative harmony, a situation favorable to the work of translation.[49]

In the eleventh century, a Benedictine monk at Monte Cassino known as Constantine the African was disseminating knowledge of scientific works in Arabic, many of them translations from Greek scholars such as Galen and Hippocrates. More influential in this regard was Adelard of Bath, active in the twelfth century and sometimes called the first English scientist. He studied at a school founded by Charlemagne in Tours, and later traveled extensively in Greece, Sicily, Italy, Asia Minor, Spain, and probably North Africa. Adelard translated Euclid's *Elements,* on geometry and mathematics, from two Arabic translations that had been made in the eighth and ninth centuries; no Latin version had survived. Adelard's translation was used by Roger Bacon in the thirteenth century and became the basis of all editions in Europe until 1533. Adelard also translated al-Khwarizmi's astronomical tables and the *Liber ysagogarum alchorismi,* on arithmetic and geometry. In the thirteenth century, Leonardo Fibonacci of Pisa acquired a knowledge of Arabic mathematics while he was in North Africa, and thus paved the way for the Hindu-Arabic numerals to become widely known in the West.[50]

Western scholars learned much from Arabic-writing philosophers and scientists, but also subjected their work to critical scrutiny. The West institutionalized the study of Greek and Arabic writers—Euclid, Avicenna, Averroës, al-Khwarizmi, and others—by incorporating their works into the university curriculum. One of the reasons why the scientific tradition died out in Islamic civilization was an inability to pass on knowledge through independent educational institutions like those that developed in Europe. There were deeper reasons for this decline as well. Early Islamic civilization had been open to outside influences, deriving much of value from the legacy of the Greeks and Romans, Persians and Indians; but then, at a crucial point, "foreign sciences" were rejected. The result was intellectual stagnation and decay.

Muslim authorities such as the leading theologian al-Ghazali (1058–1111) strongly emphasized the priority of faith and tradition over human reason, and discouraged the pursuit of knowledge for its own sake. All learning was to be subordinated to religious learning, the highest and worthiest form of knowledge.[51] The good Muslim must refrain from investigating nature and from questioning the Koran or the hadith; those who strayed from the pure faith of Allah and his messenger to embark on scientific research were in danger of going to hell.[52] In his *Deliverance from Error*, al-Ghazali accused the two Islamic philosophers who most influenced Western science and philosophy, Avicenna and al-Farabi, of being in thrall to the "vicious unbelief" of Plato, Socrates, and Aristotle.[53] The idea that human reason could be a source of law or ethics was considered blasphemous.

This essentially antihumanist philosophy stands in stark contrast to the outlook that was emerging in Europe during the eleventh century, marked by a heightened confidence in human powers and in the ability of reason to gain knowledge of the world.[54] William of Conches (ca. 1090–c. 1154) identified different powers of the mind and their functions:

> *Intelligence is the force of the intellect whereby man perceives the immaterial, after reason has made him certain of the cause of its existence. Reason—that force or function by which the mind is able to compare and contrast that which exists with other existent things. Memory is that function which allows man firmly to retain what he has thus previously understood.*[55]

Medieval Christian philosophers believed that the rational faculties not only came from God, but represented the likeness of God in man. John of Salisbury (c. 1120–1180) described reason as a special gift that lifted man above other creatures: "All who possess real insight agree that nature, the most loving mother and wise arranger of all that exists, elevated man by the privilege of reason, and distinguished him by the faculty of speech." This rational capacity enables man to investigate the mysteries of the world around him: "While grace fructifies nature, reason looks after the observation and examination of facts, probes the secret depths of nature and estimates all utility and worth."[56]

It appears that only the West cultivated the notion of man as a rational creature able to understand the universe without the aid of revelation or spiritual agencies, and to describe the laws that govern it. While Islamic theologians rejected the very concept of rational agency and denied that the universe was orderly, Christian thinkers viewed the natural world as a rationally ordered place and thus accessible to understanding by reason. This idea, which had some grounding in Judeo-Christian theology, gained further support when medieval scholars read Plato's work, particularly the *Timaeus*. Here they found an image of man as a creature elevated by virtue of reason within the cosmic order, and a picture of the cosmos itself as an integrated whole, orderly in design and function, governed by laws of cause and effect. They also found a set of ideas that helped them develop a model for the investigation of nature, including the principle of causality, the idea of process in nature, an awareness of mathematical structure in the physical world, the necessity of empirical observation, the joining of inductive and deductive reasoning, the use of hypothesis, and an acceptance of the uncertainty that surrounds "merely probable knowledge."[57]

Platonism influenced many areas of inquiry in the Middle Ages, even the study of scripture. One of the philosophers inspired by Plato, Hugh of Saint Victor (c. 1096–1141), saw a rational principle connecting everything in the universe: "The ordered disposition of things from top to bottom in the network of this universe . . . is so arranged that, among all the things that exist, nothing is unconnected or separable by nature, or external to it."[58] Thierry of Chartres (c. 1100–c. 1150) described how the world appeared to have come into being through a predictable sequence of cause and effect, adding, "This existence and this order can be shown to be rational."[59] For Adelard of Bath, God's creation is "the product of a rational nature," and therefore "it is possible for men to achieve an understanding of this rational order inherent in nature, an understanding as complete as the extent that human knowledge [*scientia*] progresses."[60]

These philosophers believed that all activity of reason honors the glory of God. Rational pursuits made one a better Christian, thought William of Conches, and therefore scientific research was a religious activity.[61] The investigation of nature came to be understood as a way to celebrate the glory of God's work and show gratitude for the gift of the universe.[62]

Twelfth-century thinkers in the West asserted that rational inquiry was a better source of truth than unquestioning acceptance of authority. According to Peter Abelard (1079–1142), "Authority is inferior to reason because it deals with opinions about the truth rather than with truth itself, while reason concerns the thing itself and can settle the question."[63] Adelard of Bath explained that "authority alone cannot create belief in the thought of a philosopher nor even lead one towards such belief, and this is why logicians agree that citing authority does not even necessarily add probability to a given argument." Authority was a poor substitute for reason, a point he illustrated by declaring, "I am not a man who can satisfy his hunger from a picture of a steak!"[64]

For some philosophers, there were no limits to the subjects that reason could examine or the authorities that could be submitted to rational scrutiny. William of Conches fearlessly asserted that it was permissible to disagree with the greatest thinkers of the past, including the church fathers, "for even though they were greater men than we are, yet they were men."[65] Berengar of Tours (c. 999–1088) held that doctrines of the church should be examined through the rational process of dialectic, "which is superior to all authorities and which was used by Augustine and even by Christ himself. Whatever is illogical, notably, the doctrine of transubstantiation, is necessarily false." Truth is attained, he said, "not by decrees of the Church . . . but by reason, which is the image of God in man."[66]

The Pauline notion of conscience (*synderesis*)[67] also supported the liberation of reason from external authorities, so that man could arrive at moral truths unaided by scripture, and the individual conscience could even become the judge of scripture. Thierry of Chartres introduced one of his biblical commentaries as "an exegetical study of the first portion of Genesis from the point of view of an investigator of natural processes and of the literal meaning of the text."[68] William of Conches likewise examined the Bible in a scientific manner and declared that its irrational elements should not be taken literally. These medieval scholars may be called the fathers of biblical criticism, setting a precedent for the more radical critiques of Spinoza in the seventeenth century.

SCIENCE AND INTELLECTUAL FREEDOM

The natural philosophers of the twelfth-century renaissance contributed important concepts and attitudes to the scientific revolution in the sixteenth and seventeenth centuries. First, they had confidence in the ability of reason to fathom the world around them. They recognized the importance of observation and verification, and of mathematics as a tool for measuring their observations and formulating results. The outcome of these efforts, remarked Herbert Butterfield, was to transform "the whole diagram of the physical universe and the very texture of human life," as well as changing "the character of men's habitual mental operations." This was a true revolution, an event of such consequence that it "outshines everything since the rise of Christianity and reduces the Renaissance and Reformation to the rank of mere episodes, mere internal displacements, within the system of medieval Christendom." The scientific revolution, in Butterfield's view, was "the real origin both of the modern world and of the modern mentality."[69]

From the medieval revival to the beginning of the scientific revolution, new ideas could spread easily through Europe largely because Latin served as a common language of learning. Scholars and scientists corresponded with each other across Europe, aided by improving mail service. They founded societies of learning, which published their own periodical journals. One important network for the exchange of scientific ideas centered around Marin Mersenne (1588–1648), a theologian, philosopher, mathematician, music theorist, and defender of Galileo who helped translate some of his works. "The sciences have sworn inviolable friendship to one another," said Mersenne, a view that encouraged the fruitful exchange of ideas with other scholars in several countries.[70]

While intellectual freedom permitted scholars to probe the secrets of nature and even criticize religious doctrine, it also resulted in a great increase in literacy that had no parallel elsewhere in the world. For example, Lawrence Stone found that by 1640, "over half the male population of London was literate," and the proportion of adult males across the country who could read was also growing.[71] Protestantism gave momentum to a broadening of literacy and the ideal of universal education, in part because Protestant reformers starting with Martin Luther believed that reading the Bible was a religious duty for every Christian and that it should be made available in the vernacular. According to some economic historians, the encouragement of literacy accounts for "the entire Protestant lead in economic outcomes."[72] But literacy rates were rising all across Europe, along with a dramatic increase in the rate of book production following the invention of the printing press and the shift toward the vernaculars as scholarly languages. The printing press also gave birth to the daily newspaper, the first appearing in London in 1666. As Toby Huff put it, "There is hardly a more visible symbol of the intellectual freedom assumed to go along with a public sphere than the daily press."[73] By contrast, newspapers did not appear in the Islamic world until the nineteenth century, and literacy rates remain low even in the twenty-first century.

Intellectual freedom also involved learning to see an issue from different angles. In the twelfth century, Peter Abelard wrote a remarkable work for his students called *Sic et Non*, "Yes and No," in which he posed 158 questions that present a theological assertion followed by its negation. For example: "Must human faith be completed by reason, or not?" This format cultivated an ability to argue on both sides of a question and to see someone else's point of view, which is the basis of tolerance. Ramon Lull (1232–1315) once discussed the idea of unifying the three monotheistic religions, revealing an intellectual acceptance of differing beliefs. In a worked titled *De pace fidei*, "On the Peace of Faith," Nicolas Cusanus (1401–1464) imagined a summit meeting in heaven among representatives of all nations and religions, treating other religions with respect. In *Cribratio Alchorani*, "Sifting the Koran," Nicolas credited both Judaism and Islam with sharing some measure of the truth.

The long road from intellectual tolerance to critical pluralism led through humanists such as Marsilio Ficino in the fifteenth century, Guillaume Postel and Jean Bodin in the sixteenth, Locke and Milton in the seventeenth, Voltaire and Kant in the eighteenth, and J. S. Mill in the nineteenth. These and other European thinkers recognized the power of human reason but also its limitations, and they came to understand that the remedy for these limitations could be found in the freedom to criticize.

ᘒᘓ

CONSENT OF THE GOVERNED

In an Islamic theocracy, sovereignty belongs to God. Subjects are to obey unquestioningly the dictates of those who interpret the holy book. In a democracy, sovereignty rests with the people, who freely participate in their own governance, in making and enacting law. The ideals of popular sovereignty and freedom, supported by charters of rights and liberties, developed only in the West.[74] Democracy was nourished over the centuries by uniquely European principles and institutions such as the rule of law and a sense of individual autonomy.

The Middle Ages are often viewed in the popular imagination as a time of despotism, yet significant contributions to modern democracy grew out of that era. There is a democratic element in *The Rule of Saint Benedict* (c. 530), a book of precepts for monks living communally under the authority of an abbot. Besides being deeply consequential in shaping medieval monasticism, it was more widely influential in the formation of Europe, embodying the concepts of a written constitution and the rule of law, and bestowing dignity on manual labor. The Venetian Republic and other city-states in medieval Italy, some of them modeled on the Roman Republic, fostered the idea of citizens as participants in their own governance. In England, the Charter of Liberties issued when Henry I acceded to the throne in 1100 set limits on the king's powers regarding the treatment of church officials and nobles. The Magna Carta of 1215 was an effort to limit royal power by law, as well as protect the traditional privileges of the barons.

The sixteenth century produced some important anti-absolutist theories of government, while an influential school of theologians and jurists at the University of Salamanca developed ideas of natural rights, popular sovereignty, the separation of powers, and international law. During the English Civil War in the seventeenth century, the Levellers' manifesto, "Agreement of the People," emphasized popular sovereignty, equality before the law, and religious tolerance. From England's upheavals came republican political theorists—such as John Milton, James Harrington, and Algernon Sidney—who profoundly influenced the American Founding Fathers. Sidney recognized that a political order had to account for human fallibility: "Our inquiry is not after that which is perfect, well knowing that no such thing is found among men; but we seek that human Constitution which is attended with the least, or the most pardonable inconveniences." Friedrich Hayek used this statement as an epigraph to *The Constitution of Liberty.*

One of the most basic elements of Western-style democracies is freedom of conscience, which is necessary for achieving true consent of the governed. And freedom of conscience, as Roger Scruton has argued, can be guaranteed only under a secular government.[75] The roots of secularism go back to the biblical distinction of priestly and kingly authority, which inspired medieval Christians to elaborate theories of the relationship between spiritual and temporal powers. The religious wars in Europe between 1540 and 1650 prompted many calls for a stricter separation of civil and ecclesiastical powers, from people like Spinoza, Milton, and Locke, as well as dissident Protestant sects.[76] Many Anabaptists, who had suffered persecution under both Protestant and Catholic authorities, argued that the state should not interfere in religious affairs, and vice versa. Leonard Busher, an Anabaptist, made a case for the separation of church and state in a tract he addressed to King James I of England, *Religious Peace: or, a Plea for Liberty of Conscience,* where he asserted that "as kings and bishops cannot command the wind, so they cannot command faith."[77]

John Locke, echoing certain church fathers such as Tertullian, likewise maintained that sincere religious belief must be freely adopted; it cannot result from the coercion that comes with state promotion of a particular religion. "Such is the nature of the understanding, that it cannot be compelled to the belief of any thing by outward force," wrote Locke. "Confiscation of estate, imprisonment, torments, nothing of that nature can have any such efficacy as to make men change the inward judgment that they have framed of things."[78]

Thomas Paine once presented a simple argument for why government by consent of the governed must be secular, beginning with the observation that if "something has been revealed to a certain person, and not revealed to any other person, it is revelation to that person only," while it is "hearsay to every other, and consequently they are not obliged to believe it."[79] In Paine's argument, as Thomas Nagel fleshes it out, the reasons given for political decisions must meet a certain standard of "higher-order impartiality" or objectivity, since they must appeal to all members of society, or specifically to all citizens who participate in the process of government. One should be prepared to present one's case to others in such a way that all can assess the argument on the same basis. The standard of impartiality is not met when "personal faith or revelation" is a part of the argument, because "to report your faith or revelation to someone else is not to give him what you have, as you do when you show him your evidence or give him your arguments." Without objective evidence, political debate degenerates into a "clash between irreconcilable subjective convictions" rather than a disagreement in the public domain.[80]

Secular law is made legitimate by the consent of those who must obey it.[81] Consent, in turn, grows from a climate of intellectual freedom. It is the ideal of freedom that fundamentally distinguishes Western societies from others, as Roger Scruton argues: "Without freedom there cannot be government by consent; and it is the freedom to participate in the process of government, and to protest against, dissent from, and oppose the decisions that are made in my name, that confer on me the dignity of citizenship. Put very briefly, the difference between the West and the rest is that Western societies are governed by politics; the rest are ruled by power."[82]

THE ENLIGHTENMENT

The secularizing of Western institutions is most strongly linked to the Enlightenment of the eighteenth century, but the "intellectual backbone" for the Enlightenment project everywhere in Europe came from a courageous Dutch Jew of the seventeenth century, Baruch Spinoza.[83] His *Tractatus Theologico-Politicus,* first published anonymously in Amsterdam in 1670, did more than any other work to spark this revolution in human history. Spinoza did not regard theology as an independent source of truth. Treating the Bible as a purely human text, he formulated "a new science of contextual Bible criticism . . . using reason as an analytical tool but not expecting to find philosophical truth embedded in Scriptural concepts," as Jonathan Israel explains.[84] Spinoza rejected the possibility of miracles and denounced the clergy for exploiting the credulity of the masses. His *Tractatus* set out a subtle theory on the nature of religion, but many of his ideas were easy to grasp even by the unlettered: "the identification of God with the universe, the rejection of organized religion, the abolition of Heaven and Hell, together with reward and punishment in the hereafter, a morality of individual happiness in the here and now, and the doctrine that there is no reality beyond the unalterable laws of Nature, and consequently, no Revelation, miracles or prophecy."[85]

While secular humanists tend to downplay the role of Christianity in the making of the West, emphasizing classical antiquity as the wellspring of Western civilization, there is an equal tendency on the other side to blame the Enlightenment for all the ills of the modern world, including the excesses of the French Revolution and fascism in the twentieth century. In his magisterial studies of the Enlightenment, Jonathan Israel highlights its positive legacy in promoting the equal dignity of all humans and liberation from superstition and oppression:

> *The Enlightenment—European and global—not only attacked and severed the roots of traditional European culture in the sacred, magic, kingship, and hierarchy, secularizing all institutions and ideas, but (intellectually and to a degree in practice) effectively demolished all legitimation of monarchy, aristocracy, woman's subordination to man, ecclesiastical authority, and slavery, replacing these with the principles of universality, equality, and democracy.*[86]

Israel distinguishes two broad tendencies running through the Enlightenment, one radical and democratic, the other moderate and antidemocratic, and he sees an unbridgeable chasm between them. Radical philosophers such as Diderot, d'Holbach, and Helvé-tius promoted a set of universal moral values: "democracy; racial and sexual equality; individual liberty of lifestyle; full freedom of thought, expression, and the press; eradication of religious author-ity from the legislative process and education; and full separation of church and state." The radicals judged all cultures by these prin-ciples. Moderate Enlightenment philosophers such as Voltaire, and those influenced by them, were more relativistic in their judgments. For example, according to Sir William Jones, a figure of the mod-erate Enlightenment, the British judiciary in Calcutta in the eigh-teenth century would ensure that British subjects were governed by British laws, while the natives would be "indulged in their own prejudices, civil and religious, and suffered to enjoy their own cus-toms unmolested." This relativism meant "preserving the caste system, among much else," notes Israel. "That such hierarchies of customs, morality, and law were being extended in the world was anathema to the radical thinkers."[87] Today, cultural relativism in the West discourages cross-cultural judgments, thus impeding the reform of injustices around the world and inhibiting the defense of Western civilization.

ECONOMIC LIBERALISM

Liberal democracy in the West was supported by a scientific study of economics that resulted in theories emphasizing freedom and individual autonomy. Modern concepts of money came down from Aristotle via the great Scholastics of the thirteenth century, such as Thomas Aquinas and Albertus Magnus. In sixteenth-century Spain, economists from the School of Salamanca promoted the view that individuals have a right to own property and to benefit exclusively from it. They also argued that private property stimulates economic activity, which in turn increases the general well-being. These ideas were further developed in the eighteenth century by economists such as Adam Smith, David Ricardo, and Jean-Baptiste Say (1767–1832), with their emphasis on free enterprise and competition, free trade and unrestricted circulation of capital. In short, liberty was the key to producing an "economic order more complex but also superior in performance to traditional orders or managed orders."[88]

In the twentieth century, Friedrich Hayek and other representatives of the Austrian School refreshed the fundamental ideals of classical liberalism against the backdrop of menacing totalitarian experiments. Hayek argued that spontaneous order emerges in a society through the combined efforts of individuals who are free to exercise initiative and benefit from their own efforts. It is not a pre-existing natural order, nor can it be artificially established by an external authority. Rather, it is a self-organizing order that arises from pluralism and freedom.

Spontaneous order and freedom have had enemies on both the left and the right end of the political spectrum. On the right have been those who envision a natural order embodied in feudal and monarchic regimes, ruling over an agricultural and crafts-based society. On the left are those who fervently believe they can impose a more just and rational order upon society—a belief that has resulted in the totalitarian systems of Nazism and communism, and the offshoots that persist today. These regimes betrayed and scorned the Western values that had grown and matured over a period of centuries: the notions of the civic state, private property, Roman law, Christian charity, the autonomous person, and the individual conscience. The totalitarian regimes misunderstood or mistrusted the spontaneous order of complex modern societies; and having destroyed it, they created only misery in its place, sacrificing millions of lives on the altar of an artificial ideal. The horrific experiments of Nazism and communism served mostly to demonstrate the superiority of liberal democracy.[89]

⚘
EXPLOITATION THEORY

According to the doctrines of communist totalitarianism, the prosperity of Western industrial societies rests in large measure on exploitation of the rest of the world. Invoking the legacy of colonialism is a standby for Marxist-Leninists. V. I. Lenin argued that capitalism needs imperialism in order to survive, since it has to find new markets for its surplus in the less-developed nations, which it meanwhile drains of resources. England, for example, is alleged to have benefited enormously by the accumulation of capital through theft of natural resources and the exploitation of slave labor from its colonies in Asia, Africa, and the Americas.

Dependency theory, which originated in the late 1940s and was further developed in the 1950s by American Marxists, holds that resources flow from a "periphery" of poor and underdeveloped states to a "core" of wealthy states, enriching the latter at the expense of the former, which are said to be deliberately kept in a state of dependency. In this theory, it is because of exploitation that rich nations are rich—and poor nations are poor.[90] Jared Diamond explains the poverty of Africa partly by saying that much of the continent is "still struggling with its legacies from recent colonialism."[91] But even African economists do not believe that nonsense.[92] If colonialism could explain the wealth and poverty of nations, it would be difficult to account for the impressive prosperity of the former British colonies of Hong Kong and Singapore, and the onetime Japanese colonies of South Korea and Taiwan.[93]

Another theme in the exploitation school is that the use of slaves and profits from the slave trade supported Western prosperity. But David Richardson, a leading historian of the slave trade, has argued that slave-trading profits "could have contributed at best only small amounts to financing early British industrial expansion."[94] The economic historians Stanley Engerman and Patrick O'Brien have shown that the trade in slaves, which was only a small fraction of Britain's or Europe's trade, did not generate big profits.[95] Robert Paul Thomas and Richard Bean found that the greatest profits in the trade were most likely earned by those Africans who captured the slaves in the interior.[96] The Arab or Ottoman participation in the slave trade predated the Atlantic slave trade by centuries, yet it did not spark an industrial revolution in Arab or Ottoman lands.

David Eltis and Stanley Engerman have argued that the slave trade constituted "a relatively small share of the Atlantic trade of any European power. Its direct contribution to the economic growth of any nation was trivial."[97] They found that sugar cultivation depending on slave labor was not high in value added or in strategic linkages compared with other British industries.[98] Moreover, the beginning of the industrial revolution occurred well before the most intensive period of the British slave trade.[99]

Similarly, Western nations had already produced key innovations of the industrial revolution, such as steam power and steel ships, before they became imperial powers.[100] British India did not yield any economic benefit to the average person in Britain, according to Deirdre McCloskey, although some individuals did become immensely rich.[101] The British public paid for the British Empire and got little out of it. The same applies to other European colonial empires. "The glorious Spanish and Portuguese empires," notes McCloskey, "left Spain and Portugal at the last among the poorest countries in Europe."[102] By contrast, France's prosperity rested on "French law, French style, French labor, French banking, French education, French originality, French openness to ideas," rather than on "lording it over poor Muslims in Africa and poor Buddhists in Vietnam."[103]

After the British India Company was dissolved in 1874, Britain continued to trade with India, but this trade was smaller than

Britain's trade with rich European countries or the United States. Moreover, contrary to Marxist notions, "trade is trade, not looting," notes McCloskey.[104] Far from stifling India's home industries, British imperialism allowed the Indian cotton textile factories to grow. Om Prakash, an Indian economic historian, comments that "India's cotton-mill history seems paradoxical: it flourished despite competing against the most important, the most internationally aggressive and politically most powerful industry in Britain," so that "by 1910 the Indian industry had become one of the world's largest."[105]

A leading figure of the Latin American dependency school, Fernando Henrique Cardoso, after becoming the finance minister of Brazil, came to the bitter realization that his country needed trade with other countries, especially those rich, capitalist nations he had previously regarded as enemies. Unless Brazil became a part of the global economy, it would be unable to compete. "It is not an imposition from outside. It's a necessity for us," wrote Cardoso.[106]

Thus we can no longer defend the notion that Western prosperity is founded on the exploitation of poor people in the Third World. The rich countries are rich because of their practices at home, and because of their readiness to adopt and adapt new things, such as Chinese inventions or New World crops.[107] Jared Diamond concluded that the "proximate factors" in Europe's ascendance were "its development of a merchant class, capitalism, and patent protection for inventions, its failure to develop absolute despots and crushing taxation, and its Greco-Judeo-Christian tradition of empirical inquiry."[108] Ironically, given other pronouncements by Diamond, some readers disparaged this as ethnocentric, or "utterly conventional Eurocentric history," in James M. Blaut's words.[109] But Diamond, in fact, was pointing to some key ingredients of Western success; and behind those proximate factors were culture, ideas, and attitudes.

BOURGEOIS VIRTUES

Addressing the question of what happened at the end of the eighteenth century that enabled first Britain and then the rest of western Europe to increase their wealth sixteenfold, Deirdre McCloskey summed up the answer in the title of her book, *Bourgeois Dignity: Why Economics Can't Explain the Modern World.* "A change in rhetoric about prudence, and about the other and peculiarly human virtues, exercised in a commercial society, started the material and spiritual progress," she contends.[110] A new respect for "bourgeois virtues" in combination with liberty resulted in the "innovation backed by liberal economic ideas that has made billions of poor people pretty well off, without hurting other people."[111]

The industrial revolution also depended on a store of knowledge and knowhow that had been accumulating since the Middle Ages, and on the intellectual freedom that allowed for science and experimentation. Europeans broke away from tradition, cultivating a vogue for the new and a sense of progress. They learned to experiment, and they invented instruments to aid their observation and measurement. The industrial revolution in Europe "would not have been possible without the scientific revolution" and the resulting Newtonian view of the world, says Toby Huff.[112] A combination of scientific curiosity and entrepreneurial energy prompted Europeans to explore the world and make contact with Asia and America. The same energy and curiosity led Europeans to expand their sum of knowledge as fast as possible. Europeans were eager to adopt new ideas, improve upon them, and put their knowledge to practical use. By 1600, Joel Mokyr notes, Europeans "knew better than anyone else how to sail the globe, make clocks, compute interest using logarithms, pump water from mines."[113]

Europeans were also "far better than any other society in dissem-inating the knowledge among themselves as well as transmitting it from generation to generation."[114] The development of modern aca-demic institutions owed much to the vision of Wilhelm von Hum-boldt (1767–1835), the minister responsible for educational reform in Prussia. Humboldt was the founding father of the University of Ber-lin, which became the model for universities throughout Europe and the United States. His treatise *On the Internal and External Organi-zation of the Higher Scientific Institutions in Berlin* presents knowl-edge as an end in itself and makes the case for academic freedom.

Over the centuries, the West built up a defining set of institutions and ideals. They are not the exclusive property of the West, however; anyone can rationally choose to live by them without feeling he is thereby betraying his tribe. These values include religious tolerance, freedom of conscience, freedom of speech, respect for the individual, protection of human rights, the rule of law, equality before the law, separation of church and state, representative democracy, separation of powers, constitutional limits on state power, freedom of trade, honoring of contracts, private property rights, academic freedom, the encouragement of skeptical and critical thinking, and the meth-ods of scientific research.[115] These are the reasons for the success of the West. We have a moral responsibility to be grateful for this legacy and to defend it.

DRUGS, SEX, AND ROCK 'N' ROLL; OR, THE MYTH OF EASTERN SPIRITUALITY AND WESTERN MATERIALISM

In *The Enemy at Home,* Dinesh D'Souza argues that one of the causes of the September 11 terrorist attack was the way the American cultural left exported "a decadent American culture that angers and repulses traditional societies, especially those in the Islamic world that are being overwhelmed with this culture." The left, he charges, "is waging an aggressive global campaign to undermine the traditional patriarchal family and to promote secular values in non-Western cultures. This campaign has provoked a violent reaction from Muslims who believe that their most cherished beliefs and institutions are under assault."[1] It is as though Britney Spears had conspired with Hollywood to foist an irreligious, sexually licentious, antifamily culture onto the Muslim world.

D'Souza's thesis is morally dubious, however. First of all, the West is not imposing its culture on anyone. Part of the genius of Western and particularly American popular culture is its appeal to millions of people—across national, religious, and ethnic boundaries—who seek it out and pay for it willingly. Second, Western popular culture is a manifestation of cultural, intellectual, and political freedom, and its excesses are the price we pay for the joyful expressions of its more enduring creations, such as the songs of Bob Dylan or the Beatles, and cinematic classics such as *It's a Wonderful Life, Some Like It Hot,* and *Casablanca.* Far from being uniformly bad, Western popular culture often surprises by its inventiveness. To watch Fred Astaire is to witness a committed creative artist in total control of his gifts, performing his art with elegance and with infectious, life-affirming exhilaration, like a bright lantern in dreary times. The charm and wit of *The Thin Man*—based on Dashiell Hammett's novel, with screenplay by Albert Hackett and Frances Goodrich, starring William Powell and Myrna Loy—is as good as anything by Sacha Guitry, and certainly better than the affected plays of Noel Coward.

Rock 'n' roll, suggested Tom Stoppard, has functioned not just as entertainment but as a potent weapon against totalitarian ideologies. Fun for the sake of fun, music for the sake of music, any activity for its own sake is something that totalitarian regimes cannot cope with, as F. A. Hayek long ago argued. In "The Power of the Powerless," Vaclav Havel wrote that attending a rock concert was a way to rebel "against being manipulated by the Communist regime," a way of "living in truth."[2] On hearing the songs of a Czech rock group called the Plastic People of the Universe, Havel remarked, "There was disturbing magic in the music, and a kind of inner warning. Here was something serious and genuine. . . . Suddenly I realized that, regardless of how many vulgar words these people used or how long their hair was, truth was on their side." The music conveyed "an experience of metaphysical sorrow and a longing for salvation."[3] When the members of the band were imprisoned, it struck Havel as "an attack by the totalitarian system on life itself, on the very essence of human freedom and integrity." These were only young people who wanted to express themselves truthfully.[4]

As Stoppard explained, "The band was not interested in bringing down Communism, only in finding a free space for itself in the Communist society. But of course there was no such space." The authorities were unable to comprehend these "pagans" who were apolitical, who didn't care how they looked, but only cared about their music, and who were uncompromising in their demand for freedom to write and perform whatever they wanted. The rock 'n' roll underground became, in effect, "an attack on the official culture of Communist Czechoslovakia."[5]

If Stoppard is right, then we need more "decadent" rock bands, not fewer, to bring down the latest totalitarian threat to our freedoms. D. H. Lawrence would undoubtedly have approved of the rockers, for he once pleaded:

If you make a revolution, make it for fun,
don't make it in ghastly seriousness,
don't do it in deadly earnest,
do it for fun.
Don't do it because you hate people,
do it just to spit in their eye.
Don't do it for the money,
do it and be damned to the money.

This embrace of fun may be rejected by the authorities in the Islamic world, but it is a mistake to believe that we in the West are hated because of something we have done and that we must therefore change our behavior to appease those who hate us. "The illusion that we are to blame, that we must confess our faults and join our cause to that of our enemies, only exposes us to a more determined hatred," as Roger Scruton eloquently put it. "The truth is that we are not to blame; that our enemies' hatred of us is entirely unjustified; that their implacable enmity cannot be defused by our breast-beating."[6] Islamists have been unable to cope with the modern world that was created principally by Western institutions and cultural values, by the ingenuity, creativity, intellectual curiosity, and energy of Western civilization. The failures of their own civilization at every level have left them full of dangerous resentment, so they try to impose a rival ideology on the rest of the world. Their expressed grievances may change, but the underlying ideology remains the same.[7]

∽

MUSLIM FAMILY VALUES

In his effort to accuse the American cultural left of provoking the Islamic world by undermining its values, Dinesh D'Souza betrays a romantic, idealized vision of Muslim domestic life. He would have us believe that strong families are particularly valued in Islamic culture. But the Qatar Statistics Authority, for instance, reported that eighty divorces a month were recorded in 2009, and around half of all marriages ended in divorce. The lawyer Rashid Al-Marri revealed that "80% of divorces in Qatar see the husband accused of beating his wife." An article published by an Italian news agency painted a grim picture for divorced women in Qatar, where sharia governs family matters: "While the man is able to find another partner easily, the woman is branded for life. . . . Indeed, divorced women are stigmatised in this part of the world and are considered outsiders to Islam." They suffer "defamation and indifference from society as a whole," and many develop psychiatric illnesses.[8]

A number of scholars, including Muslims, have written about the traumatic effects of Muslim childrearing practices on both men and women.[9] Tawfik Hamid, who once belonged to the inner circle of the Egyptian Muslim Brotherhood, holds Islamic social and family dynamics responsible for the creation of terrorists. In *The Roots of Jihad,* he explains his thesis:

> *Islamic terrorism stems from personality changes which occur in those who try to be sincere followers of their religion. These changes initially affect the relationship of a Muslim to his children, his wife and his neighbours. But the change becomes greater and greater until, at the end, a person becomes quite evil. It is not hard to understand how beating your children to force them to pray, beating your wife to discipline her, and thinking that your neighbor's house deserves to be burned because he does not go to the mosque to pray, can become consuming dimensions in a Muslim's personality, and part of the religious duties to be followed.*[10]

Howard Bloom similarly attributes the violence of Arab societies to the character of their family relationships. In *The Lucifer Principle,* he refers to Lila Abu-Lughod's research on the Bedouin, who outlaw "close, warm relationships between men and women" and regard romantic love as "immoral."[11] He also cites the observations of Hisham Sharabi, who was a professor at Georgetown University, on the intolerable repression of Arab children, and of Halim Barakat, a sociologist of Syrian origin raised in Beirut, who blamed the plight of the Muslim Levant on the structure of its families.[12] Bloom concludes:

> *Islamic mothers tend to be warm and nurturing, but Islamic fathers treat their children harshly, acting cold, distant, and wrathful. Their justification is an old religious proverb: "Father's anger is part of God's anger." When he reaches puberty, an Arab boy is expelled from the loving world of his mother and sisters into the realm of men. There, hand-holding between males is still allowed, but physical affection between men and women is frowned upon. A vengeful masculinity stands in its place. The result: violent adults.*[13]

In 1995, Bloom offered this prophetic analysis: "In much of Arab society, the unmerciful approach of fathers to their children continues, and public warmth between men and women is still considered an evil. Perhaps thus is why a disproportionate number of Arab adults, stripped of intimacy and thrust into a life in which vulnerable emotion is a sin, have joined extremist movements dedicated to wreaking havoc on the world."[14]

℘

SEX AND DRUGS IN THE EAST

. . . if way to the Better there be, it exacts a full
look at the Worst . . .
—THOMAS HARDY, "IN TENEBRIS II"

There is indeed decadence in the West, as Dinesh D'Souza says. But does he really believe that Muslim societies are free of immodest sexual behavior and drug abuse, not to mention alcoholism? Let me offer some sobering statistics:

- The highest numbers of drug addicts in the world are to be found not in New York but in Pakistan, according to Al Jazeera English news.[15]
- Reuters reported in 2009 that Iran has 130,000 new drug addicts each year.[16]
- A report published in the *Guardian* in 2010 said that approximately one million people in Pakistan have a drinking problem.[17]
- Child prostitution is found throughout Asia, including Afghanistan, Pakistan, and Bangladesh; and 95 percent of the teenage prostitutes in Islamabad, Rawalpindi, and Lahore were sexually abused by close relatives, friends, or teachers before they entered the trade.[18]

- There are between 15,000 and 20,000 child sex workers living near bus stands and railway stations in Lahore. Male child prostitution is more common than any other form of commercial sexual exploitation in Pakistan.[19]
- Practically every city in Pakistan, from Peshawar to Quetta, has child prostitution, and the abuse of children generally is rising.[20]
- Banafsheh Zand-Bonazzi uncovered a remarkable advertisement that documents the Iranian regime's approval of a brothel at Imam Reza's shrine in the holy city of Mashad. It refers to the institutionalized prostitution called *muta,* or "temporary marriage," in Shia Islam, whereby a man marries a woman for a specific length of time in return for a sum of money.[21]

The excesses of Western popular culture—a price we pay for our freedom—can make a person cringe and render the defense of Western civilization more difficult. But the freedom and openness of Western societies mean that our ills are exposed publicly, while some of the worst aspects of Islamic societies are hidden from the outside world. Notions of shame and honor forbid the public display of one's own shortcomings. In recent years, however, Asian political leaders and the media have openly acknowledged the problems of drug abuse, HIV infection, child abuse, child labor, forced prostitution, and the plight of women. Nonetheless, the extent of these problems is not well known in the West.

Drug abuse is the first accusation hurled at the West by self-righteous Muslims, as though such a problem could not exist in the lands where Islam predominates. But in 2000, the BBC reported that Pakistan was "amongst the world's top countries for the numbers of addicts." The story quoted a UN official saying that "A particular problem [is] the rising number of injecting heroin abusers," and referred to a nongovernmental organization's estimate that the number of heroin addicts was increasing at a rate of 100,000 per year.[22] In 2010, Al Jazeera reported that Pakistan had "the highest number of drug addicts in the world," with at least five million people using heroin, opiates, or other mind-altering substances.[23] About 25 to 30 million lives are adversely affected by the addiction of relatives.[24] Two Pakistani parliamentarians cited the ban on alcohol as the reason for the growing rate of drug addiction.[25] On the other hand, the *Guardian* reported in 2010 that approximately ten million people drank alcohol in Pakistan.[26]

Drug use is a problem in Iran, too. A report by the United Nations found that in 2005 Iran had the highest rate of drug addiction in the world, involving 2.8 percent of the population over age fifteen. "With a population of about 70 million and some government agencies putting the number of regular users close to 4 million, Iran has no real competition as world leader in per capita addiction to opiates, including heroin," said the *Washington Post* story. The director of the Iranian National Center for Addiction Studies estimated that 20 percent of Iran's adult population was "somehow involved in drug abuse."[27] On April 7, 2005, Akbar Alami, a member of Iran's parliament, stated publicly that the actual number of drug users in Iran was close to 11 million.[28] Drug addiction is also the main cause for the spread of HIV/AIDS in Iran.

According to some analysts, a high unemployment rate and a lack of social freedom are among the main reasons for drug use by Iran's young people. A twenty-year-old resident of Tehran said that many of his friends used drugs as a way to escape. "We don't have entertainment here, and drugs are very cheap and easy to get," Amir explained, adding that "whenever young people get together, the only thing they think about is getting and using drugs because it makes them happy. And also because of the problems they have, they want to get rid of these problems for some time. They have no hope in the future. They think there is no future for them in Iran."[29] Under the theocratic regime, Iran's youth get heavy doses of Islam, which clearly does not keep them away from drugs. Perhaps a little rock 'n' roll might make the drug situation better rather than worse.

While drug addiction is a major problem among young men in Iran, the number of female drug users is also said to be growing, and it is linked with prostitution. Iranian newspapers estimated in 2005 that about 300,000 women were working the streets. Many had run away from abusive families. An Iranian filmmaker, Nahid Persson, won several international awards for her courageous clandestine documentary on the plight of young prostitutes and the problem of drug abuse in Iran. *Prostitution Behind the Veil* follows Fariba and Minna, two young women on the streets of Tehran who are close friends. Both acquired a heroin addiction through a drug-addicted husband. "Their life was about finding clients and getting money so that they could buy an egg or some food for their children," said Persson. "And because of their addiction, they had to buy heroin. They didn't have a normal life. When one becomes addicted to drugs, one forgets about [real] life."[30]

Another reason why many women become prostitutes in Iran is poverty. Statistics released by the Iranian government show that at least half the population live below the poverty line, and the deputy health minister admitted that 20 percent of Iranians were going hungry daily. Only 11 percent of Iranian women are employed, and girls are twice as likely as boys to be deprived of education.[31]

It is women, along with non-Muslim minorities, who suffer most in Islamic societies. The constitution of the Islamic Republic of Iran explicitly reduces women to second-class citizens. A segregated healthcare system means that many women receive inadequate attention because there are not enough well-trained female doctors and nurses. A raped woman is liable to be executed or stoned to death on grounds of fornication.

Since the mullahs took power in 1979, tens of thousands of Iranian women, including dozens of pregnant women, have been executed for opposing the regime's policies. Many more have been imprisoned and tortured, usually raped repeatedly in prison; some have body parts amputated. Women were arrested and imprisoned just for participating in a demonstration of forty thousand teachers outside the Majlis (parliament) in January 2002. At least twenty-two women were sentenced to stoning or were stoned to death during Khatami's presidency (1997–2005).[32] The election of Ahmadinejad in June 2005 was certainly no improvement. In January 2006, the Women's Forum Against Fundamentalism in Iran issued a press release saying that "Iranian women have seen a new wave of nation-wide suppression, attacks and violence sponsored by Ahmadinejad's regime. Alarmed by ongoing protests and strikes throughout the country, Mahmoud Ahmadinejad and his government are once again targeting and escalating violence against women to instill fear in society."[33]

Not surprisingly, the rate of mental illness is very high among women, as is the rate of suicide. In Ilam, a western province of Iran, for example, about 70 percent of those who commit suicide are reported to be women, most of them between seventeen and thirty-five years old. According to the World Health Organization, Iran has the third highest rate of suicide in the world.[34]

Children also are subjected to various kinds of mistreatment in the Islamic world. The sexual abuse of children is widespread in the Muslim East, where girls as young as nine can be married off to middle-aged men. Girls ages ten to seventeen are the main victims of sexual slavery in Iran; 90 percent of runaway girls become prostitutes or are sold in the human-trafficking market of the Persian Gulf.[35] Approximately 700,000 children ages ten to fourteen work in black-market labor in Iran.[36]

The United Nations Children's Fund (UNICEF) reported in 2005 that less than 30 percent of adolescents (ages eleven to nineteen) in Pakistan were enrolled in school. Many Pakistani children work in the streets, on farms, as domestic workers, or as industrial labor-ers, particularly in brick kilns and the carpet-weaving industry. An estimated 3.6 million children under the age of fourteen are doing hazardous or exploitative labor. Only one-third of all Pakistani children under the age of five have been registered at birth; those without an official identity are the most vulnerable to abuse and exploitation. In Pakistan, the age of criminal responsibility is seven. Children are sometimes jailed together with adults and are physically and sexually abused. From 2000 to 2004, the media in Pakistan reported more than 17,000 cases of child abuse, along with murder, rape, honor killing, and police torture of women and children.[37]

The West does not need lectures on moral virtue from societies in which vulnerable people are routinely abused and exploited in so many ways.

THE NOBLE SAVAGE AND OTHER MYTHS

Many Western intellectuals are quick to criticize the West for its failings, real or imagined, while they exaggerate the virtues of other cultures, which they paint as being guided by primordial wisdom and superior ethics. Sometimes the efforts to glorify preindustrial societies can be rather comical. In *The Handbook of North American Indians* (1911), Franz Boas provided four Eskimo words for snow, noting the distinct roots of *aput* (snow on the ground) and *gana* (falling snow). Benjamin Lee Whorf expanded the list in 1940, proposing at least seven distinct Eskimo words for snow in an article that appeared in the MIT journal *Technology Review*. From there the number grew steadily, reaching almost four hundred in some popular accounts—implying an extraordinary degree of verbal nuance. In fact, one could perhaps find fourteen words in an Eskimo language to describe different kinds of snow or snowy and icy conditions; but one could find more in English (avalanche, sleet, blizzard, slush, dusting, flurry, frost, hail, powder, hardpack, spindrift, icicle, iceshockle, berg, growler, calf, serac, nieve, glacier, firn, slob ice, graupel, rime, hoar, permafrost, etc., along with various compound words: snowflake, snowstorm, snowball, snowman, snowbank, and the like).[38]

In the introduction to his Pulitzer-winning book *Guns, Germs, and Steel: The Fates of Human Societies,* Jared Diamond displays the muddled thinking and clichés that can result from the effort to establish the superiority of non-Westerners. On the one hand, he rejects racially based explanations for disparities in economic achievement—how brave of him!—and calls such ideas "loathsome" and "wrong." Diamond says that "Sound evidence for the existence of human differences in intelligence that parallel human differences in technology is lacking."[39] Then, with a breathtaking jump in logic, he claims in the very next sentence that "modern 'Stone Age' peoples are on the average probably more intelligent, not less intelligent, than industrialized peoples."[40] So, it is "loathsome" and "wrong" and "racist" to suggest that whites are more intelligent than aborigines, but one can assert with impunity that the aborigines are more intelligent than industrialized peoples. "From the very beginning of my work with New Guineans," he writes, "they impressed me as being on the average more intelligent, more alert, more expressive, and more interested in things and people around them than the average European or American is."[41] This assertion seems to leave open the possibility of a genetic difference in IQ between ethnic groups, but it is clearly a subjective impression. How many New Guineans did Diamond actually know? A hundred? A thousand? Why is it not racist and loathsome and wrong to make a sweeping claim of New Guinean superiority to Westerners on such a slender basis?

One might also question the grounds for Diamond's conclusion that most Westerners—850 million or so—are "privately and subconsciously" racist.[42] Europeans are brought on the stage as "colonialists" who seem to contribute little to civilization except for the subjugation and extermination of indigenous peoples in Australia, the Americas, and Africa. The fact that Native Americans and black Africans were killing each other long before the Europeans arrived is apparently of no concern to Diamond.

One popular myth is that Native Americans and other primitive cultures lived in harmony with nature before the white man's arrival among them. Unfortunately, the reality is more sobering. As Shepard Krech has shown, the American Indians often indulged in overkilling of wildlife and allowed overgrazing of the land.[43] Researchers have found that the inhabitants of Polynesia were no more environmentally sensitive. The Polynesian peoples originally came from the islands of Southeast Asia in outrigger canoes, bringing along "dogs, pigs, breadfruit seedlings, taro, and inevitably, rats to islands that had never seen the like," writes Nathaniel Philbrick. "Once on a new island, the Polynesians set to work re-creating an agricultural society similar to the one they had left behind, a process that led to the extinction of countless indigenous species of animals and plants." Archaeologists working on Upolu, an island of Samoa, concluded that it once held "between 100 and 242 people per square kilometer—a density that would have had a disastrous effect on the island's ecology." Another result of this overpopulation was "culturally sanctioned methods of population control—from infanticide to ritual sacrifice to cannibalism."[44] Herman Melville, particularly in *Omoo,* vividly described the limitations of life in the South Seas, in a way that evokes Marx and Engels' pronouncements about "the idiocy of rural life." The notion of ecological balance is, in reality, a modern Western construct.

Another myth that could be the subject of whole monographs is that of Eastern spiritual wisdom. Its origins can be found as early as Herodotus and the historians who followed Alexander the Great to India. Westerners are generally not familiar with the important place of atheistic and naturalistic traditions in Indian history. After examining the various early schools of Indian philosophy, Dale

Riepe found some that were "clearly naturalistic" or materialist, such as the Carvaka, with no room for a deity, immortality, a soul, or karma, and where the universe was seen as perpetually evolving. Several others were "certainly strong in some naturalistic elements." For example, "Theravada and Vaibhasika Buddhism and Jainism find no teleological principle in the world; they find no deity. They are, consequently, humanistic systems in which the individual man achieves the highest ethical goals without nonhuman aid."[45]

Riepe adds that since India gained independence, naturalism has again raised its ancient and honorable standard. Today there is a flourishing Atheist Centre in southern India. Undoubtedly the majority of the people of India are religious believers, but they are no more "spiritual," however defined, than the average Christian in the United States. They are mainly struggling to survive and trying to acquire the material benefits that Westerners take for granted. Many despair of ever having the worldly comforts that are flaunted in their faces in the cinema and in the richer parts of their cities, so they understandably find solace in religion.

Much has been made of Eastern mysticism. But Islamic mysticism, specifically Sufism, derived almost entirely from Gnosticism and eastern Christian mysticism, which themselves drew upon Neoplatonic ideas.[46] The West has a long tradition of mystical writings that rival anything in Buddhism or Hinduism. Here are a few of the Western Christian mystics: Saint Bernard of Clairvaux, Saint Francis of Assisi, Saint Bonaventura, Ramon Lull, Meister Eckhart, Jan van Ruysbroeck, Walter Hilton, Julian of Norwich, Saint Catherine of Siena, Margery Kempe, Thomas à Kempis, Saint Teresa of Avila, and Jacob Boehme.[47] But those disillusioned with "Western materialism" apparently find it more fulfilling to seek mystical experience in a tradition remote from Christianity—*ex oriente lux*. Heaven forbid that they admit that religious ecstasy of the mystical kind was equally available in the elegant verses of Saint John of the Cross.

As for mainstream Islam, can one seriously take its vision of the afterlife as "spiritual" when it offers only a crass materialism with all the delights of a celestial bordello? Rachid Boudjedra, an Algerian novelist and essayist, makes some scathing remarks about religion in Algeria and assails the hypocrisy of the majority—80 percent of the so-called believers is his figure—who pray (or pretend to pray) only in the month of Ramadan, who go on pilgrimage for the social prestige, who drink wine and fornicate yet claim to be good Muslims.[48] Many Muslims are impelled to pray now and then by a fear of hell and a desire to reserve a place for themselves in heaven, but in the rest of their lives they are no more "spiritual" than anyone else who lives for creature comforts.

"Spiritual" has become a hopelessly vague term, employed to mean an outpouring of emotion in the presence of the sentimental object of one's choosing. But if we take it to mean "relating to spirit, the mind, the higher faculties; highly refined in thought and feeling, habitually or naturally looking to things of the spirit,"[49] then I suggest that the person who saves up money for a pilgrimage to Bavaria to hear Wagner's operas at the Bayreuth Festspielhaus is probably more spiritual than the average "believer" of whatever faith who makes a pilgrimage to absolve his worldly sins or to have his body cured of some biological malady. The performance and appreciation of Western classical music are spiritual activities. Even the smallest of French villages takes pride in its annual music festival. The display of visual arts, the preservation of ancient monuments, the activities of the New York Historical Society, the meetings of the Poetry Society at Barnes & Noble, a visit to the Fra Angelico exhibition at the Metropolitan Museum of Art, a night at the opera—all are spiritual endeavors, involving the higher faculties. The West does show an interest in spiritual matters in the more conventional sense of going to church, for example, but also nurtures the life of the spirit and the mind in more varied ways than are available in the rest of the world.

✑
RELATIVISM OR UNIVERSAL VALUES?

The history of codifying human rights goes through the Greeks and the Bible, through various Western charters and philosophers—the Magna Carta, the English Declaration of Rights and Bill of Rights that followed the Glorious Revolution of 1688, John Locke, Montesquieu, the U.S. Constitution with its Bill of Rights—and eventually to the Universal Declaration of Human Rights in 1948. This document came out of the West after the defeat of Nazism and Fascism, a moment of moral clarity that suggested the necessity of proclaiming a universal set of ethical values. At the discussion stage, however, it became clear that Muslim states were not happy with all the articles, and particularly Article 18, which defended the right of an individual to change his religion.

Moreover, the executive board of the American Anthropological Association refused to endorse the Universal Declaration of Human Rights on the grounds that it was "ethnocentric." It went against the fashionable doctrine of cultural relativism, which eventually led to the disasters of "multiculturalism." Western anthropologists and other intellectuals, including Jean-Paul Sartre, along with Third World thinkers such Frantz Fanon, elaborated a concept of "Third-Worldism," in which the underdeveloped world could not be held responsible for its troubles. Encased in their provincialism and supported by Western intellectuals, Third World leaders blamed the West for the failures of their own cultures. Instead of asking themselves "What did we do wrong? How can we put it right?" they asked "Who did that to us?" This combination of relativism and victimhood has made it difficult to address various problems in an effective way.

Many British administrators in India were shocked by the Hindu custom of suttee (or sati), the burning of widows on the funeral pyres of their husbands, and by the practice of infanticide. Eventually, steps were taken to suppress them. But some British Orientalists were so sympathetic to Indian culture that they could not bring themselves to criticize any aspect of it. While attempting to see local customs from the perspective of the locals is commendable, it can lead to the kind of moral relativism that inhibits any reform. Moreover, uncritical acceptance of another's culture smacks of insincerity or even condescension. "We must not judge them by our standards" implies "They are not up to our standards," and thus, "They are not ready for reform." By contrast, the controversial Indian scholar Javed Majeed defends *The History of British India* by James Mill, which conveys nothing but contempt for Hindu culture, as a healthy antidote to Orientalist romanticism.[50]

It is surely legitimate to criticize many aspects of non-Western cultures. In the past, this could be done without drawing sullen accusations of "racism" or of "Orientalism" in Edward Said's pejorative sense. The philosopher Bernard Williams commented on a book by Bernal Díaz del Castillo, who accompanied Cortés to Mexico, and described their response to seeing the sacrificial temples. "This morally unpretentious collection of bravos was genuinely horrified by the Aztec practices," Williams remarked. "It would surely be absurd to regard this reaction as merely parochial or self-righteous. It rather indicated something which their conduct did not indicate, that they regarded the Indians as men rather than as wild animals."[51] Postmodernist relativism has discouraged this kind of frank cross-cultural judgment and even the ability to see our common humanity. As a result, we ignore the suffering and deny the rights of large sections of humankind.

Recently, a number of scholars from the Third World have acknowledged the primacy of culture in explaining the success or failure of nations, thereby suggesting that cultural changes within the Third World are the way to alleviate its difficulties. These scholars include Mariano Grondona, professor of government at the National University Buenos Aires; Carlos Alberto Montaner, author of several books on the economy of Latin American countries, and Daniel Etounga-Manguelle, a development expert from Cameroon. Certain Western scholars, such as Richard Shweder, professor of human development at the University of Chicago—who agreed with the decision of the American Anthropological Association to oppose the Universal Declaration of Human Rights—dubs these non-Western scholars "cosmopolitan intellectuals" who are not truly representative of their societies.[52]

Daniel Etounga-Manguelle put Shweder in his place with superb, withering sarcasm:

> We Africans really enjoy living in shantytowns where there isn't enough food, health care, or education for our children. Furthermore, our corrupt chieftaincy political systems are really marvelous and have permitted countries like Mobutu's Zaire to earn us international prestige and respect. Moreover, surely it would be terribly boring if free, democratic elections were organized all over Africa. Were that to happen, we would no longer be real Africans, and by losing our identity—and our authoritarianism, our bloody civil wars, our illiteracy, our forty-five year life expectancy—we would be letting down not only ourselves but also those Western anthropologists who study us so sympathetically and understand that we [Africans] can't be expected to behave like human beings who seek dignity on the eve of the third millennium [1998]. We are Africans, and our identity matters! So let us fight for it with the full support of those Western scholars who have the wisdom and courage to acknowledge that Africans belong to a different world.[53]

This is an eloquent reply to all the cultural relativists who refuse to see our common humanity, who view certain cultures as biological specimens that must be kept in quarantine lest they be contaminated by the outside world, and who regard all those who break free and criticize those cultures as traitors. There is nothing sacrosanct or fixed about a culture's customs and traditions; they can and do change with circumstances or transform under examination. As Daniel Patrick Moynihan once put it, "The central conservative truth is that it is culture, not politics, that determines the success of a society. The central liberal truth is that politics can change a culture and save it from itself."[54]

Janadas Devan, a journalist from Singapore, has argued that one must be skeptical of Asian leaders who justify tyranny by appealing to "Asian values."[55] In the late 1990s, the Asian Human Rights Commission issued an Asian Human Rights Charter that fully endorses the Universal Declaration of Human Rights along with other international instruments for the protection of rights and freedoms, including the International Covenant on Economic, Social and Cultural Rights, and the International Covenant on Civil and Political Rights.[56] There is no reason to think there are inherent psychological barriers to Asians accepting the principles of human rights as recognized in the West.

EAST VERSUS WEST?

Oh, East is East and West is West, and never the twain shall meet,
Till Earth and Sky stand presently at God's great Judgment
Seat; . . .

We are all familiar with these lines from Kipling's "Ballad of East and West." They seem to imply that "the peoples on opposite sides of the globe are so different that they will never understand each other until the Day of Judgment," as one of Kipling's biographers put it.[57] Less familiar are the following lines, which assert that differences of class, race, nation, or continent are irrelevant between two men of equal courage:

But there is neither East nor West, Border, nor Breed, nor Birth,
When two strong men stand face to face,
tho' they come from the ends of the earth!

Indeed, the divide between East and West is not unbridgeable, as the case of India demonstrates. John Strachey once invoked cricketing and parliamentary terminology to make the point: "To know a no ball from a googly and a point of order from a supplementary question is genuinely to have something in common."[58] India today is a democracy with a constitution inspired by Western models. For the educated Indian at least, there is no clash of civilizations. Christians, Hindus, Buddhists, or Jains of Indian origin tend to prosper in the West in all fields—as economists, entrepreneurs, artists, scientists, and the like. They have no problems integrating into Western societies, where they can practice their faith in private while enjoying freedom and opportunity, and while contributing much to the intellectual and artistic life of the West.

The protections of human rights in India's modern constitution reflect Western patterns, but one can find a precedent in the ancient history of India. In the third century BCE, the emperor Asoka had fourteen edicts inscribed on rocks and cave walls, declaring principles such as religious tolerance. The rock edicts may be read as one of the earliest bills of human (and animal) rights.[59] Iranians too can find adumbrations of a human rights philosophy in their own heritage, specifically in the famous proclamation by Cyrus the Great in 538 BCE. Hirad Abtahi, a legal adviser at the International Criminal Court, described the proclamation as a pioneering document, with "theoretical principles which foreshadow the core principles of present days [*sic*] human rights, that is: freedom of thought, conscience and religion, protection of civilians, protection of property, and more generally, the idea of peace."[60] Abtahi quotes Plato's encomium to Persia in Cyrus's time:

[T]he Persians, under Cyrus, maintained the due balance between slavery and freedom, they became, first of all, free themselves, and after that, masters of many others. For when the rulers gave a share of freedom to their subjects and advanced them to a position of equality, the soldiers were more friendly towards their officers . . . and if there was any wise man amongst them, able to give coun-sel—since the king was not jealous but allowed free speech and respected those who could help at all by their counsel, such a man had the opportunity of contributing to the common stock the fruit of his wisdom. Consequently, at that time all their affairs made progress, owing to their freedom, friendliness and mutual inter-change of reason.[61]

Plato's admiration for the Persian culture under Cyrus is echoed in the modern ties between Persians and Westerners in promoting human rights. Many organizations in the West are recording the daily violations of human rights in Iran and trying to improve the situation.[62] There are also many courageous Iranians working in the West to bring human rights to their native land—the same rights taken for granted by Westerners. For these Iranians, there is no clash of civilizations. In the United States today there are an estimated one and a half million Iranians, a large percentage of whom are said to be secularists. The Iranians I have addressed in Paris, Stockholm, Washington D.C., Chicago, and Los Angeles have all been ferociously anti-Khomeini and pro-democracy, and largely secular. My first book, *Why I Am Not a Muslim*, was trans-lated into Persian soon after its publication in the United States. On September 12, 2001, two hundred thousand Iranians had a spontaneous candlelight vigil and march in Tehran as a show of solidarity with the United States and the families of the World Trade Center victims. It was a moment that called to mind these lines from Goethe's *West–östlicher Divan:*

God has made the Orient!
God has made the Occident!
North and South his hands are holding,
All the lands in peace enfolding.

Is it accurate to talk about a clash of civilizations? The situation is evidently more complex than West versus East. Even so, it will not do to pretend, in a rush of ecumenical sentimentality, that we all adhere to the same values. While all humans—every Hottentot and Eskimo, Semite and Indo-European, Polynesian and Native American—belong to the same species, we do not all live under the same customs or institutions. Is it reprehensible to have cultural and aesthetic preferences? The cultural relativist can hardly object if I opt for my own cultural customs. I am not a racist in doing so.

William Empson once wrote, "I think it is true to say that European music is a much larger creature than Far Eastern music, it is fresh air."[63] Empson's judgment is borne out by many Asian artists and writers. For example, the Chinese American writer Amy Chua comments, "The Chinese never achieved the heights of Western classical music—there is no Chinese equivalent of Beethoven's Ninth Symphony."[64] It is remarkable how many violinists, pianists, cellists, and conductors from East Asia can be heard performing in major Western venues. Chen Kaige, a Chinese film director, observes that "Western classical music has elements of love and forgiveness that come from religion. Chinese music is very intellectual, very exotic, but there is no love. You don't feel warm after you listen to it."[65] As Steve Sailer explains, classical music in the West emerged from a culture shaped by a theology that "valued each unique soul," and Chen hopes that this music "can educate his people in spirituality and individualism."[66] Western music reflects a particular culture, and yet, like other gifts of the West, it also touches upon universal values.

✑✑

CHAPTER FOUR

SLAVERY, RACISM, AND
IMPERIALISM

It is commonplace among intellectuals and opinion-makers to
see non-Western cultures as victims of exploitation by Western
imperialism and racism. Chapter Two made the case that the West's
success did not rest on exploiting other peoples; this chapter shows
that slavery and racism and imperialism are far from being Western inventions. Racism flourishes openly in some places outside
the West today, and even slavery is still practiced. As scholars from
Albert Camus to Pascal Bruckner have argued, it is unfair for the
West alone to bear the burden of the past injustices of the slave trade
and colonialism. This is especially so since it was the West that first

took steps to abolish slavery; that took legal measures to end institutionalized racism; and that voluntarily withdrew from its colonial
possessions and abandoned any imperial ambitions.

❳❴

SLAVERY

Slaves have been employed by the majority of settled societies at one
time or another. The practice of slavery is known to have occurred
in most ancient civilizations, including Sumer, the Akkadian empire,
Egypt, India, China, Greece, Rome, Islamic domains, black Africa,
and pre-Columbian America. One of the first written law codes, that
of Hammurabi, included clear provisions for slavery.

I was born in the western Indian state of Gujarat in 1946. My
family, being Muslim, moved a year later to Karachi, then the capital
of newly created Pakistan. One of my earliest memories is of being
amazed at the sight of Makranis, sometimes called Sidis (or Sid-
dhis, or Habshi), probably descended from black slaves brought over
in medieval times or those imported from Mozambique in the late
eighteenth century. My grandfather was a true Gujarati merchant
and trader who had moved to Mozambique in the 1920s, settling
in and around the northern port town of Quelimane. My father,
who joined his brother in Quelimane in 1959 after the death of their
father, is buried there.

These bits of autobiography were dramatically revived in memory not long ago when I learned about the role of Gujarati merchants, both Muslim and Hindu, in financing the East African slave
trade. Sir Bartle Frere, who was governor of Bombay in the 1860s,
estimated that almost half the slave trade from Somalia to Madagascar was financed by Indians, mainly from Gujarat. There is also
evidence that those Indian merchants were more directly involved
in the shipping of black slaves to India (especially to the state of

Gujarat) and to the Persian Gulf, with Quelimane serving as a major trading port.[1]

Reading about the participation of the Gujaratis in the slave trade brought home to me its vast geographical extent. It was not confined to the Atlantic, as many in America seem to think. Many different societies and groups—ethnic, linguistic, religious—were not immune from the moral corruption inherent in a commerce that treated fellow humans as merchandise.

Black-on-Black Slavery

Western scholars and intellectuals have accustomed us to think of black Africans only as passive victims in the Atlantic slave trade. Sheldon Stern, who taught African American history for a decade before becoming the historian at the John F. Kennedy Library and Museum, remarks that the truth is quite different: "The history of the slave trade proves that virtually everyone participated and profited—whites and blacks; Christians, Muslims, and Jews; Europeans, Africans, Americans, and Latin Americans."[2] Yet when Stern examined the requirements for courses on American history in forty-nine states, he discovered that not one of the curriculum guides mentioned the key role of Africans in supplying slaves for the Atlantic trade.

Professor Stern points out that the slave trade is taught differently in Africa today. As an example, he quotes this passage from a Nigerian textbook:

Where did the supply of slaves come from? First, the Portuguese themselves kidnapped some Africans. But the bulk of the supply came from the Nigerians. These Nigerian middlemen moved to the interior where they captured other Nigerians who belonged to other communities. The middlemen also purchased many of the slaves

from the people in the interior. . . . Many Nigerian middlemen
began to depend totally on the slave trade and neglected every other
business and occupation. The result was that when the trade was
abolished [by England in 1807] these Nigerians began to protest.
As years went by and the trade collapsed such Nigerians lost their
sources of income and became impoverished.[3]

Samuel Sulemana Fuseini, an educator and politician in Ghana, acknowledged that his Asante ancestors became wealthy by abducting other Africans and selling them on the slave market. Kofi Awoonor, a Ghanaian diplomat, has written that "there is a great psychic shadow over Africa, and it has much to do with our guilt and denial of our role in the slave trade. We too are blameworthy in what was essentially one of the most heinous crimes in human history."[4] The president of Benin in 2000, Mathieu Kerekou, apologized for his country's participation in the slave trade.[5] Senegal's president in 2001, Abdoulaye Wade, called for a recognition of shared responsibility for the Atlantic slave trade among Africans, Europeans, and Americans.[6]

In the United States, there are also budding signs of candor about the slave trade, as Stern reveals by quoting from a recent college textbook written by three African American historians. Here we read that Europeans and Americans "did not capture and enslave people themselves. Instead they purchased slaves from African traders," who "restricted the Europeans to a few points on the coast, while the kingdoms raided the interior to supply the Europeans with slaves." European traders provided firearms for African aggressors, but did not initiate their wars.

Sometimes African armies enslaved the inhabitants of conquered
towns and villages. At other times, raiding parties captured iso-
lated families or kidnapped individuals. As warfare spread to the
interior, captives had to march for hundreds of miles to the coast
where European traders awaited them. The raiders tied the captives

together with rope or secured them with wooden yokes around their necks. It was a shocking experience, and many captives died from hunger, exhaustion, and exposure during the journey. Others killed themselves rather than submit to their fate, and the captors killed those who resisted.[7]

As Robert Paul Thomas and Richard Bean have pointed out, certain Africans themselves "were the ones with the bright and horrible and profitable idea of seizing their fellow Africans at low cost and selling them to Arabs or Europeans."[8]

John Thornton of Boston University, a leading historian of slavery, likewise dispels a number of myths about the slave trade in his book *Africa and Africans in the Making of the Atlantic World, 1400–1680*. Thornton argues that Africans, far from being passive, were firmly in control of their continent's destiny and their interactions with Europeans. They were active participants in trade with Europe, including the slave trade. "Europeans did not possess the military power to force Africans to participate in any type of trade in which their leaders did not wish to engage. Therefore all African trade with the Atlantic, including the slave trade, had to be voluntary," Thornton explains.[9] Europeans did not conquer and pillage Africa. Instead, they engaged in a peaceful, well-regulated trade, tapping into an existing slave market.

Thornton notes that slavery had a long history in African societies, where "relatively large numbers of people were likely to be slaves at any one time."[10] These societies were inegalitarian, and slavery was deeply rooted in their legal and institutional structures. Since there was no private ownership of land, African entrepreneurs bought slaves as "the only form of private, revenue-producing property recognized in African law."[11] Slaves were the major form of private investment and a sign of wealth and social prestige. Many worked in agriculture or in mines; some performed administrative duties or military service. Thus, economic growth in Africa was closely tied to slavery.

Africans began exporting slaves as soon as they discovered there was an outside market for them. Thornton notes that the rapid growth of Congo's slave trade with Europeans "had to draw on a well-established and developed system of slavery, slave marketing, and slave delivery that pre-existed any European contact." Such a system was in place because "the capture, purchase, transport, and sale of slaves was a regular feature of African society." This reality, Thorton argues, was "as much responsible as any external force for the development of the Atlantic slave trade."[12] African leaders were not forced into participating in the slave trade. The African slavers had total control of the entire operation from the moment of capture to the delivery of the slaves to European ships.

This is "the *whole* story of the Atlantic slave trade" that Sheldon Stern says must be taught to young Americans if we are to preserve "civic unity and belief in the historical legitimacy of our democratic institutions." Teaching half-truths about history, including the history of slavery, is divisive. "Once we recognize the shared historical responsibility for the Atlantic slave trade, we can turn our attention to 'transforming the future' by eradicating its corrosive legacy."[13]

The Arab Slave Trade

A number of African Americans, both Muslim and Christian, have demanded reparations from the United States for its part in the slave trade, as has Dieudonné, a French comedian of Cameroonian origin. They conveniently forget that black Africans were willing participants in the slave trade, and they do not demand reparations from the Arabs, even though Arabs were engaged in the slave trade for thirteen centuries and shipped far more black slaves across the Sahara and the Red Sea than were sent across the Atlantic. Feelings of guilt over its participation in the Atlantic slave trade are undoubtedly one reason why the West has lavished more than $400 billion in aid on sub-Saharan Africa over the past few decades. The Arabs have done nothing similar. The Saudis have instead spent millions on spreading anti-Western propaganda and an intolerant form of Islam around the world.

African Americans who convert to Islam regard Christianity as unforgivably linked to the history of slavery and racism. They are unaware that the Christian conscience of individuals like William Wilberforce played a central part in the eventual abolition of the slave trade. Moreover, they have only a vague knowledge of Islamic history or theology, even of the foundational texts. They have been taught a tendentious version of Islamic culture, one that is painted as being free of racism, colonialism, imperialism, and slavery. But the Koran accepts the existence of slavery and regulates its practice. Among African Americans there is little awareness of the Muslim Arab participation in the black African slave trade, both trans-Saharan and East African, or of the antiblack racism of major Muslim thinkers.

A tenth-century Persian treatise on world geography described black Africans as "people distant from the standards of humanity." A thirteenth-century Persian writer asserted that "the ape is more teachable and more intelligent than the Zanji," a term used either for the Bantu-speaking black population of East Africa south of Ethiopia, or for black Africans more generally. According to the celebrated fourteenth-century sociologist Ibn Khaldun, "the Negro nations are, as a rule, submissive to slavery, because [they] have little [that is essentially] human and have attributes that are quite similar to those of dumb animals."[14]

Tidiane N'Diaye, a Senegalese anthropologist and historian, wrote a passionate account of the role that Muslim Arabs played in the black African slave trade, with the pointed title *The Veiled Genocide*.[15] He demonstrates that although slavery existed in Africa long before the Arabs arrived there, the Arab slave trade was larger in scope and more deadly in its effects. Muslim Arabs captured, enslaved, and castrated millions of black Africans, resulting in death for hundreds of thousands. *The Veiled Genocide* is a courageous book, bluntly stating the facts no matter how politically incorrect. N'Diaye lays to rest many myths of slavery, documenting that both Muslim Arabs and black Africans had been enslaving other humans for centuries before the white man arrived in Africa. In a forthright fashion that would be virtually unthinkable for a Western historian, N'Diaye writes:

[The Arabs] brought with them an avalanche of sorrows. As the Arabs advanced, mere survival was a real challenge for the people. Millions of Africans were victims of raids, were massacred or captured, castrated and sent to the Arabo-Muslim world. And that in inhuman conditions, by caravans across the Sahara or by sea, from trading posts dealing in human flesh from East Africa. Such was in reality the major occupation of the majority of Arabs who Islamized the African people, all the while posing as pillars of the faith and exemplary believers. They often went from region to region, the Koran in one hand, and the knife for castrating in the other, leading a hypocritical "life of prayer," never uttering a word without invoking Allah or a saying or deed of the Prophet.

Beautiful and noble principles but which were trampled upon—with such joy, such indignity, such dishonesty—by these Arab slavers, who submitted Africa to fire and sword. For, behind this religious pretext, they committed the most revolting crimes and the most atrocious cruelties. . . .

The Atlantic Slave Trade lasted four centuries, whereas the Arabs raided Sub-Saharan Africa for thirteen centuries without interruption. The majority of men shipped disappeared because of their inhuman treatment and systematic castration. . . . For, even though there are no degrees of horror nor a monopoly of cruelty, one can argue, without risk of contradiction, that the slave trading and jihad carried out by Arab Muslims to procure captives for these predators without pity was far more devastating than the Atlantic Trade. And it is still being carried on under our noses.[16]

Olivier Pétré-Grenouilleau, a specialist on the history of slavery, concludes that between the seventh century and the 1920s, Arab merchants handled more than seventeen million black slaves, of which more than one and a half million died en route, many across the Sahara.[17] In the nineteenth century alone, over a million slaves were exported from eastern ports of Africa to Yemen, Saudi Arabia, and the Persian Gulf; millions more were transported around the African interior and along the eastern coast.[18] A large number of slaves were used in East Africa itself, on clove plantations in Zanzibar or on plantations growing cereals, oilseeds, sugar, and cotton. Others were set to work digging up gum copal or collecting orchilla lichens, which were used for making dyes.[19] Many of the slaves transported across the Red Sea and the Gulf of Aden were eventually sent to Anatolia, Iran, northern India, or back to Egypt. Eunuchs were especially prized by wealthy Turkish and Iranian families.[20]

Jan Hogendorn has documented the plight of the young black males who were captured to be sold as eunuchs, in what has been called "the hideous trade." Slave eunuchs, mainly from sub-Saharan Africa, were in demand primarily to supervise the harems of wealthy men in the Muslim Mediterranean region, since they "could be trusted with large numbers of nubile women."[21] They were usually castrated in boyhood, when they had the best chance of surviving the very risky operation, usually a total removal of the testicles and penis. The first danger was hemorrhaging, which could cause a very quick death. Another danger was the high risk of infection in tropical climes, which could result in death within a few days. Death rates could reach 90 percent or even higher. This mortality rate made the surviving eunuch slaves especially valuable: "Turkish merchants are said to have been willing to pay 250 to 300 (Maria Theresa) dollars each for eunuchs in Borno (north-east Nigeria) at a time when the local price of young male slaves does not seem to have exceeded about 20 dollars."[22] Although the British ended the use of eunuchs in Egypt and India, the demand persisted in

Iran. Eunuchs were still being exported from East Africa in the early twentieth century.[23]

White Slaves

Not well known to the general public is the enslavement of Europeans and North Americans by Arabs, especially during the seventeenth and eighteenth centuries. According to Robert C. Davis, "almost certainly a million" and possibly many more white Europeans were taken into slavery by Muslims of the Barbary Coast between 1530 and 1780.[24] The coasts of Portugal, Spain, France, Italy, Ireland, and England, especially Cornwall, were all targets of Muslim raids for centuries.

English slaves suffered terrible cruelty and indignities at the hands of Muslim masters, particularly the vicious Moulay Ismail ibn Sharif, who ruled Morocco from 1672 to 1727. "We were driven like beasts thither and exposed to sale," wrote William Okeley, who had been auctioned at Algiers. Of the Arab slave masters he said, "Their cruelty is great, but their covetousness exceeds their cruelty."[25] The slaves were held in underground dungeons, "filthy, stinking and full of vermin," and often were forced to sleep in their own excrement.[26] Slave drivers would amuse themselves by waking the white slaves at night and forcing them to do more hard labor. Many died from their maltreatment, or from dysentery or the plague, or from the ravages of forced labor. They were frequently beaten and tortured in an effort to make them convert to Islam. Conversion did not bring freedom, however, but only long days of work at building Moulay Ismail's endless palaces. Those who fell ill were sometimes executed on the spot. One English slave recalled seeing other slaves dragged before Moulay Ismail, and seven of them were too weak to stand, so he immediately killed them, "making their resting place a slaughter house."[27]

The wanton cruelty of Moulay Ismail terrified the white European slaves. "One of his common diversions," observed a French padre, was "at one motion, to mount his horse, draw his cimiter and cut off the head of the slave who holds his stirrup."[28] When a Spanish slave walked past him without removing his hat, Moulay Ismail "darted his spear at him," piercing deep into the man's flesh, and then ripped the barbed tip out of his skin.[29] When a mason was found guilty of shoddy work, Moulay Ismail ordered his black guard to break fifty bricks over the mason's head and then throw him into jail.[30] "He was of so fickle, cruel and sanguine a nature that none could be even for one hour secure of life," wrote Thomas Pellow, another English slave. Just as cruel were the black slave drivers appointed to oversee the white captives, whom they often flogged. Pellow lamented that they "immediately punish the least stop or inadvertency, and often will not allow the poor creatures time to eat their bread." A slave thought to be slacking in his labors would be struck on the head by the overseer, who, "when he had broke it, counterfeited the charitable surgeon, applying unslacked lime to stanch the bleeding," wrote Germain Mouette, a French slave.[31]

After a crushing British naval victory in 1816 and the total destruction of Algiers, more than fifteen hundred slaves were freed and the Barbary corsairs ceased to be a menace to European shipping, for a while at least.

Abolition and Resistance

The abolition of slavery was very much a Western initiative. It was Europe that "first decided to set the slaves free: at home, then in the colonies, and finally in all the world," as Bernard Lewis said.[32] Abolitionism was a concept that did not resonate well either in black Africa, where slavery was not opposed in principle, or in the Islamic world, where it was believed to be supported by religion.[33]

In black Africa, slavery was a mainstay of local economies. Thus, some African chiefs reacted with disbelief to news that trafficking in slaves would be illegal as of May 1, 1807, and the announcement led to riots on the Gold Coast. The slave trade had shaped and supported too many African societies for it to be ended without resistance. The king of Bonny told an English captain, "We think that this trade must go on. That is the verdict of our oracle and the priests. They say that your country, however great, can never stop a trade ordained by God himself."[34] As late as 1840, the king of Dahomey said that he dealt in about nine thousand slaves each year, selling three thousand himself and giving the others to his troops to sell. The king received a sizable income from these transactions and taxes on exports. He was willing to do anything the British government asked of him "except to give up the slave trade," for which nothing else was considered an adequate substitute. "The slave trade has been the ruling principle of my people," he said. "It is the source of their glory and wealth. Their songs celebrate their victories and the mother lulls the child to sleep with notes of triumph over an enemy reduced to slavery. Can I, by signing . . . a treaty, change the sentiments of a whole people?"[35]

The abolitionist movement was resisted for a longer time in the Islamic world, in large part because slavery is accepted in the Koran. In 1872, Sir Bartle Frere was sent by the British foreign office to Zanzibar to negotiate a treaty with the sultan, Barghash bin Said, to end the slave traffic. Barghash first insisted that abolishing slavery would ruin Zanzibar's agriculture and that slavery was approved in Islamic law. Eventually, in 1873, he signed a treaty agreeing to close all public slave markets and prohibit the transport of slaves over water.[36]

In the Ottoman Empire, slavery was taken for granted: "Accepted by custom, perpetuated by tradition and sanctioned by religion," as Ehud R. Toledano put it. Abolitionism was considered a foreign idea, barely understood and vigorously resisted.[37] The Turkish historian

Y. H. Erdem confirmed that no antislavery movement ever emerged from Ottoman society; there were no abolitionist tracts to spotlight the suffering of slaves or bring the subject to wide attention. In modern Turkey, the abolition of slavery is not a part of the educational curriculum.[38]

"The anti-slavery measures of European colonial powers were generally viewed by Muslims not only as a threat to their very livelihood but also as an affront to their religion," said John Azumah, a Ghanaian with a doctorate in "Islam and Slavery" from the University of Birmingham. "Muslims therefore resisted all abolition efforts and chattel slavery persists in Muslim countries today."[39] A United Nations report in 1995 highlighted "the abduction and traffic of young boys and girls from Southern Sudan to the northern part of the country for sale as servants and concubines."[40] In 2006, John Eibner described the ongoing practice of slavery in Sudan:

Black women and children in Darfur continue to be enslaved by government-backed janjaweed militiamen, especially for sexual purposes. In the far south, Khartoum's longtime ally, the Lord's Resistance Army, still perpetrates atrocities against civilians, including enslavement. Moreover, tens of thousands of Dinka and Nuer women and children captured before the government made peace with the Sudan People's Liberation Army remain in bondage. Officials at the Committee for the Eradication of the Abduction of Women and Children estimate the presence of at least 40,000 such slaves in northern Sudan, and have documented the names and locations of more than 8,000.[41]

Slaves can still be found in northern Nigeria and Mauritania, and there is evidence to suggest that it still exists in Saudi Arabia too. The death of slavery, in short, "has been a protracted one and is still not over."[42]

⦿⦿
RACISM

Western countries have taken substantive legal measures to ban discrimination on the basis of race in all aspects of society—to the extent of condoning "reverse discrimination" against whites. But open, unapologetic racism persists in much of the rest of the world, including some East Asian societies and many Muslim countries.

Islamic Anti-Semitism

We have already seen evidence of an Arab prejudice against black Africans and its role in perpetuating slavery. More widely known is the hatred of Jews that is widespread in the Islamic world, often encouraged by the state—for instance, in government funding of a film based on *The Protocols of the Elders of Zion,* a proven forgery that is nonetheless taken seriously by virtually all Muslims. Hitler's *Mein Kampf* is also very popular in the Muslim world today. The official Egyptian daily newspaper *Al-Akhbar,* on April 29, 2002, featured a column by Fatma Abdallah Mahmoud titled "Accursed Forever and Ever," saying of the Jews:

> *They are accursed in heaven and on earth. They are accursed from the day the human race was created and from the day their mothers bore them. They are accursed also because they murdered the Prophets. They murdered the Prophet John the Baptist and served up his head on a golden platter to the singer and dancer Salome. Allah also cursed them with a thousand curses when they argued with and resisted his words of truth, deceived the Prophet Moses, and worshiped the golden calf that they created with their own hands!! These accursed ones are a catastrophe for the human race. They are the virus of the generation, doomed to a life of humiliation and wretchedness until Judgment Day.[43]*

116

He continued in this vein for another fifteen lines. One cannot imagine a Western newspaper publishing such a vitriolic screed.

It is also difficult to picture a Western politician surviving in office after making the kind of overtly racist comments that Maha-thir Mohamad regularly did in his long tenure as Malaysia's prime minister. For example, in October 2003 he said to an Islamic confer-ence: "The Europeans killed 6 million Jews out of 12 million, but today the Jews rule the world by proxy. They get others to fight and die for them."[44] If any Western politician made similar remarks about Arabs, there would be an outcry both at home and around the world. The standards of behavior in the West are indeed higher. Trent Lott was forced to resign as the U.S. Senate majority leader in December 2002 over a single statement that was interpreted as being supportive of segregation, although it was not explicitly so.

Many In the West claim that Islamic Jew-hatred is a product of the Arab-Israeli conflict. Some Western scholars have tried to argue that Islamic anti-Semitism is only a recent phenomenon learned from the Nazis and that Jews lived safely under Islamic rule for cen-turies, especially in medieval Spain. These assertions are not sup-ported by the evidence. Yet there is a palpable eagerness to accept romantic clichés about the "Golden Age" of Muslim Spain as histori-cal fact. Those whom we expect to have done their own research on the subject often disappoint us.

Consider the case of Amartya Sen, a celebrated economist and winner of the Nobel Prize. In recent years, Sen has written on sub-jects outside his area of expertise. Unfortunately, he seems not to have checked his history, something that would have been easy given the resources available. For example, he perpetuates a myth about Mai-monides in his book *Identity and Violence*. Here, Sen tells us twice that when "the Jewish philosopher Maimonides was forced to emi-grate from an intolerant Europe in the twelfth century, he found a tolerant refuge in the Arab world."[45] I do not know how to character-ize this misinterpretation of history—willful? grotesque? dishonest?

117

or perhaps typical. It is certainly an indication that in today's intellectual climate one can denigrate Europe any way one wishes, to the point of distorting history, without any of the distinguished scholars who blurb one's book raising an eyebrow.

The one reviewer who did object to Sen's "potted history" was Fouad Ajami, who described it as something "tailored for interfaith dialogues," but which "will not do as history." Writing in the *Washington Post*, Ajami reminded Sen that

> *Maimonides, born in 1135, did not flee "Europe" for the "Arab world": He fled his native Córdoba in Spain, which was then in the grip of religious-political terror, choking under the yoke of a Berber Muslim dynasty, the Almohades. . . . Maimonides and his family fled the fire of the Muslim city-states in the Iberian Peninsula to Morocco and then to Jerusalem. There was darkness and terror in Morocco as well, and Jerusalem was equally inhospitable in the time of the Crusader Kingdom. Deliverance came only in Cairo—the exception, not the rule, its social peace maintained by the enlightened Saladin.*[46]

The Almohades, who conquered Córdoba in 1148, persecuted the Jews and presented them with the choice of conversion to Islam, death, or exile. Maimonides' family chose exile, along with other Jews. Even then, they had to be constantly on the move to avoid the all-conquering Almohades. Maimonides eventually settled in Egypt, where he was physician to the grand vizier Alfadhil and to Saladin, the Kurdish sultan and celebrated foe of the Crusaders.

Maimonides' *Epistle to the Jews of Yemen* was written in about 1172 in reply to questions from Jacob ben Nathanael al-Fayyami, head of the Jewish community in Yemen.[47] The Jews of Yemen were being subjected to a campaign of persecution designed to convert them to Islam. Maimonides provided them with guidance and encouragement:

You write that the rebel leader in Yemen decreed compulsory apostasy for the Jews by forcing the Jewish inhabitants of all the places he had subdued to desert the Jewish religion just as the Berbers had compelled them to do in Maghreb [northwest Africa]. Verily, this news has broken our backs and has astounded and dumbfounded the whole of our community. And rightly so. For these are evil tidings, "and whosoever heareth of them, both his ears tingle" (I Samuel 3:11). Indeed our hearts are weakened, our minds are confused, and the powers of the body wasted because of the dire misfortunes which brought religious persecutions upon us from the two ends of the world, the East and the West, "so that the enemies were in the midst of Israel, some on this side, and some on that side" (Joshua 8:22).[48]

Maimonides worried that the relentless persecution of the Jews by Muslims would cause many "to drift away from our faith, to have misgivings, or to go astray, because they witnessed our feebleness, and noted the triumph of our adversaries and their dominion over us."[49]

Maimonides asserted that Muhammad, "the Madman" (a term used by many other medieval Jewish writers), had invented his own religion with the aim of "procuring rule and submission."[50] At the same time, Muslims alleged that the Jews had falsified their own scripture, the Torah, and "expunged every trace of the name of Mohammed therefrom."[51] Maimonides lamented, "Never did a nation molest, degrade, debase and hate us as much as they," adding that the Jews "were dishonored by them beyond human endurance."[52] Maimonides described how the Jews had tried to remain at peace with their persecutors:

We have acquiesced, both old and young, to inure ourselves to humiliation, as Isaiah instructed us "I gave my back to the smiters, and my cheeks to them that plucked off the hair" (50:6). All this notwithstanding, we do not escape this continued maltreatment which well nigh crushes us. No matter how much we suffer and elect to remain at peace with them, they stir up strife and sedition, as David predicted, "I am all peace, but when I speak, they are for war" (Psalm 120:7).[53]

The Jew-hatred that Maimonides refers to is, like slavery, deeply ingrained in Islamic culture, sanctioned by the Koran, and encouraged by the example of Muhammad. Anti-Semitism is found in what I will call Islam 1, the Islam of the texts: the Koran, the hadith, and the Sira (the biography of Muhammad). It is also found in Islam 2, the Islam elaborated from these texts by early commentators and jurists, and then set in stone more than a millennium ago. And it is found in Islam 3, meaning Islamic civilization, or what Muslims have done in history. All three Islams have been anti-infidel, viewing Christians and others with disdain and contempt, but reserving a special animus for Jews.

The Koran describes both Jewish and Christian religious leaders as devious moneygrubbers:

O you who believe! Lo! many of the Jewish rabbis and the Christian monks devour the wealth of mankind wantonly and debar men from the way of Allah; they who hoard up gold and silver and spend it not in the way of Allah, unto them give tidings of painful doom. (IX.34)

It presents Jews as base and rebellious murderers of prophets:

Wretchedness and baseness were stamped upon them [that is, the Jews], and they were visited with wrath from Allah. That was because they disbelieved in Allah's revelations and slew the prophets wrongfully. That was for their disobedience and transgression. (II.61)

It also accuses the Jews of willfully perverting the truth and going astray, thus earning Allah's curse:

*Have you not seen those who have received a portion of the Scrip-
ture? They purchase error, and they want you to go astray from the
path. . . . Some of the Jews pervert words from their meanings, and
say, "We hear and we disobey," and "Hear without hearing," and
"Heed us!" twisting with their tongues and slandering religion. If
they had said, "We have heard and obey," or "Hear and observe us"
it would have been better for them and more upright. But Allah
had cursed them for their disbelief, so they believe not, except for a
few. (IV.44–46)*

The oldest extant biography of Muhammad reveals the prophet's
frequent attacks on Jews; he would have them assassinated if he felt
they had insulted or disobeyed him. When Muhammad gave the
command "Kill any Jew that falls into your power," one of his followers, Ibn Mas'ud, assassinated a Jewish merchant, Ibn Sunayna.[54]
Other followers of Muhammad were happy to obey similar orders.[55]
From the hadith comes an account of a vindictive attack on a Jewish
critic of Muhammad:

*Then occurred the "sariyyah" [raid] of Salim Ibn Umayr al-Amri
against Abu Afak, the Jew, in [the month of] Shawwal in the
beginning of the twentieth month from the hijrah [immigration
from Mecca to Medina in 622 AD], of the Apostle of Allah. Abu
Afak was from Banu Amr Ibn Awf, and was an old man who had
attained the age of one hundred and twenty years. He was a Jew,
and used to instigate the people against the Apostle of Allah, and
composed (satirical) verses [about Muhammad].*

*Salim Ibn Umayr, who was one of the great weepers and who
had participated in Badr, said, "I take a vow that I shall either kill
Abu Afak or die before him." He waited for an opportunity until
a hot night came, and Abu Afak slept in an open place. Salim Ibn
Umayr knew it, so he placed the sword on his liver and pressed it
till it reached his bed. The enemy of Allah screamed and the people*

who were his followers, rushed to him, took him to his house and interred him.[56]

Muhammad also instigated massacres of Jewish tribes. All the men of the Banu Qurayza tribe, between six hundred and eight hundred men, were exterminated.[57] The tribe of Banu'l-Nadir were also attacked, and the survivors were banished.[58] The narrator of the biography boasts, "Our attack upon God's enemy cast terror among the Jews, and there was no Jew in Medina who did not fear for his life."[59]

After the September 11 terrorist attack, many Muslims and apologists of Islam glibly came out with the following Koranic passage in an effort to show that Islam disapproves of violence: "Whoever killed a human being shall be looked upon as though he had killed all mankind" (V.32). Unfortunately, these wonderful-sounding words, which came from a Jewish text (Mishnah Sanhedrin 4:5),[60] are often quoted out of context, for the next verse changes the meaning considerably. Here are the two verses in full:

That was why We laid it down for the Israelites that whoever killed a human being, except as a punishment for murder or other villainy in the land, shall be looked upon as though he had killed all mankind; and that whoever saved a human life shall be regarded as though he had saved all mankind. Our apostles brought them veritable proofs: yet it was not long before many of them committed great evils in the land. Those that make war against God and His apostle and spread disorder shall be put to death or crucified or have their hands and feet cut off on alternate sides, or be banished from the country. (V.32–33)

The noble sentiments of the first (Jewish) verse, abjuring violence, are entirely undercut by what follows: a command for any who oppose the prophet to be banished or mutilated or crucified. Indeed, the Koran charges believers to fight against the infidels until they have submitted:

> *Fight against such of those to whom the Scriptures were given as believe neither in God nor the Last Day, who do not forbid what God and His apostle have forbidden, and do not embrace the true faith, until they pay tribute out of hand and are utterly subdued. (IX.29)*

Thus, Muhammad himself set the pattern for hatred of infidels, especially Jews, and for violence against them. Contempt for Jews is promoted in the Koran and demonstrated in Islamic history. For example, hundreds of Jews were killed near Córdoba and other parts of Muslim Spain between 1010 and 1013, during the so-called "Golden Age." More than six thousand Jews were massacred in Fez, Morocco, in 1033. The entire Jewish community of roughly four thousand in Granada was exterminated during the Muslim riots of 1066. "This was a disaster, as serious as that which overtook the Rhineland Jews thirty years later during the First Crusade, yet it has rarely received much scholarly attention," writes Robert Wistrich. He also records the persecution, expulsion, and forced conversion of Jews in Tunisia, and a massacre of Jews in Marrakesh in 1232. In short, "the looting and killing of Jews, along with punitive taxation, confinement to ghettos, the enforced wearing of distinguishing marks on clothes (an innovation in which Islam preceded medieval Christendom), and other humiliations were rife" from Spain to the Arabian peninsula.[61]

So it is not surprising that in the twentieth century, the grand mufti of Jerusalem, Haj Amin al-Husseini, met with Adolf Hitler to ask for German help in exterminating the Jews of the Muslim world. Some scholars recently have highlighted this alliance in order to emphasize a Nazi influence in modern Islamic anti-Semitism. But even they have been obliged to acknowledge how deeply entrenched that prejudice already was in the Muslim world. In his superbly researched and highly original *Nazi Propaganda for the Arab World*, Jeffrey Herf notes that Islamic anti-Semitism may have been reinforced by Nazism, but also long predated it:

> *A simple-minded optimism seeks to convince us that contact and communication between people from different cultures will invariably foster international understanding, peace, and good-will. Sometimes it has. In this case, the collaboration of officials of the Nazi regime with Arab allies in wartime Berlin demonstrated that the opposite was also possible. The more these political allies exchanged ideas, the more they reinforced, renewed, and accentuated some of the worst elements of their respective civilizations, namely, hatred of Jews and of Western political modernity.*[62]

East Asian Prejudice

The prevalence of racist views among the Chinese and the Japanese is not frequently discussed, though it is amply documented historically and still in evidence today. When Condoleezza Rice visited China as the U.S. secretary of state in April 2005, she was subjected to repugnant racist attacks.[63] Frank Dikötter's introduction to *The Construction of Racial Identities in China and Japan: Historical and Contemporary Perspectives* makes for eye-opening reading on the subject of racism against black Africans in East Asia. It is an essential corrective to the politically correct posture that deliberately ignores the phenomenon of "racialized identities" in East Asia and the discrimination that results.[64]

Dikötter quotes Kang Youwei, a celebrated Chinese philosopher of the late nineteenth century, describing black Africans as having "iron faces, silver teeth, slanting jaws like a pig, front view like an ox," and as being "stupid like sheep and swine." Kang recommended that they be whitened by intermarriage—provided that anyone could persuade a light-skinned girl to marry such a "monstrously ugly black." Similar attitudes have prevailed to this day:

> [O]fficial policies endorsing racial discrimination and leading to abuses of human rights can be found in most East Asian states. Myths of origins, ideologies of blood and theories of biological descent have formed a central part in the cultural construction of identity in China and Japan since the nationalist movements of the late nineteenth century. Naturalised as a pure and homogeneous "Yamato race" in Japan, or as a biological descent group from the "Yellow Emperor" in China, political territories have been conflated with imaginary biological entities by nationalist writers.[65]

Both Japan and China created their own binary oppositions between "advanced" and "backward" peoples, a racialized version of "civilization" versus "barbarism." Both created rankings of population groups according to the characteristics attributed to them. The Japanese saw themselves as the "leading race," marked by "spiritual and physical purity," and carrying out a divine mission in their colonial expansion into Korea and China. "In war-time Japan, a sense of unique purity—both moral and genetic—was central to the notion of racial separateness in which other population groups were dehumanised as beasts and ultimately as demons."[66]

Pseudoscientific racial theories were disseminated by the state through means such as school textbooks and anthropology exhibitions. These theories contributed to social self-definition, as Dikötter remarks, but also produced racially marginalized groups, notably "Blacks" and "Jews," neither of them very numerous in China or Japan yet both prominent in the racial taxonomics of those countries.[67] In modern Japan, where an influx of foreign workers has stoked fears of racial contamination, essays like "We Cannot Marry

Negroes" by Taisuke Fujishima promote the idea of blackness as a symbol of the savage. Talk of Japanese biological uniqueness and purity remains commonplace. In China, African students are periodically attacked on university campuses because they are imagined to belong to an inferior species; and theories of racial purity are invoked to justify discrimination against non-Han peoples such as the Tibetans and the Uighurs.[68]

Writing in the 1990s, Dikötter saw no clear evidence that racial hierarchies were being challenged by cultural authorities in East Asia. He concluded on a somber note:

> *In an era of economic globalisation and political depolarisation, racial identities and racial discrimination have increased in East Asia, affecting both the human rights of marginalised groups and collective perceptions of the world order. Official policies endorsing racial discrimination and leading to abuses of human rights can be found in most East Asian states.*[69]

A United Nations special rapporteur on racism and xenophobia, Doudou Diène, reinforced Dikötter's conclusions, finding "deep and profound" racism in Japan, without sufficient recognition of the problem by the government. Racial discrimination affects national minorities—the Buraku people, the Ainu, the people of Okinawa— along with ethnic Koreans and Chinese, and foreigners from other Asian countries.[70] The Burakumin are descendants of people who were outcasts in feudal Japanese society because of their association with occupations considered unclean: leatherworking, the butcher's trade, and disposing of dead cattle. Historically, the Burakumin have faced considerable bigotry and persecution. Today they are still considered socially inferior, and on average they earn substantially less than the rest of the Japanese workforce. Many influential Japanese public figures conceal their Buraku origins lest they lose their positions. The parallels to the "untouchables" of India are obvious.[71]

South Asian Discrimination

On university campuses in India, black African students often face overt discrimination, as do students from the northeast of India, with their East Asian features. Dr. Renu (Gupta) Naidu recalled how her friends at Delhi University in the early 1990s treated Northeastern students with disdain and sometimes threw obscenities at them. "Any Northeastern student entering a college campus earns the epithet 'Chinky' on day one, and has to live with being looked at as, at the very least, an oddity, for the rest of her or his stay," Naidu said. "Students told me about being asked questions like whether they eat rats." In her research on the lives of Northeastern tribal girls at Delhi University, Naidu found that Northeastern students had a dropout rate of around 50 percent, and higher for girls, which she attributed to sociocultural friction. As a "non-Marathi" student doing postgraduate work at Nagpur, Naidu herself had felt the sting of prejudice.[72]

Discrimination against Dalits, formerly called untouchables, remains pervasive in India, and semantic games do not change the fact that it is a kind of racism. The National Campaign on Dalit Human Rights reports that nearly 170 million Dalits suffer from caste discrimination in India today.[73] The Delhi Declaration in August 2005 on behalf of the Dalits indicated that about 300,000 cases of persecution were registered with the police between 1981 and 2001, and specified many varieties of discrimination that Dalits face in modern India.[74] A major episode of caste rivalry occurred at the end of August 2005, in the village of Gohana, about forty-seven miles from New Delhi. A dispute between Dalits and the higher-caste Jat community led to a mass exodus of Dalits, after which a violent mob of about 1,500 to 2,000 Jats—armed with spears and axes, petrol and kerosene—went on a looting and arson spree, destroying nearly sixty Dalit houses in about four hours. The police stood by as spectators; according to some accounts, they even gave assistance to the mob.[75] For several decades, Dalits have received "affirmative action" set-asides in schools and workplaces, but still they encounter deep-seated prejudice, hate campaigns, rape and murder, along with daily injustices such as being required to use segregated public facilities in many parts of India.[76]

Racism toward anyone with darker skin is widely reported throughout South Asia. Cricketers from the West Indies are often subjected to insults from spectators in India. Discrimination regularly manifests itself on the job, from airports to factories: higher up the managerial ladder, you are likely to find lighter-skinned people. Parents boast about their children's light skin, or emphasize a fair complexion when they advertise a prospective bride. Skin lighteners are sold everywhere and advertised at sports venues.[77] Clearly it is false to suggest that prejudice against darker skin is a distinctly Western sin.

IMPERIALISM

The West is often portrayed as uniquely imperialistic, but this too is a myth that falls before the historical record. For example, the emperor Wu-ti (r. 140–87 BCE) doubled the size of China with his numerous military expeditions. Under Wu-ti, the Han Chinese pushed southward, subjugating and absorbing non-Han peoples. After the Han occupied the Shuofang region, to cite just one case, it was immediately settled with 100,000 Chinese colonists. Han China became "the most aggressive imperialist colonial power in Asia," writes Chun-shu Chang, a professor of history at the University of Michigan.

> The Han Empire in the East was matched in power and ambition only by the Roman Empire in the West in the ancient world. While the latter controlled the Mediterranean world and the land extending to the Atlantic Ocean, the Han hegemony over the Asian

*continent extended east to west from Korea on the Pacific Ocean
to Uzbekistan, and south to north from Vietnam and Kashmir to
Mongolia. It was Pax Romana on one side of the globe and Pax
Sinica on the other.*[78]

The history of Southeast Asia is marked by imperial ambition
and warfare among the many kingdoms that sprouted up there. For
example, what came to be called Burma (or Myanmar) was first colonized by the Mon and the Pyu peoples. The Pyu, who established
eighteen kingdoms centered on cities in the first century BCE, are
described in Chinese histories as humane and peaceful. Their city-
states were destroyed in the ninth century by the warlike Nanzhao
people, from what is now Yunnan. The Nanzhao had rebelled against
the Tang dynasty and then expanded into Burma, Laos, Thailand,
and north into Sichuan, before their dynasty was overthrown in 902.
The Mon people had established a kingdom centered on Thaton in
lower Burma by around 300 BCE. It was overrun in 1057 by the Pagan
kingdom, which had been founded by Burmans in the ninth century.
The Mon also established the prosperous kingdom of Dvaravati, in
what is now Thailand, in the sixth century. Dvaravati came to be
increasingly dominated by the Khmer Empire from the eleventh
century on, until it was finally incorporated into the Thai kingdom.
From the mid-twelfth century, most of mainland Southeast Asia was
controlled by two great imperial powers, the Pagan kingdom and
the Khmer Empire, the latter ruling over parts of modern-day Laos,
Thailand, Vietnam, Myanmar, and Malaysia.[79]

Greater Japan

The Japanese conquered their home islands from the Ainu tribes,
reducing them to a minority confined to the far north. The Japanese empire can be said to have existed from the Meiji Restoration in 1868 until 1947, when a new constitution was enforced by

the Americans. After the Sino-Japanese War of 1894–95, the Japanese controlled Taiwan and part of Manchuria. Korea was formally annexed in 1910, resulting in exploitation and a curtailment of civil liberties for the Korean people. During the early 1940s, the Japanese were able to seize Hong Kong, British Malaya, the Philippines, Singapore, Burma, parts of Borneo, Central Java, Malang, Cepu, Sumatra, Dutch New Guinea, and many key islands of the Pacific. At the height of its power in 1942, imperial Japan ruled over an area of nearly three million square miles, making it one of the largest maritime empires in history.[80]

The Imperial Japanese Army and Imperial Japanese Navy were responsible for crimes against millions of civilians and prisoners of war. According to Chalmers Johnson of the Japan Policy Research Institute, "the Japanese slaughtered as many as 30 million Filipinos, Malays, Vietnamese, Cambodians, Indonesians and Burmese." Johnson adds that imperial Japan and Nazi Germany both "looted the countries they conquered on a monumental scale, though Japan plundered more, over a longer period, than the Nazis. Both conquerors enslaved millions and exploited them as forced labourers—and, in the case of the Japanese, as prostitutes for front-line troops." If you were an Allied prisoner of war held by the Nazis, you had a 4 percent chance of not surviving the war, whereas the chance of dying in Japanese custody was nearly 30 percent.[81]

Rudolph Rummel estimates that approximately 3.9 million Chinese, mostly civilians, were killed as a direct result of Japanese actions in China between 1937 and 1945.[82] The most brutal episode has come to be called the Rape of Nanking (or Nanjing Massacre), now well known through Iris Chang's book of the same name. The Japanese army committed many atrocities as it advanced from Shanghai to Nanking in 1937. After capturing Nanking on December 13, the Japanese killed at least 200,000 civilians and disarmed soldiers, and raped tens of thousands of women and girls, over a six-week period.[83]

Japanese soldiers systematically searched door to door for young women and girls, many of whom were gang-raped and often killed immediately afterward with a bayonet jabbed into the vagina. Young children were cut open to allow Japanese soldiers to rape them. There are many firsthand accounts of these atrocities written by American or European doctors, missionaries, or businessmen. Reverend James M. McCallum, for example, wrote in his diary on December 19, 1937:

> *Never I have heard or read such brutality. Rape! Rape! Rape! We estimate at least 1,000 cases a night, and many by day. In case of resistance or anything that seems like disapproval, there is a bayonet stab or a bullet. . . . People are hysterical. . . . Women are being carried off every morning, afternoon and evening. The whole Japanese army seems to be free to go and come as it pleases, and to do whatever it pleases.[84]*

Robert O. Wilson, a surgeon at the American-administered University Hospital in the Safety Zone, described the outrages in letters to his family. Here are excerpts of letters dated December 15 and 18:

> *The slaughter of civilians is appalling. I could go on for pages telling of cases of rape and brutality almost beyond belief. Two bayoneted corpses are the only survivors of seven street cleaners who were sitting in their headquarters when Japanese soldiers came in without warning or reason and killed five of their number and wounded the two that found their way to the hospital.*
>
> *Let me recount some instances occurring in the last two days. Last night the house of one of the Chinese staff members of the university was broken into and two of the women, his relatives, were raped. Two girls, about 16, were raped to death in one of the refugee camps. In the University Middle School where there are*

8,000 people the Japs came in ten times last night, over the wall,
stole food, clothing, and raped until they were satisfied. They bayo-
neted one little boy of eight who have [sic] *five bayonet wounds*
including one that penetrated his stomach, a portion of omentum
was outside the abdomen. I think he will live.[85]

Leading up to these events, the emperor Hirohito had approved a proposal from the army to cast off the dictates of international law regarding the treatment of prisoners of war. Japanese staff officers were advised not even to use the term *prisoner of war.* A direct result was the Straw String Gorge massacre of December 18. After the fall of Nanking, the Japanese rounded up Chinese soldiers and took them to the Yangtze River, tied their hands and feet together, placed them in four columns, and opened fire. Finally they bayonetted each one before dumping the bodies into the river. An estimated 57,500 Chinese prisoners of war were killed.

None of the territories conquered by the Japanese was spared from similar depredations. Here are some examples:

- Approximately 100,000 civilians were massacred in Manila, about 10 percent of the city's population. Japanese soldiers killed men, and raped and murdered women and children indiscriminately.
- In the Sook Ching massacre, the Japanese systematically exterminated the Chinese of Singapore, between 50,000 and 90,000 people, soon after its capture on February 15, 1942.
- The Imperial Japanese Army rounded up the population of Kalagong, Burma, and raped the women and children in an effort to get information. When the Japanese failed to extract anything of value, the entire village of about 600 was massacred and the bodies dumped in wells.[86]

- The Imperial Japanese Navy executed 300 Australian and Dutch prisoners of war on the island of Ambon in the Dutch East Indies.
- Japanese soldiers machine-gunned twenty-two Australian nurses on Bangka Island, also in the Dutch East Indies.
- The Japanese tormented and physically abused 161 Australian prisoners at Parit Sulong, on the west coast of Malaya, before throwing gasoline on them and igniting it.
- On Wake Island, in the North Pacific, the Japanese killed 98 American civilians on October, 7, 1943.
- At Puerto Princesa in Palawan province, Philippines, the Japanese Fourteenth Area Army herded 150 prisoners of war into three covered trenches, doused them with gasoline, and then set them on fire. Those who tried to escape were shot down. Eleven men did manage to get away.
- A Japanese submarine sank a Dutch freighter on March 26, 1944. The crew collected the 105 surviving sailors and killed all but twenty of them, who were then tied with rope and pushed off the submarine before it submerged again.
- The Bataan Death March was perpetrated in the Philippines in 1942, when 75,000 American and Filipino prisoners of war were forced to march sixty miles and treated with great cruelty along the way. Those unable to keep up were shot or run over with trucks. As many as 11,000 may have died.
- At Sandakan POW camp on North Borneo, over 2,500 POWs were held, mostly Australian. "Only six survived the depredation of forced labor, starvation, mass execution, lack of medical treatment, and two death marches in which prisoners were forced to walk 260 kilometers."[87]

Torture was frequently used to extract information from prisoners of war, who often were subsequently executed.[88] Special Japanese military units, such as the infamous Unit 731 under Shiro Ishii, conducted experiments of the most horrific kind possible on POWs and civilians in China.[89] The Japanese also conducted biological warfare with agents and diseases including anthrax, bubonic plague, smallpox, and cholera. The death toll from Japanese experimentation and germ warfare is around 580,000, according to the 2002 International Symposium on the Crimes of Bacteriological Warfare.[90]

Yoshiaki Yoshimi, a professor of history at Chuo University in Tokyo and founding member of the Center for Research and Documentation on Japan's War Responsibility, has studied the use of chemical weapons during the war. Along with Kentaro Awaya, he determined that the Imperial Japanese Army was employing chlorine, phosgene, lewisite, and nausea gas extensively beginning in spring 1938 and mustard gas from summer 1939 against Chinese troops.[91] Together with Yuki Tanaka of the Hiroshima Peace Institute, Yoshimi found documents in the Australian National Archives showing that cyanide gas was tested on Australian and Dutch prisoners on the Kai Islands of Indonesia in 1944.[92]

Many amply confirmed eyewitness testimonies and written reports attest to acts of cannibalism against natives and Allied prisoners of war committed by Japanese personnel in many parts of Asia and the Pacific. The Australian section of the Tokyo War Crimes Tribunal gathered much of this evidence. "Cannibalism was often a systematic activity conducted by whole squads and under the command of officers," wrote Yuki Tanaka.[93] Hatam Ali testified that flesh was cut from living people in New Guinea.[94]

More than ten million Chinese civilians were mobilized for forced labor.[95] About 270,000 Javanese laborers were brought to various parts of Southeast Asia under Japanese command, but only 52,000 ever returned—a death rate of over 80 percent.[96] The Japanese forced about 180,000 Asian laborers and 60,000 Allied prisoners of war to build the Burma Railway linking Rangoon and Bangkok, a distance of about 258 miles. Nearly 90,000 Asians and 16,000 Allied POWs died as a direct result of the project.[97]

Yoshiaki Yoshimi has argued that as many as 200,000 women were forced into Japanese military brothels. Most were from Korea and China, while others came from the Philippines, Burma, the Dutch East Indies, the Netherlands, and Australia.[98]

Islamic Jihad Conquest

Professor Hugh Kennedy, from the School of Oriental and African Studies in London, published a book in 2007 titled *The Great Arab Conquests: How the Spread of Islam Changed the World We Live In.*[99] One wonders if a publisher today would promote a book titled *The Great British Empire, and How It Changed the World.* Many a modern introductory book on Islam begins by singing the praises of a people who conquered half the civilized world in an incredibly short period of time; in glowing terms it will recount an era when Muslims ruled over a vast population of diverse peoples and cultures, in an empire stretching from the banks of the Indus to the shores of the Atlantic. One can hardly imagine a contemporary British historian getting away with similar eulogies to the British Empire, nostalgically recalling a time when three-quarters of the world was colored red in English atlases to indicate the British Empire and Possessions. European colonialism and imperialism (both being terms of abuse by now) are blamed for all manner of problems on earth, and treated as a matter of shame for all Europeans; but Arab imperialism is held up as something admirable and a justifiable source of Muslim pride. While Europeans are castigated for having imposed their language and culture on the Third World, few care to point out how Islamic armies and colonizers trampled many ancient, advanced civilizations.

Professor Speros Vryonis has described in detail how the Byzantine civilization, an essentially Hellenic and Christian way of life, was annihilated by the Turkish invasions of the eleventh century.[100] Magnificent monasteries were ravaged; large numbers of people were massacred or enslaved if they could not flee. To illustrate the violence and devastation in the Turkish conquest of Byzantine Anatolia, Vryonis quotes from the lament of Anna Comnena, daughter of the Byzantine emperor:

> *Swords and spears were whetted against the Christians, and also battles, wars, and massacres. Cities were obliterated, lands were plundered, and the whole land of the Rhomaioi was stained by blood of Christians. Some fell piteously [the victims] of arrows and spears, others being driven away from their homes were carried off captive to the cities of Persia. Terror reigned over all and they hastened to hide in the caves, forests, mountains, and hills. Among them some cried aloud in horror at those things which they suffered, being led off to Persia; and others who yet survived (if some did remain within the Rhomaic boundaries), lamenting, cried, the one for his son, the other for his daughter. One bewailed his brother, another his cousin who had died previously, and like women shed hot tears. And there was at that time not one relationship which was without tears and without sadness.[101]*

Vryonis lists eighty towns and villages, thirty-four environs of towns and villages, and thirteen provinces that were "pillaged, enslaved, massacred, or besieged" by the invading Turks. He also quotes a fourteenth-century account by Demetrius Cydones of Turkish depredations in Anatolia:

> *They took from us all the lands which we enjoyed from the Hellespont eastward to the mountains of Armenia. The cities they razed to the ground, pillaged the religious sanctuaries, broke open the graves, and filled all with blood and corpses. They outraged the souls of the inhabitants, forcing them to deny God and giving to*

them their own defiled mysteries. They abused their [Christians']
souls, alas, with wanton outrage! Denuding them of all property
and their freedom, they left the [Christians as] weak images of
slaves, exploiting the remaining strength of the wretched ones for
their own prosperity.[102]

Sultans gave the wealth and lands confiscated from Christians to their own Muslim followers. Mosques and madrassas sprang up all over Anatolia, often in buildings taken from the Greek Orthodox Church.[103] By the end of the fifteenth century, the Byzantine Empire was obliterated.[104]

The Muslim conquests were achieved at "extraordinary cultural costs."[105] It is both sad and ironic that all teaching in the French language was discontinued in Algeria because it was considered a symbol of French imperialism. This policy is sad because it has cut a whole generation off from the rich cultural heritage of another civilization; it is ironic because Arabic itself was imposed on a people whose mother tongue was Berber. Arab imperialism even convinced those people that they were ethnically Arab (which they were not) and brainwashed them into accepting a religion that was alien to their own tradition. Muslims despise any coreligionists who accept what they regard as alien Western values, yet fail to consider that they themselves could justifiably be seen as "traitors" to the culture of their ancestors. Muslims in present-day India are descendants of Hindus; in Iran, of Zoroastrians; in Syria, of Christians. A vast number of Muslims throughout the world have been persuaded to accept a religion that originated thousands of miles away and to bow toward Arabia five times a day—a vivid symbol of cultural imperialism. Before they can read or write their national language, they are taught to recite a book in a language they do not understand. These Muslims learn more about the history of a people remote from them geographically and ethnically than about their own countries before the advent of Islam.

Islamic dominance has cut millions of people off from their own non-Muslim heritage, as V. S. Naipaul observed during his travels in Pakistan:

> *The time before Islam is a time of blackness: that is part of Muslim theology. History has to serve theology. The excavated city of Mohenjodaro in the Indus Valley—overrun by the Aryans in 1500 BC—is one of the archaeological glories of Pakistan and the world. The excavations are now being damaged by waterlogging and salinity, and appeals for money have been made to world organizations. A featured letter in* Dawn *[a daily Pakistani newspaper] offered its own ideas for the site. Verses from the Koran, the writer said, should be engraved and set up in Mohenjodaro in "appropriate places": "Say (unto them, O Mohammed): Travel in the land and see the nature of the sequel for the guilty. . . . Say (O Mohammad, to the disbelievers): Travel in the land and see the nature of the consequence for those who were before you. Most of them were idolaters."[106]*

The Arabs turned out to be the most successful imperialists of all time, since so many of those conquered by Arabs came to believe they were thereby saved and that their whole prior cultural heritage was worthless. "History, in the Pakistan schoolbooks I looked at, begins with Arabia and Islam," Naipaul reports. "In the simpler texts, surveys of the Prophet and the first four caliphs and perhaps the Prophet's daughter are followed, with hardly a break, by lives of the poet Iqbal, Mr Jinnah, the political founder of Pakistan, and two or three 'martyrs,' soldiers or airmen who died in the holy wars against India in 1965 and 1971."[107]

A contempt for the pagan past still limits the historical imagination and narrows the intellectual horizons of most Muslims. It was left to Western archaeologists to recover and give back to mankind a part of its glorious past. The sciences of Egyptology, Assyriology, and Iranology were initially the exclusive concerns of European and American scholars.

India under the Arabs and the British

The British Empire is typically characterized as an overwhelmingly negative force in history, but a comparison with the rival imperialism of Islam provides a corrective to this view. The Islamic conquest of India brought the destruction of Hindu and Buddhist temples, sculptures, and art; forced conversions; taxes demanded by Islamic law; reduction of the Hindu population to second-class status and slavery.

K. S. Lal analyzed demographic data for India from 1000 to 1525—from Mahmud of Ghazni to the end of the Delhi sultanate— half a millennium of invasion and jihad by Muslim warriors who are celebrated in Muslim chronicles as "killers of *lakhs*" of Hindus. A *lakh* equals a hundred thousand. Lal estimates that the number of Hindus who perished as a result of these jihad campaigns was approximately eighty million.[108]

Sir Jadunath Sarkar wrote about the dreadful consequences of Islamic imperialism for the peoples of India, the inferior status imposed on non-Muslims, the discriminatory taxes, the constant humiliation of Hindus and others.[109] There was a period of Mughal tolerance, especially under Akbar the Great—who, significantly, did not consider himself a Muslim.[110] But the long-term result of Islamic rule in India was cultural stagnation. "The barrenness of the Hindu intellect and the meanness of spirit of the Hindu upper classes are the greatest condemnation of Muhammadan rule in India," wrote Sir Jadunath. "The Islamic political tree, judged by its fruit, was an utter failure."[111]

Several hundred years of Muslim rule did not result in anything comparable to the splendid institutions that emerged after two hundred years of a British presence. Indeed, the British influence is credited for sparking a Bengal Renaissance. "The greatest gift of the English, after universal peace and the modernization of society, and indeed the direct result of these two forces, is the Renaissance which marked our nineteenth century," wrote Sir Jadunath. "Modern India owes everything to it."[112]

Similarly, the Indian historian R. C. Majumdar contrasts the lack of Hindu cultural advancement under the long period of Muslim colonial rule with the great achievements made during the much shorter interval of British rule: "Judged by a similar standard, the patronage and cultivation of Hindu learning by the Muslims, or their contribution to the development of Hindu culture during their rule . . . pales into insignificance when compared with the achievements of the British rule."[113]

It is instructive to compare Islamic and British attitudes toward the monuments of other civilizations: contempt and vandalism on the one hand, respect and preservation on the other. Here is how Vincent Smith described the Muslim assault on all traces of Buddhism in Bihar, northeast India:

> *The ashes of the Buddhist sanctuaries at Sarnath near Banares still bear witness to the rage of the image-breakers. Many noble monuments of the ancient civilisation of India were irretrievably wrecked in the course of the early Muslim invasions. Those invasions were fatal to the existence of Buddhism as an organized religion in northern India, where its strength resided chiefly in Bihar and certain adjoining territories. The monks who escaped massacre fled, and were scattered over Nepal, Tibet, and the south.[114]*

The art historian J. C. Harle remarked that the *furor islamicus,* the urge to destroy the idols of the infidels, is a main reason for the paucity of early art and architectural remains in Bihar.[115]

Thousands of Hindu temples were also razed to the ground. Sita Ram Goel compiled evidence from more than eighty Muslim sources to catalogue the devastation. Here are some examples:

So the temples were attacked "all along the way" as the armies of Islam advanced; they were "robbed of their sculptural wealth," "pulled down," "laid waste," "burnt with naptha," "trodden under horse's hoofs," and "destroyed from their very foundations," till "not a trace of them remained." Mahmûd of Ghazni robbed and burnt down 1,000 temples at Mathura, and 10,000 in and around Kanauj. One of his successors, Ibrâhîm, demolished 1,000 temples each in Hindustan (Ganga-Yamuna Doab) and Malwa. Muhammad Ghûrî destroyed another 1,000 at Varanasi. Qutbu'd-Dîn Aibak employed elephants for pulling down 1,000 temples in Delhi. Alî I 'Âdil Shâh of Bijapur destroyed 200 to 300 temples in Karnataka. A sufi, Qâyim Shâh, destroyed 12 temples at Tiruchirapalli. Such exact or approximate counts, however, are available only in a few cases. Most of the time we are informed that "many strong temples which would have remained unshaken even by the trumpets blown on the Day of Judgment, were levelled with the ground when swept by the wind of Islam."[116]

Lord Curzon, the British viceroy of India (1898–1905), was shocked to see the decay and neglect of India's monuments, whether from Muslim and Sikh conquests, or Indian indifference, or the disrespectful way that the British had turned empty palaces into barracks in addition to constructing their own eyesores. The viceroy believed that his country had since "purged itself of the spirit of stupid and unlettered vandalism," and should now atone by taking vigorous action to preserve India's magnificent cultural heritage, "an elementary obligation of government." The British could not afford "to allow the memorials of an earlier and superior art or architecture to fall into ruin."[117] Lord Curzon told the Asiatic Society of Bengal:

> *If there be any one who says to me that there is no duty devolving upon a Christian Government to preserve the monuments of a pagan art, or the sanctuaries of an alien faith, I cannot pause to argue with such a man. Art and beauty, and the reverence that is owing to all that has evoked human genius or has inspired human faith, are independent of creeds, and, in so far as they touch the sphere of religion, are embraced by the common religion of all mankind. . . . There is no principle of artistic discrimination between the mausoleum of the despot and the sepulchre of the saint. What is beautiful, what is historic, what tears the mask off the face of the past, and helps us to read its riddles, and to look it in the eyes— these, and not the dogmas of a combative theology, are the principle criteria to which we must look.[118]*

Lord Curzon carried out his preservationist mission with fervor and thoroughness. He had an English club cleared out of the royal palace in Mandalay, and a post office removed from a beautiful Islamic building. He had cobwebs and insects cleaned out, and cracked plaster repaired. Minarets were rebuilt, fountains restored, trees planted. Craftsmen were trained to re-create seventeenth-century work in marble and sandstone. Curzon found a mosaicist from Florence to revive the ancient art of *pietra dura* inlay and repair the marble panels of the Red Fort in Agra that were damaged in the Mutiny. He also devoted special care to the Taj Mahal and other sites in Agra, which he believed to have the loveliest architectural remains in the world. He called his considerable expenditures on Agra "an offering of reverence to the past and a gift of recovered beauty to the future."[119]

Said's Orientalism

In the view of Edward Said, the Arabs and "Orientals," by which he seems to mean only Muslims, were always the victims of European imperialism. His hugely influential *Orientalism* does not mention the inconvenient fact that Jews were a significant part of the population of Middle Eastern countries and made great contributions to them, but were chased out or persecuted, especially during moments of intensified Arab nationalism or Muslim fervor. A great number of the Sephardic Jews fleeing from Muslim persecution ended up in Israel, where they now constitute about 50 percent of the population. It makes no sense to talk of Israel as a European colony—nor to reduce everything to an East-versus-West anti-imperialist struggle, as Said did.

Said claimed that the Islamologists were all colluding with imperialists. But he left out any reference to the German Islamologists, since that would have undermined his argument. Germans were the greatest scholars of Islam in the nineteenth century, but Germany had no colonies to speak of in the Islamic world. Said clearly preferred to forget that imperial Germany encouraged Muslims to revolt against the British and the Russians during World War I, and that Arab leaders allied themselves with the Nazis during World War II. Arab philo-Nazism came to be redefined as progressive because it was anticolonialist.

Another curious omission from Said's *Orientalism* is the "Orientals" themselves. Complaining that Orientals were never given a voice, Said opened with an epigraph from Karl Marx: "They cannot represent themselves; they must be represented."[120] But Orientals have in fact been representing themselves for many centuries: in art and literature, in philosophical and historical writings. For Said, however, they seem to exist only when Orientalists write about them.

Surely that is a truly "Orientalist" position, by Said's own pejorative definition. Orientals could not be autonomous individuals or moral subjects with their own desires, in charge of their destiny, but only passive subjects or helpless victims of Western conspiracies. Said could not acknowledge that they were actively and politically engaged with the world, for it would destroy the main thrust of his argument. As C. A. Bayly noted in *The Oxford History of the British Empire,* one of the many unfortunate consequences of Said's influence was the proliferation of histories that denied to Asians or Africans or Polynesians any agency in their own histories "more thoroughly than had the nineteenth-century Imperial writers. Some even espoused the view that history could only represent the view of the white conqueror; we can never know the mind of the 'native.'"[121]

Christopher Hitchens has noted that the "reverse-Orientalist dogma" of Said and his acolytes cannot explain "the alliance of the Turkish empire with imperial Germany, any more than it can account for the current colonization by post-Ottoman Turkey of Christian and European Cyprus."[122] Orientals were not passive in their exchanges with the West in the age of imperialism, as Susan Bayly observes: "Throughout the nineteenth century there was much debate, exchange, and 'resistance' across the realm of culture, rather than any one-sided transfer of values or institutions. Indeed, it was Asians as much as Britons who shaped these developments in faith, knowledge, and perception."[123]

☙❧

CONCLUSION

Europe has been guilty of terrible crimes, but what civilization has not? In the twentieth century, the sins of the West were no worse than the crimes and follies of Asia: for example, the Rape of Nanking, when Japanese soldiers killed more than 300,000 unarmed civilians;[124] the crimes of Mao, resulting in the deaths of well over

70 million Chinese in peacetime;[125] Pol Pot's bloody rein in Cambodia, which killed 1.7 million people, one-fifth of the population;[126] or the massacre of more than a million Muslims in East Pakistan (now Bangladesh) by the Muslims of West Pakistan.[127] Nor were they worse than those of Africa: an estimated 300,000 people killed under Idi Amin's regime in Uganda;[128] the massacres in Rwanda that left 800,000 people dead; the slaughter of two million in southern Sudan,[129] and a further 400,000 in Darfur.[130] Neither were they worse than crimes of the Middle East: the genocidal massacre of more than a million Armenians by the Turks;[131] the atrocities of Saddam Hussein;[132] Hafez Assad's attack on the city of Hama in 1982, which left 30,000 to 40,000 civilians dead or missing;[133] the massacre at Palmyra (Tadmur) Prison in Syria;[134] the repressive policies of the Islamic Republic of Iran, which have killed as many as one million people since 1979.[135]

A profound difference between the West and the Rest lies in the way that Western intellectuals, writers, historians, and politicians have themselves chronicled the follies of the West, challenging Westerners to rethink their ideas and alter their policies and social behavior. Self-assessment and courageous acts of self-criticism have resulted in successful movements to abolish slavery, to dismantle empires, to protect the human rights of women and minorities in law, and to defend freedom of inquiry and expression.[136]

CHAPTER FIVE

IRONY, SELF-CRITICISM, AND OBJECTIVITY

Humans are rational beings endowed with powers of reflection and self-reflection, "a perpetually turning feed-back process"[1] that enables them to reinterpret changing data, adjust their beliefs, and change their situation accordingly, instead of passively accepting their lot. A capacity to submit even the most cherished beliefs and traditions to critical scrutiny has been particularly well developed in Western man. Sir Ernst Gombrich argued that this is what explains why the West "so rapidly overtook the great civilizations of the East" after the Middle Ages:

In the venerable civilizations of the East, custom was king and tradition the guiding principle. If change came it was all but imperceptible, for the laws of Heaven existed once and for all and were not to be questioned. That spirit of questioning, the systematic rejection of authority, was the one invention the East may have failed to develop. It originated in ancient Greece. However often authority tried to smother this inconvenient element, its spark was glowing underground. It was that spark, perhaps, that was fanned into flame by the awareness that our ancestors did not have the monopoly of wisdom, and that we may learn to know more than they have if only we do not accept their word unquestioned. As the motto of the Royal Society (dating from 1663) has it, Nullius in verba—By nobody's word. *In pre-war years, when the Warburg Institute was housed next door to the Imperial Institute of Science, I overheard two students at lunch. "How does he know it is a wave?" I venture to think that this kind of question was not often heard in ancient China or India.*[2]

The "spirit of questioning" and the "systematic rejection of authority" were applied not only to science, but to every other aspect of culture and society. The result was a long tradition of self-criticism that had no equivalent outside the West. Questioning and cultural self-criticism often came in the form of irony, which reflects the ability to acquire distance from one's assumptions and view them as though from the outside—in effect, more objectively.

IRONY AND SATIRE

I shall begin with a joke, and it is essential that you be able to laugh at this joke. Time: the 1950s. Place: the Holy Land.

Two archaeologists are working on a site they believe is the true location of the crucifixion of Jesus Christ at Golgotha (Calvary), just outside ancient Jerusalem. After months of careful digging, they come across two skeletons six feet apart. Thinking that perhaps these are the bones of the thieves crucified at the same time as Jesus, they shift their attention to a spot where Jesus himself would have been crucified. Sure enough, they find some bones and the remains of a wooden cross. With more excavation and carbon-dating analysis, they conclude that the archaeological details are consistent with the Gospel accounts of the crucifixion, and that they have found the bones of Jesus.

Realizing the implications of their discovery, they decide to discuss it with some eminent theologians before releasing the news to the public. They immediately think of Rudolf Bultmann (1884–1976), a pioneer of "form criticism." Bultmann was convinced that the Gospel narratives of Jesus' life were not intended as history but rather as theology in an accessible story form, told in the language of myth.[3]

Our archaeologists phone Bultmann and breathlessly explain their discovery. Bultmann listens patiently, and then, after a long silence, he finally says (cue the thick German accent), "You mean he really existed!"

Your laughter is the difference between a democracy that guarantees freedom of expression, and a theocracy that stifles discussion of religion and any other subject it considers taboo. The West is able to submit its own founding texts to scrutiny, and willing to face up to the consequences of this examination. The West is a culture able to laugh at itself, even at its most cherished beliefs. It is a culture capable of irony.

The sense of irony is a subtle state of mind that distinguishes the West from other cultures. The word derives from the Greek *eironeia,* a term of reproach closely associated with Plato's Socrates, meaning dissimulation, dissemblance, feigned ignorance, mock modesty,[4] or sly deception with overtones of gentle mockery.[5] It has acquired a deeper meaning over the centuries, although there is no firm agreement on what is encompassed by the term, a fact that in itself may be a manifestation of irony.

The American philosopher Willard Quine once said that it didn't matter what one believed as long as one was insincere—a witticism that is almost a definition of irony. I would contend that irony is the capacity to look at one's own central beliefs through the eyes of others and recognize their contingency. Irony also encompasses self-deprecation and self-mockery, revealing a humility that enables us to show solidarity with others. "I too have my foibles and weaknesses," it says. Thus, irony can be seen as a form of self-criticism and self-awareness. Behind it are the Christian notions of forgiveness and tolerance, which permit the West to accept man's weaknesses, though without relinquishing moral imperatives or the ability to pass moral judgments. Irony in memorable art holds ideals up before our eyes, but does not allow them to cloud our perception of realities. Great art helps us understand how man aspires to ideals, but falls short.

Here is another joke, which I found at the Ironic Catholic, a website that announces: "We're just having a good-natured chuckle at our human foibles as Christians, with an occasional spicy zinger from left field. Or right field. Or center."[6] This joke features three "dialectical theologians" who tried to achieve some accommodation with critical inquiry and the historical methodology that were putting so much "knowledge" in doubt. In addition to Rudolf Bultmann, the cast includes Paul Tillich, who dismissed biblical literalism, and Karl Barth, perhaps the most orthodox of the three.

The joke goes like this: Barth, Tillich, and Bultmann are fishing on Lake Geneva. They are having a lovely time, smoking their pipes and chatting idly. But it's getting warm and they are thirsty. So Barth stands up, steps out of the boat, and walks across the water to the shore, where he gets some beers and then returns to the boat. The drinks don't last long. So Barth says to Tillich: "Your turn, Paul." Tillich steps out of the boat, walks across the water, and fetches some more beers. It is really hot now, and the drinks are soon finished.

Bultmann is sweating profusely, so finally Barth tells him: "Come on, Rudolf, it's your turn now." With a slight tremor in his knees, Bultmann gets up, steps out of the boat—and sinks like a rock. Fortunately he manages to swim to the surface and drag himself back into the boat. As Bultmann sits sulking at the far end, Tillich turns to Barth and asks: "Do you think we should have told him where the stepping stones are?" Barth looks at him in puzzlement and says: "What stones?"

Irony helps us resolve our differences and diffuse the tensions that inevitably arise in civic and political life. A sense of irony can be acquired, and it may be, as Norman D. Knox observed, what "frees the political activist from fanatical attachment to any one cause, thereby keeping the door to progress open."[7] Or in Friedrich Schlegel's argument, irony takes the user or observer from a "closed" to an "open" state of mind.[8] Always lurking under the ironic stance, however, are certain moral and political dangers, as Hegel pointed out. Irony can lead to a feeling of superiority, accompanied by contempt for ordinary mortals, or it can result in a denial of the great and noble in man. It can lead to cynicism and nihilism, a form of subjectivism that Hegel called "evil through and through" since it was destructive of moral truth.[9] But we can cultivate an ironic attitude that is not totally skeptical or relativistic, one that allows for cross-cultural judgments and promotes moral objectivity. We can be meliorists without being absolutists; we can argue that certain ways of viewing the world are indeed better or truer than others.

The Islamic fundamentalist with his murderous certainties cannot bear the ironic outlook. He hates to be criticized and laughed at; he will kill if he thinks you have insulted his religion, or his prophet or holy book. He certainly does not question his central beliefs or cultivate the reflective attitude that would enable him to see his religion from the outside.

Irony and satire have a central place in the Western tradition of cultural self-criticism that goes back to classical antiquity. As Matthew

Arnold famously said, much of Western literature from the Greeks to the present can be seen as a criticism of life. There is a rich vein of satire in Western writing, from Archilochus and Hipponax, through the comedies of Aristophanes and the hexameters of Lucilius, to Varro and Persius, then through Horace, the picaresque novel of Petronius, the invectives of Seneca, Juvenal, and Lucian—all of whom used ridicule and irony to puncture the pretensions and complacency of various contemporaries and of society as a whole. This vein was further mined by Boccaccio's *Decameron,* Chaucer's *Canterbury Tales,* William Langland's *Vision of Piers Plowman,*[10] Rabelais's *Gargantua and Pantagruel,* and by those eighteenth-century masterpieces of satire, *Gulliver's Travels* (Swift), *Candide* (Voltaire), *Rameau's Nephew* (Diderot), and so on. These works questioned the foundations of contemporary beliefs, every system of thought—religious, philosophical, political, social, or scientific.

‿‿
CULTURAL SELF-CRITICISM

Self-criticism is not just the chance tenor of scattered writings in the Western canon, and it is not confined to some minor genre such as satire; it is the entire warp and woof of Western civilization. One could argue that the European novel, ever since Cervantes' *Don Quixote,* has in some way addressed the difference between life as it is and life as it ought to be. Thus, what I mean by "self-criticism" is both broader and subtler than strident denunciation or the crude social realism of Upton Sinclair's *The Jungle,* for example.

Matthew Arnold defined culture as "the disinterested endeavor after man's perfection," an effort that depends on self-criticism. Education itself is, in essence, a nurturing of the critical spirit. In the preface to *Culture and Anarchy,* Arnold explained his notion of culture as something that is, "above all, an inward operation":

The whole scope of the essay is to recommend culture as the great help out of our present difficulties; culture being a pursuit of our total perfection by means of getting to know, on all the matters which most concern us, the best which has been thought and said in the world; and through this knowledge, turning a stream of fresh and free thought upon our stock notions and habits, which we now follow staunchly but mechanically, vainly imagining that there is a virtue in following them staunchly which makes up for the mischief of following them mechanically.[11]

The ability to turn "a stream of fresh and free thought upon our stock notions and habits" is truly the distinctive, redemptive grace of Western civilization, running through it as a basso ostinato.

The sharpest critiques of the Western tradition are to be found in the West. Modern denunciations of the West by Third World intellectuals such as Frantz Fanon and Edward Said rely on analyses provided by Western thinkers, including Karl Marx, Sigmund Freud, Friedrich Nietzsche, Antonio Gramsci, Jacques Derrida, Michel Foucault, Jacques Lacan, and Jean-Paul Sartre. The method of critical analysis developed in the West, said Arthur Schlesinger Jr., is testimony to "the internally redemptive potentialities of the Western tradition."[12]

The movement to end slavery began with cultural self-criticism in the West, and was inspired by Christianity. In 1783, a group of three hundred Quakers presented the British Parliament with the first petition calling for the suppression of the slave trade. This initiative resulted in the formation of a nondenominational Committee for the Abolition of the Slave Trade. Nine of the twelve founding members were Quakers and the remaining three were evangelical Anglicans: Granville Sharp, Thomas Clarkson, and William Wilberforce.

Before this time, many British writers and intellectuals had already started to bring about a change in public opinion with their denunciations of the slave trade. Daniel Defoe castigated the trade in humans in his *Life of Colonel Jacque* (1722).[13] Thomas Day called slavery "a crime so monstrous against the human species that all those who practise it deserve to be extirpated from the earth."[14] He also wrote an antislavery poem called "The Dying Negro" (1773). Joseph Priestley argued that slavery reduced men and women to "mere brutes," leaving them "deprived of every advantage of their rational nature."[15] Jeremy Bentham described the colonies where slavery flourished as "a disgrace and an outrage upon humanity."[16]

The sermons of Laurence Sterne expressing pity for slaves touched the heart of a slave named Ignatius Sancho, who became a friend of many learned men in London. Sterne and Sancho exchanged moving letters, such as one in which Sterne wrote:

> [B]ut 'tis no uncommon thing, my good Sancho, for one half of the world to use the other half of it like brutes, and then endeavour to make 'em so. For my own part, I never look Westward (when I am in a pensive mood at least) but I think of the burdens which our brothers and sisters are there carrying—& could I ease their shoulders from one ounce of 'em, I declare I would set out this hour upon a pilgrimage to Mecca for their sakes.[17]

Samuel Johnson pointed out the irony that "Slavery is now no where more patiently endured, than in countries once inhabited by the zealots of liberty."[18] Besides criticizing Americans, he denounced his own English compatriots who were complicit in the trade, saying: "Of black men the numbers are too great who are now repining under English cruelty."[19] Johnson dictated a long argument against slavery to James Boswell.[20] He also assisted Boswell in preparing a brief for the advocate of Joseph Knight, an African-born slave sold in Jamaica who was seeking freedom from his Scottish master. Knight was encouraged by a ruling of 1772 in which England's Lord Chief

Justice, Lord Mansfield, had called slavery "odious," a ruling taken by many to mean that slavery was outlawed in England, although its actual focus was narrower. Lord Kames and his fellow judges on the Scottish Court of Session wrote in their judgment on the Knight case: "The dominion assumed over the negro, under the law of Jamaica, being unjust, could not be supported in this country to any extent." They pronounced slavery to be against the law in Scotland and granted Knight his freedom.[21]

Richard Brinsley Sheridan, a playwright and member of Parliament, spoke against slavery in the House of Commons in 1807, when Lord Percy proposed a bill to phase out the institution in the West Indies.[22] Sheridan would influence the great African American abolitionist Frederick Douglass, who at the age of twelve found another speech of his in *The Columbian Orator,* a collection of speeches and dialogues from various periods of Western history compiled in New England by Caleb Bingham. Douglass read the book at every opportunity, he wrote in his autobiography. He was particularly influenced by John Aikin's "Dialogue Between a Master and Slave," in which the slave refutes every argument for slavery that his master brings forward, and finally the master emancipates the slave. "It is unnecessary to say that a dialogue with such an origin and such an end, read by me when every nerve in my being was in revolt at my own condition as a slave, affected me most powerfully," Douglass wrote. In the same book he also found "one of Sheridan's mighty speeches, on the subject of Catholic Emancipation," among other inspiring orations.

These were all choice documents to me, and I read them over and over again, with an interest that was ever increasing . . . . The reading of these speeches added much to my limited stock of language, and enabled me to give tongue to many interesting thoughts which had often flashed through my mind and died away for want of words in which to give them utterance. The mighty power and

heart-searching directness of truth penetrating the heart of a slave-
holder, compelling him to yield up his earthly interests to the claims
of eternal justice, were finely illustrated in the dialogue; and from
the speeches of Sheridan I got a bold and powerful denunciation of
oppression and a most brilliant vindication of the rights of man.[23]

There is surely something moving about an African American abolitionist being inspired by the self-criticism of dead white males.

Douglass also took inspiration from the Declaration of Independence and the U.S. Constitution, where he found statements and
implications of universal values that he drew upon to argue for the
abolition of slavery:

[T]he constitution of the United States—inaugurated "to form a
more perfect union, establish justice, insure domestic tranquillity,
provide for the common defense, promote the general welfare, and
secure the blessings of liberty"—could not well have been designed
at the same time to maintain and perpetuate a system of rapine
and murder like slavery. Especially, as not one word can be found
in the constitution to authorize such a belief. . . . [T]he constitu-
tion of our country is our warrant for the abolition of slavery in
every state in the American Union.[24]

The distinguishing institutions of the West, with their inherited wisdom, are its chief glory, even though Westerners have not always
lived up to them. The eighteenth century was the high tide of the
Atlantic slave trade, yet it also brought a revival of the Western ideals of freedom, equality, and human rights, eventually leading to the
abolition of the degrading traffic in humans.

Critics of the European colonial empires, such as Edward Said,
have contended that egregious acts of brutality against the indigenous peoples represented the very nature of Western culture, not just

aberrations. But as Keith Windschuttle reminded them, the West itself had produced its own anti-imperialist, anticolonialist tradition:

Many of them write as if they believe the critique of imperialism first emerged among its colonized subjects as a protest at their bondage. The most they concede to the Western side of the equation is that anti-imperialism also arose within Marxism especially Lenin's book Imperialism: The Highest Stage of Capitalism *(1917). (Marx himself, some are aware, was in favour of British rule in India, which he thought would hasten the world revolution.) But in fact the merits of imperialism have been debated in the West since the Middle Ages.*[25]

Surely one factor in the hasty and unseemly abandonment of British India was the hostile climate generated by critics of empire such as John Stuart Mill, H. G. Wells, George Bernard Shaw, and John Galsworthy. In advancing various reasons —from the humanitarian to the economic—for Britain to disengage from its colonies and desist from empire building, they could draw upon the critiques offered by earlier generations. John Locke denied any natural right of conquest. Jonathan Swift, in that supreme work of self-criticism and redemptive grace, *Gulliver's Travels,* appealed to humanitarian considerations in calling the practice of colonization into question:

To say the truth, I had conceived a few scruples with relation to the distributive justice of princes upon those occasions. For instance, a crew of pirates are driven by storm they know not whither, at length a boy discovers land from the topmast, they go on shore to rob and plunder, they see an harmless people, are entertained with kindness, they give the country a new name, they take formal possession of it for the king . . . they murder two or three dozen of the natives . . . return home, and get their pardon. . . . Ships are sent

with the first opportunity, the natives driven out or destroyed, their
princes tortured to discover their gold . . . and this execrable crew
of butchers employed in so pious an expedition, is a modern colony
sent to convert and civilize an idolatrous and barbarous people.[26]

In a similar spirit, Samuel Johnson grumbled, "I do not much wish
well to discoveries for I am always afraid they will end in conquest
and robbery." Jeremy Bentham advised the French revolutionaries to
emancipate France's colonies.[27] Adam Smith raised pragmatic arguments against empire in *The Wealth of Nations.*[28]

Soon after the Great Mutiny of 1857, when the British public was
clamoring for some sort of revenge for the deaths of the British citizens during the uprising, John Malcolm Ludlow, a Christian social-
ist, had the courage to paint an unflattering portrait of the principal
actors who shaped British policy, Robert Clive and Warren Hastings:
"To play fast and loose with the plighted word of state, to sell the
mercenary sword to whoever might bid high enough for it, to help
wrong and fleece the wrong-doer, such was English custom in those
days."[29] Ludlow held the British Parliament and the British people
ultimately responsible for the judicial inequities, the oppressive fiscal
system, and the lagging economy of India. In his view, the establishment and maintenance of English power in India was an ugly story:
"It begins in feebleness and cowardice; it is pervaded by rapacity; it
closes with a course of fraud and falsehood, of forgery and treason, as
stupendous as ever lay at the foundation of a great empire."[30]

These anti-imperialist and abolitionist themes were characteristic of the Western capacity for self-criticism and self-correction. By
contrast, self-criticism remains elusive in Islamic cultures. Regarding
the Arab Islamic world, David Pryce-Jones argues that the "acquisition of honour, pride, dignity, respect and the converse avoidance
of shame, disgrace, and humiliation are keys to Arab motivation,
clarifying and illuminating behaviour in the past as well as in the
present." The imperatives of honor and shame "enforce identity and

conformity of behaviour."[31] In such a value system, it is impossible to admit publicly that one is wrong, for doing so would bring shame on the individual, the family, the country, or even his religion. Taslima Nasrin, an apostate from Islam (now an atheist) and a human rights advocate who was forced out of her native Bangladesh, once gave a talk in Germany criticizing Islam for its treatment of women and non-Muslim minorities. After her talk, an Arab warned her never to insult Islam in public again; he felt totally humiliated, especially in front of an infidel audience, even though in private he agreed with many of her strictures on his nominal religion.[32] Western-style satire would be very difficult to try in Arab society, for it would risk the humiliation of one's own culture.

A pervasive worry about cultural shame is intensified by the conspiracy theories that are rife throughout the Middle East. "By filtering reality through a distorting prism," writes Daniel Pipes in *The Hidden Hand,* this conspiracy thinking "fosters anti-Western, anti-Israeli, anti-democratic, antimoderate, and antimodern actions. At the same time, and almost paradoxically, it infuses the region's peoples with a sense of passivity."[33] An obsession with conspiracies leads to fatalism, a refusal to take charge of one's own destiny or to take responsibility for the manifest backwardness of one's culture. Instead, everything wrong is blamed on the West, with ostentatious self-pity: "If only the wicked West and those Zionists would leave us alone, we would be great again as in the time of our forefathers, when one Muslim could fell ten infidels with a stroke of the sword!" In a culture so defensive and shame-averse, any cultural self-criticism takes courage and is rather rare.

Another possible reason for the dearth of self-criticism in Islamic countries may be conjectured from Czeslaw Milosz's analysis in *The Captive Mind.* He devotes a chapter to how people in totalitarian societies develop means to cope publicly with all the contradictions of everyday life. One cannot openly admit to such contradictions; officially they do not exist. Hence people learn to dissimulate their thoughts and emotions, never revealing their true beliefs publicly. Milosz sees a striking analogy in Islamic civilization, where it goes under the name *ketman,* the Persian word for concealment. Milosz found its description in Gobineau's *Religions and Philosophies of Central Asia.* "The people of the Mussulman East," wrote Gobineau, "believe that 'He who is in possession of truth must not expose his person, his relatives or his reputation to the blindness, the folly, the perversity of those whom it has pleased God to place and maintain in error.' One must, therefore, keep silent about one's true convictions if possible." If silence does not suffice, one may resort to all kinds of ruses by which "one acquires the multiple satisfactions and merits of having placed oneself and one's relatives under cover, of not having exposed a venerable faith to the horrible contact of the infidel, and finally of having, in cheating the latter and confirming him in his error, imposed on him the shame and spiritual misery that he deserves."[34] *Ketman* is practiced equally in front of infidels and other Muslims of a different sect or tribe. Gobineau gives the example of Hadzhi-Sheikh-Ahmed, the founder of a sect, who never openly advanced the heretical ideas that were attributed to him, even in his books, though in private he was more daring.[35]

In the late nineteenth and early twentieth centuries, a liberal class was emerging in some Muslim countries, and it seemed for a breathless and magical while that the Islamic world would finally step into the modern age. In Egypt, Qassem Amin called for the emancipation of women; Taha Hussein advocated free schooling and the use of reason; Salama Moussa founded the Egyptian Association of Scientific Culture. Barry Rubin summarizes how these liberal thinkers joined a capacity for self-criticism with an appreciation for non-Arab traditions:

> *During the 1920s and 1930s, such thinkers and political figures— especially, but not exclusively, in Egypt—declared themselves*

rationalists, patriots of their own countries rather than pan-Arab nationalists, part of a Mediterranean people whose history was rooted in all those who had lived on that soil and not just the Arabs or Muslims among them. They dreamed of making Egypt a modern state along European lines while at the same time preserving its own traditions. The view of one such man, Tawfiq al-Hakim, could well stand as a contemporary liberal credo: the highest priority was to understand past mistakes to avoid repeating them; the biggest task was to expose truth no matter who was offended or what established ideas were challenged.[36]

And yet something went wrong; the liberal train was derailed. From the 1950s onward, talk of freedom, democracy, and representative government was no longer being heard, and the idea of taking responsibility for society's problems lost out to blaming them on foreigners.[37] Thus it is all the more important to acknowledge the exceptions—the liberal Arab intellectuals like al-Afif al-Akhdar and Tarek Heggy.

Al-Akhdar, a Tunisian who lives in France, wrote a blistering critique of Arab societies, lamenting that while the rest of the world was embracing modernity and globalization, the Arabs were regressing to the Dark Ages. Why was human knowledge growing everywhere else, he asked, while the Arab mind was gripped by illiteracy and ideological paralysis? asked al-Akhdar.

Why do expressions of tolerance, moderation, rationalism, compromise, and negotiation horrify us, but [when we hear] fervent cries for vengeance, we all dance the war dance? Why have the people of the world managed to mourn their pasts and move on, while we have . . . our gloomy bereavement over a past that does not pass? Why do other people love life, while we love death and violence, slaughter and suicide, and call it heroism and martyrdom?

Arabs suffer from an inferiority complex and a "national humiliation whose shame can be purged only by blood, vengeance, and fire." At the same time, they nurture a belief in their own superiority as those chosen by Allah to lead humanity—so why should they borrow anything from their inferiors? The Koran describes the Arabs as the best nation in the world, yet their history in the last two centuries is a chronicle of failures. The result is "a fixated, brooding, vengeful mentality" that is inimical to "farsighted thought and self-criticism." Al-Akhdar suggests that Arabs could learn from the Japanese, who understood the "vital necessity to emulate the enemy . . . becoming like him in modern knowledge, thought and politics, so as to reshape the traditional personality and adapt it to the requirements of the time."[38]

Another bold critic from within the Arab world is Tarek Heggy, an Egyptian who studied law and management and worked at the Shell Oil Company for many years. "We have dug ourselves into a cave, cut off from the rest of humanity thanks to a static mindset that ignores the realities of our time and the new balances of power," wrote Heggy. He continued: "We remain locked in a fantasy world of our own making . . . a world in which anachronistic slogans are still widely regarded as sacrosanct, immutable constants." The result has been isolation and alienation from the outside world, and at home "a pattern of lost opportunities and a climate inimical to democracy and development." Egyptian intellectuals have created "an intellectually barren and culturally stagnant landscape which has moved Egypt further away from its dream of catching up with the developed world."[39]

Unfortunately, candor of this kind is rare in the Arab world, where the few liberal intellectuals to be found are kept in check by the political powers through control of the media and other cultural institutions.[40] Arab liberal thought is thus "fragmented, advocated by largely isolated individuals," notes Barry Rubin, and consequently "the liberal case is heard by only a tiny portion of Arabs, its small space hedged about with the thorns of its enemies."[41]

OBJECTIVITY AND CURIOSITY

And you shall know the truth, and the truth
shall make you free.
—JOHN 8:32

The attainment of truth is the common end of all the sciences in the broadest sense. Philosophers have often defined knowledge as belief that is justified by truth, yet postmodernists and other charlatans argue that the very notion of truth or objective knowledge is merely part of an imperialistic "discourse of power." To reject the notion of objective knowledge, however, is to abandon the possibility of science, or even the possibility of rational discourse on morality and politics, since ethical and political decisions often depend on having access to objective knowledge. We may only approximate the truth most of the time, but we must aim for it through a process of trial and error, conjecture and refutation, corroboration and disconfirmation.

The search for objective truth begins with curiosity, the desire for knowledge as a good in itself rather than only for instrumental purposes. Curiosity was particularly keen among the ancient Greeks, in comparison with other early civilizations. In the fifth century, Democritus declared that he "would rather discover one cause than gain the kingdom of Persia."[42] Aristotle, who had one of the most widely inquiring minds of anyone who has ever lived, defended his study of the lowliest animals, for even if some "have no graces to charm the sense, yet nature, which fashioned them, gives amazing pleasure in their study to all who can trace links of causation, and are inclined to philosophy. . . . Each and all will reveal to us something natural and something beautiful."[43] Aristotle explained why it is important to set aside utilitarian motives in the pursuit of knowledge:

> *To seek from all knowledge a result other than itself and to demand that it must be useful is the act of one completely ignorant of the distance that from the start separates good things from necessary things; for they differ completely. For the things that are loved for the sake of something else and without which life is impossible must be called necessities and joint-causes; but those that are loved for themselves, even if nothing else follows from them, must be called goods in the strict sense; for this is not desirable for the sake of that, and that for the sake of something else, and so ad infinitum—there is a stop somewhere.[44]*

In later republican Rome, Cicero likewise described the pursuit of knowledge as an activity central to the nature of man as a rational creature. "Inquiry into and searching for truth are primary characteristics of mankind," he wrote in his treatise *On Duty*. "So when we are free from business obligations and other preoccupations, we become eager to see something new, to hear and learn something; we begin to think that knowledge about the mysteries and wonders of the world is necessary to a happy life."[45] Cicero's attitude toward learning may be taken as typical of educated Romans in his day.

Cardinal Newman, in his classic defense of education as a self-justifying good, referred to Cicero's view of knowledge as the first thing we seek after our physical wants have been satisfied. The ideal of knowledge for its own sake has been obstinately holding its ground from age to age, wrote Newman in *The Idea of a University*.

> *Knowledge is capable of being its own end. Such is the constitution of the human mind, that any kind of knowledge, if it be really such, is its own reward. . . . Now, when I say that Knowledge is, not merely a means to something beyond it, or the preliminary of*

certain arts into which it naturally resolves, but an end sufficient to rest in and to pursue for its own sake, surely I am uttering no paradox, for I am stating what is intelligible in itself, and has ever been the common judgment of philosophers and the ordinary feeling of mankind. . . . [W]e are satisfying a direct need of our nature in its very acquisition; and, whereas our nature, unlike that of the inferior creation, does not once reach its perfection, but depends, in order to it, on a number of external aids and appliances, Knowledge, as one of the principle of these, is valuable for what its very presence in us does for us after the manner of a habit, even though it be turned to no further account, nor subserve any direct end.[46]

Intellectual curiosity, a thirst after knowledge as a thing of value in itself, has been a distinctive feature of Western civilization through the centuries and lies at the heart of many Western institutions. Matthew Arnold identified a certain kind of curiosity as the origin of objectivity, the ability "to see things as they are," and as an essential driver of science and culture:

For as there is a curiosity about intellectual matters which is futile, and merely a disease, so there is certainly a curiosity,—a desire after the things of the mind simply for their own sakes and for the pleasure of seeing them as they are,—which is, in an intelligent being, natural and laudable. Nay, and the very desire to see things as they are implies a balance and regulation of mind which is not often attained without fruitful effort, and which is the very opposite of the blind and diseased impulse of mind which is what we mean to blame when we blame curiosity. Montesquieu says:—"The first motive which ought to impel us to study is the desire to augment the excellence of our nature, and to render an intelligent being yet more intelligent." This is the true ground to assign for the genuine scientific passion, however manifested, and for culture, viewed simply as a fruit of this passion; and it is a worthy ground, even though we let the term curiosity stand to describe it.[47]

Islamic civilization generally did not share the Western ideal of pursuing knowledge for its own sake, as Bernard Lewis demonstrates with example after example in *The Muslim Discovery of Europe*. There was relatively little interest in the natural world or in other cultures. The prevailing attitude toward alien literature was contempt; and for a Muslim to learn a foreign language or infidel script was considered impious. We know of only a single document from eight centuries of the Islamic presence in Spain that reveals any interest in a European language. In the Muslim view, European literature provided neither aesthetic appeal nor moral guidance.[48]

Living on a small continent of many nations, Europeans found it necessary to learn different languages. They even developed scholarly tools for the study of Arabic; the first Latin-Arabic glossary was prepared in the twelfth century, opening the way to European appreciation of Arabic literature and even an attempt to translate parts of the Koran into Latin. By the sixteenth century, several Arabic glossaries and dictionaries as well as a treatise on Arabic grammar were available to Europeans.[49] As the intellectual horizons of the West opened wide during the sixteenth and seventeenth centuries, Arabic studies flourished in many European universities, along with the study of Persian and Turkish, resulting in critical editions that laid the foundations of classical Orientalism. This scholarly activity was partly connected to the needs of diplomacy and commerce, as Lewis points out, but also reflected "the boundless intellectual curiosity unleashed by the Renaissance."[50]

In the Islamic world, by contrast, Lewis finds "not the slightest sign" of interest in Western literature or languages. "We know of no Muslim scholar or man of letters before the eighteenth century who sought to learn a Western language, still less of any attempt to produce grammars, dictionaries, or other language tools." The few translations known to have been made were of works with practical purposes, and the translators were converts or non-Muslims.[51] Otherwise, Muslim scholarship was limited to "the monuments of their own faith, law, and literature." European scholars had developed sophisticated techniques of textual criticism in their examination of classical and biblical texts, which they could apply to the study of Eastern languages and literature. Muslim scholars had "nothing remotely comparable."[52] Today, Muslims have yet to learn the science of textual criticism, let alone apply it to the Koran.

From its earliest days, Christianity drew upon the wisdom of classical antiquity, and also rejected the Marcionite attempt to cut all links with Judaic history and doctrine. Consequently, Europe maintained a fruitful relationship with the past, and the traditions of both Athens and Jerusalem have continued to enrich Western civilization throughout its history.[53] Islamic countries, on the other hand, rejected their pre-Islamic past and all the ancient pre-Islamic glories—from the civilization of the Indus River to the monuments of Mesopotamia and Egypt—as belonging to a period of ignorance and barbarism, *Jāhiliyya*.

The only history considered worthy of study was that of the Islamic community, as it revealed God's purpose for mankind. Even the great fourteenth-century sociologist Ibn Khaldun displayed an indifference to European history that was typical in the Islamic world.[54] During his travels in Persia in the seventeenth century, Sir John Chardin noticed an absence of curiosity about, for example, the origins of tobacco and sugar.[55] He found that traveling for the sake of curiosity was an alien concept to the Persians, and this explained their near-total ignorance of customs and happenings in Europe.[56] Little has changed in modern times. Michael Field, a journalist for the *Financial Times* with decades of experience in the Middle East, observed in 1994:

[Arabs] may be well informed on currency movements and the latest chat on the prospects of the Western economies but know surprisingly little about how Western societies and governments operate. Even those who live in the West or visit it frequently on holiday do not have much understanding of it because, in most cases, when they are there they mix with other Arabs, principally their own relations, and take no interest in the culture, history or institutions of the countries they are in.[57]

Muhammad Talbi, a contemporary Tunisian Muslim intellectual who is involved in interfaith dialogues, who has written that "the last Muslim philosopher open to non-Muslim cultures" was Ibn Rushd (twelfth century), called Averröes by the Europeans who were so interested in his work in the Middle Ages and the Renaissance. Today those works are available primarily in Latin or Hebrew. Talbi refers to Ibn Khaldun's belief that "All the pre-Islamic sciences concerned with religious groups are to be discarded, and their discussion is forbidden."[58] This way of thinking has prevailed to this day, when few Muslims have any deep understanding of the West. Citing Maryam Jameelah, Talbi asks, "How many Muslims, for example, have mastered Greek or Latin, and how many are intellectually equipped to study Judaism and Christianity as well as the secular ideologies from a Muslim point of view? While generations of Western Orientalists have studied Islam to the extent of their needs and goals, is it not essential for some Muslim religious scholars to become Occidentalists?"[59]

∾

ISLAM AND FOREIGN SCIENCES

In F. R. Rosenthal's judgment, early Islamic civilization could have developed to the extent it did only because it absorbed part of the Greek classical tradition between the eighth and tenth centuries.[60] By implication, Islamic civilization could have made further progress by a more extensive assimilation of Greek sciences and rationalism. Ernest Renan, on the other hand, saw Islam as fundamentally incompatible with the Greek tradition and concluded that a larger infusion of Greek rationalism would have destroyed Islam. Furthermore, there was simply no such thing as "Islamic science" or "Islamic philosophy" or even "Islamic civilization." He believed it was not because of Islam but despite Islam that science had grown for a while in the early Islamic world:

> *Science and philosophy flourished on Musalman soil during the first half of the Middle Ages; but it was not by reason of Islam, it was in spite of Islam. Not a Musalman philosopher or scholar escaped persecution. During the period just specified persecution is less powerful than the instinct of free inquiry, and the rationalist tradition is kept alive, then intolerance and fanaticism win the day. It is true that the Christian Church also cast great difficulties in the way of science in the Middle Ages; but she did not strangle it outright, as did the Musalman theology. To give Islam the credit of Averröes and so many other illustrious thinkers, who passed half their life in prison, in forced hiding, in disgrace, whose books were burned and whose writings almost suppressed by theological authority, is as if one were to ascribe to the Inquisition the discoveries of Galileo, and a whole scientific development which it was not able to prevent.[61]*

G. E. von Grunebaum similarly argued that what we know as "Islamic science" was actually discouraged by Islam. The most significant achievements in mathematics and medical science within the Islamic world occurred "in areas and in periods where the elites were willing to go beyond and possibly against the basic strains of orthodox thought and feeling."[62]

For many Western scholars and for many Muslims too, the idea of an "Islamic philosophy" is a contradiction in terms. Orthodox

Sunni Islam has never welcomed philosophical thought, with its unfettered use of reason. Traditionalists have always been hostile to philosophy, regarding it as a "foreign science" that leads to heresy, doubt, and unbelief. These fears were well founded, for many of the philosophers within the Islamic world held ideas that were far from orthodox, while others only gave lip service to Islam while they followed the guidance of reason, as exemplified in Greek philosophy.

Muslims made a distinction between native or Islamic sciences and foreign sciences. The former consisted of religion (Koranic exegesis, the science of hadith, jurisprudence, and scholastic theology) and language (grammar, lexicography, rhetoric, and literature). The foreign sciences or "sciences of the ancients" were defined as those common to all peoples and religious communities, including mathematics, philosophy, zoology, botany, medicine, astronomy, music, magic, and alchemy, among others. Early Muslim scholars had contributed to perpetuating the ancient sciences, but these endeavors were always viewed with suspicion, and with growing animosity in the later Middle Ages. The ancient authorities in these sciences were not Muslims, so their works were thought to endanger the faith.[63]

Muhammad is said to have prayed for protection from useless knowledge, meaning all sciences that are not helpful for acting rightly toward Allah. Useful knowledge is that which aids the practice of religion; it can include history and geography as well as theology and language. Any effort of learning beyond that, such as the natural sciences, is not essential to the central cultural task, which is to serve Allah, and therefore it can be discarded. Reason was thus firmly subordinated to revelation and tradition.

Unfettered intellectual inquiry was deemed not only unnecessary but also dangerous. One consequence was the persecution of scientists and philosophers. An example comes from a thirteenth-century Jewish philosopher who went to Baghdad on business and recounted how the library of another philosopher was burned there. The cleric who presided over the ritual picked up a book on astronomy by Ibn al-Haytham (Alhazen), a great mathematician and physicist whose works were translated into Latin and influenced Western scientific thought in the Middle Ages. The cleric "pointed to a delineation therein given of the sphere of the earth, as an unhappy symbol of impious Atheism," and threw the book into the flames.[64] Ibn al-Haytham's works were branded heretical and forgotten in the Muslim East.

Seen from the outside, the suppression of scientific endeavor could only mean an impoverishment of Islamic civilization, but in the Muslim view there was no loss because this science did not serve an essential purpose.[65] For Muslims, as Von Grunebaum put it, scientific research "had nothing to give to their community which this community could accept as an essential enrichment of their lives."[66]

The idea of knowledge for its own sake was meaningless at best in the Muslim context. Instead, knowledge was to be viewed through the lens of theology. George Sarton gives an example in his history of science: "One can find in many Arabic and Persian writings speculations on the order of nature as far as the distribution of the three kingdoms is concerned. The Muslims, with but few exceptions, were hardly interested in the scientific aspects of these matters, but rather in their theological implications; they were not thinking so much of evolution from the human or naturalistic point of view as of creation from the divine one."[67]

This subsuming of all knowledge under the dictates of theology is similar to what Friedrich Hayek described in twentieth-century totalitarian regimes, which also attempted to control opinion on all subjects, even the seemingly nonpolitical. He gave the example of the *Journal for Marxist-Leninist Natural Sciences,* which had these slogans: "We stand for Party in Mathematics. We stand for the purity of Marxist-Leninist theory in surgery."[68] Hayek pointed out that knowledge for its own sake, or indeed "any human activity done for its own sake and without ulterior purpose," was anathema to totalitarian ideologies. In *The Road to Serfdom,* he explained why social planners opposed any "unguided activity":

> *Science for science's sake, art for art's sake, are equally abhorrent to the Nazis, our socialist intellectuals, and the communists. Every activity must derive its justification from a conscious social purpose. There must be no spontaneous, unguided activity, because it might produce results which cannot be foreseen and for which the plan does not provide. It might produce something new, undreamed of in the philosophy of the planner. The principle extends even to games and amusements. I leave it to the reader to guess whether it was in Germany or in Russia that chess-players were officially exhorted that "we must finish once and for all with the neutrality of chess. We must condemn once and for all the formula 'chess for the sake of chess' like the formula 'art for art's sake.'"*[69]

OBJECTIVITY AND THE WESTERN UNIVERSITY

The ideal of pursuing knowledge as a good in itself is enshrined in one of the greatest creations of Western civilization, the university, modeled on the Brotherhood of Pythagoras, the Academy of Plato, and the Lyceum of Aristotle. Most non-Western universities have in some way copied the principles and structure of Western universities, and many are run by scholars and administrators trained in Western universities. The modern university was created as a home for reason, free inquiry, unfettered curiosity, and the search for objective knowledge that is shareable, underlining the unity of man.

Dr. Charles Malik, a Lebanese philosopher and diplomat, contrasts the Western attitude toward knowledge—the curiosity about things outside one's own existence, without any utilitarian purpose—and the attitudes that prevail in other cultures:

172

It is interesting to ponder why Chinese or Indians or Muslims or Arabs can enter Freiburg University or the Sorbonne or Oxford or Harvard or Chicago University or Toronto University and special-ize and earn a universally respected academic degree in their own Chinese or Indian or Muslim or Arab culture, but no German or Frenchman or Englishman or American or Canadian can enter any Chinese or Indian or Muslim or Persian or Arab university and specialize and earn a universally respected academic degree in his own German or French or British or American or Canadian culture. The reason is that these non-Western universities (and therefore their own native cultures which they themselves reflect) have not yet sufficiently caught the insatiable original Greek curi-osity about all being; they are interested in others only to a degree; for the most part only utilitarianly, only to use them, only to learn from them. They are not interested in knowing their essence, their being; they are for the most part wrapped up in themselves; the oth-ers are perhaps too strange, too forbidding for them; their original, natural, wholesome curiosity is somehow inhibited.[76]

No university in any Islamic country, with perhaps the excep-tion of Turkey, offers any rigorous courses on non-Islamic civiliza-tions, certainly nothing with the depth and comprehensiveness of courses offered in Western universities on every civilization, ancient and modern. No scholar from the Islamic world writing about his own culture and history has achieved anything near the scholarship of Carl Brockelmann or Theodor Nöldeke on Islamic studies. There is certainly no Muslim scholar who has contributed anything sig-nificant to the study of European history or languages or literature, in the way that Europeans from the sixteenth century onward have done for many aspects of Islamic civilization.

As Malik observed, Western civilization is defined by openness and fearlessness toward the truth. Writing at the height of the Cold

War, he worried about how this openness was being compromised by a "virus" that came from the bogus universities of the Soviet Union, an "inhibition of original curiosity." For example:

> *Nothing authentic is known or taught in Soviet universities about Christianity; whereas practically everything is known or taught in Western universities about communist doctrine and practice. And, as we shall see, this blunting, inhibiting virus has infected Western universities themselves with respect to the knowledge of Christianity. The non-West is gradually overpowering the West! The original universal Greek curiosity is gradually becoming overwhelmed.*[71]

Today, it is the dictates and prohibitions of Islam that are infecting Western universities. The central purpose of the university—to promote the search for objective truth through impartial research—is being corrupted by a combination of political correctness and Arab money. In recent years, Saudi Arabia and other Islamic countries have established chairs of Islamic studies in prestigious Western universities, which are then influenced to present a favorable image of Islam. Critical examination of the Koran and other primary sources of Islamic doctrine and history are discouraged. Some scholars have even lost their posts for not teaching about Islam in the way approved by Saudi Arabia.[72]

In December 2005, Georgetown and Harvard universities each accepted $20 million from the Saudi prince Alwaleed bin Talal for programs in Islamic studies.[73] Grants of this kind necessarily compromise the university's purpose of seeking truth with no other agendas. Instead, we shall have only "Islamic truth" such as is acceptable to the Saudi royal family—who allegedly have financed terrorism, anti-Westernism, and anti-Semitism for more than thirty years. Previous donations from various Saudi sources included gifts of $20 million to the University of Arkansas, $5 million to the University of California at Berkeley, and another $2 million to Harvard.

More recently, the *Telegraph* (UK) reported disturbing evidence of a determined effort by Arab countries to undermine the West through its prestigious universities in the United Kingdom, by means of grants with strings attached. Sir Howard Davies, the director of the London School of Economics (LSE), resigned from the university's governing council in early March 2011 after it was revealed that the LSE had accepted money from Muammar Gaddafi. The LSE had already received £9 million from the United Arab Emirates to support its Centre for Middle Eastern Studies.[74]

The Centre for Social Cohesion published a comprehensive report in 2009 on the foreign funding of British universities, written by Robin Simcox in a calm and measured tone.[75] An updated summary followed shortly after the LSE / Libya scandal in 2011.[76] These reports revealed that countries with some of the worst human rights records on earth—including China, Iran, and Saudi Arabia—had been funding British universities for many years. China, for example, has given approximately £500,000 "to fund Confucius Institutes, cultural and language centres, at ten UK universities." The Chinese government calls them part of its "foreign propaganda strategy" and sets their curricula, while Chinese government officials sit on their advisory boards.

The money coming from Islamic countries is a greater source of worry. In 1999, the School of Oriental and African Studies at the University of London received £35,000 from Iran, which "funded two studentships over a three year period, of which one was awarded to an Iranian cleric with close links to the regime." A representative of the Iranian government was subsequently invited to deliver a lecture praising Ayatollah Khomeini's "modernisation of Islamic thought." When the University of Durham received £10,000 from Iran in 2009, it had to enter into "a Memorandum of Understanding with the Iranian government, which includes an arrangement to publish joint books, conferences, and research, as well as an exchange programme for students and members of staff," reported the Centre for Social Cohesion. "Dr Colin Turner, co-director of Durham's Centre for Iranian Studies, admitted that a subsequent event was 'monopolised by pro-regime speakers' and that 'Iranian money comes with strings attached.'"

The universities that receive money from Islamic countries are "encouraged" in various ways to teach not merely a particular brand of Islam but also a strong anti-Western message, as Stephen Pollard explained:

A study of five years of politics lectures at the Middle Eastern Centre at St Antony's College, Oxford, found that 70 per cent were "implacably hostile" to the West and Israel. A friend of mine, a former Oxford academic, felt that his time was largely spent battling a cadre of academics overwhelmingly hostile to the West, in an ambience in which students—from both Britain and abroad—were presented a world-view that was almost exclusively anti-Western.[77]

The consequences of these strings-attached donations are grave. They result in a de facto self-censorship because university faculty and staff are reluctant to criticize primary donors. In some cases, the university administration has been altered to please donors; for example, certain members of the management committees for the Islamic studies centers at Cambridge and Edinburgh were appointed by Prince Alwaleed, the principal donor. Some universities have changed the orientation of their fields of study in accordance with donors' wishes. Many Islamic studies centers have a specific political agenda that seriously compromises the principle of academic objectivity. In effect, British universities are being used as diplomatic arms of foreign governments:

Undemocratic governments with poor human rights records are given a platform at UK universities to highlight the advantages of their system of government. This often coincides with substantial donations. For example, following a donation from Saudi Arabia, the King Abdul Aziz ibn Saud Lectures, "named in honour of the founder of the Kingdom of Saudi Arabia," were established at Oxford. Members of the Saudi government regularly speak at and attend these lectures.[78]

The modern university was founded to promote the free pursuit of objective knowledge, without constraints or ulterior purposes. This institution was a great gift from the West to the world. Today, many Western universities seem only too willing to subordinate the search for truth to financial considerations. This is a truly shameful betrayal of their original, noble principles, and of the foundations of Western civilization.

CHAPTER SIX

TWO FREEDOMS

" Congress shall make no law respecting an establishment of religion, or prohibiting the free exercise thereof; or abridging the freedom of speech, or of the press; or the right of the people peaceably to assemble, and to petition the Government for a redress of grievances." This is the First Amendment to the United States Constitution because it is the most important of the ten that constitute the Bill of Rights. It guarantees the two most fundamental rights: freedom of religion, or conscience, and freedom of speech. These freedoms are closely related, and their central place in Western civilization helps explain its success.

FREEDOM OF RELIGION

The situation of religious minorities dramatically highlights a basic difference between the modern West and the Islamic world. Ahmadis and Baha'is, Hindus and Buddhists, Jews and Christians are regularly persecuted in Muslim countries, even ones that have signed the United Nations resolution against religious intolerance. According to Brian Moynahan, Muslim terrorizing of Christians who voted for East Timor's independence in 1999 resulted in tens of thousands of deaths.[1] Churches have been destroyed in Turkey and Cyprus. Christian congregations have been bombed in Pakistan and Egypt. In October 2001, gunmen on motorcycles killed eighteen members of a Christian congregation in the Punjab. In August 2002, masked gunmen killed six people at a Christian school for foreigners in Islamabad. In September 2002, terrorists entered the Peace and Justice Institute in Karachi, separated Christians from Muslims, and then executed the Christians by gunshots to the head.[2] That is just a tiny snapshot of the problem.

In Iraq, attacks on the Christian minority have increased as American forces are preparing to leave. The Christian population in Iraq has dropped to half the size it was before the war started. By UN estimates, about one and a half million Christians were living in Baghdad before 2003; now there are fewer than half a million. Nearly 40 percent of the Iraqi refugees in Syria are Christians. Joe Obayda of Iraqi Christians In Need, a British charity set up in 2007, said that religious persecution was the main reason why Christians were leaving Iraq. His own cousin was forced to flee when Muslim militants tried to convert his daughters to Islam and demanded money from him.[3] Not a word is uttered by any Muslim spokesman against this persecution.

As Raymond Ibrahim has pointed out, acts of violence against Christians are generally reported only in a tendentious and misleading way. For example, when Muslims attack Christians—Assyrians and Chaldeans in Iraq, or Copts in Egypt, or Catholics in Pakistan—this is routinely called "sectarian" strife, as if both sides were equally at fault. Even more disturbing are the many reports implying that the Christians brought their tribulations upon themselves. A story about the Christians of the Holy Land in the *National Geographic* of June 2009 exemplifies this kind of reporting.[4]

Ibrahim argues that the persecution of Copts in Egypt is not just the work of fanatical mobs, but has the backing of many in the army and the police. It is institutionalized persecution. The Egyptian government puts obstacles in the way of Copts when they try to build or repair churches, and the police forces use live ammunition against them when they demonstrate for their rights. On one such occasion, four unarmed Christians were killed.[5] If unarmed Muslims had been killed in similar circumstances in the West, the likely result would be vigorous international condemnation, the retaliatory massacre of innocent Christians throughout the Islamic world, and the pledging of billions of dollars for compulsory courses on the glories of Islamic civilization to be taught in Western schools and colleges.

In Egypt, Christians are locked out of senior positions in government, the military, and education. They are attacked in the government-controlled media. Conversions from Islam to Christianity are not officially recognized, which means that converts to Christianity may not marry those born as Christians, and the children of Christian converts must be educated as Muslims.

If we demand that Muslim countries live up to their political and moral obligations to protect the rights of beleaguered and often terrified religious minorities, we are taking steps toward freedom of conscience and pluralism *tout court*. But as long as religion is joined to the state, Islamic fundamentalism will remain a source of violence. Freedom of conscience can be guaranteed only in a secular state, where religion is a private matter.

Secularization in the West began with the application of critical reason to religious dogma and to the Bible itself, which led to de facto religious pluralism and eventually the realization that conscience cannot be coerced. Once tolerance was granted to particular groups, it could not be restricted to those groups, as Owen Chadwick explained. "You could not confine it to Protestants; nor, later, to Christians; nor, at last, to believers in God. A free market in some opinions became a free market in all opinions."[6] Tolerance of religious minorities opened the way for a more general freedom of conscience in a secularized state. "Christian conscience was the force which began to make Europe 'secular'; that is, to allow many religions or no religion in a state, and repudiate any kind of pressure upon the man who rejected the accepted and inherited axioms of society. My conscience is my own."[7]

Article 18 of the Universal Declaration of Human Rights (1948) codifies freedom of conscience this way: "Everyone has the right to freedom of thought, conscience and religion; this right includes freedom to change his religion or belief." But in speeches to Muslim audiences, President Obama and his secretary of state, Hillary Clinton, have taken to using the expression "freedom of worship," a narrower concept than "freedom of religion." I think the terminology marks a subtle shift in policy. It conveys the Obama administration's unwillingness to defend Article 18, which clearly declares the right to *change* one's religion, not just *worship* in a particular way. Indeed, the Obama administration, along with Western intellectuals and the "mainstream" media, have been shamefully silent about the persecution of religious minorities in the Islamic world, especially the Ahmadis in Pakistan and Christians in all Muslim countries.

The West continues to apologize for its colonial past, for slavery, even for the Crusades, yet Turkey refuses to acknowledge its genocide of Armenians. Western nations might at least commemorate that atrocity by allocating one date on the calendar as a day of remembrance for the Armenians. Such a commemoration might also remind us of the need to keep demanding religious freedom for the people of the Middle East. By insisting on adherence to Article 18 within Islamic societies, we can loosen the grip of fanatics, turning religion into a private matter and ultimately encouraging a "free market in all opinions."

☙ FREEDOM OF SPEECH

Honoré Daumier (1808–1879), *Liberté de la Presse: Ne vous y frottez pas,* "Freedom of the Press: Don't mess with it." (Rosenwald Collection, image courtesy of the National Gallery of Art, Washington)

The freedom to express one's beliefs and opinions, unfettered by censorship or taboos, is one of the most important principles of Western civilization. Freedom of speech is essential for weeding out errors and approaching the truth. It is a means to restrain the excesses of those in power by publicizing their mistakes and misdemeanors. It allows the corrective of criticism to be applied in the public sphere. That is why freedom of expression is indispensable to democracy, and to social, political, scientific, and religious progress.

John Stuart Mill presented a robust defense of this fundamental principle, explaining why the suppression of free speech harms not only the speaker but all of humanity:

> *But the peculiar evil of silencing the expression of an opinion is, that it is robbing the human race; posterity as well as the existing generation; those who dissent from the opinion, still more than those who hold it. If the opinion is right, they are deprived of the opportunity of exchanging error for truth: if wrong, they lose, what is almost as great a benefit, the clearer perception and livelier impression of truth, produced by its collision with error. . . . We can never be sure that the opinion we are endeavouring to stifle is a false opinion; and if we were sure, stifling it would be an evil still.*[8]

Mill's greatest modern admirer, Friedrich Hayek, made a similar case for the necessity of intellectual freedom and the unrestricted right of dissent. Even if only a small minority of society is directly affected, Hayek observed, this freedom benefits the whole society:

> *To deprecate the value of intellectual freedom because it will never mean for everybody the same possibility of independent thought is completely to miss the reasons which give intellectual freedom its value. What is essential to make it serve its function as the prime mover of intellectual progress is not that everybody may be able to think or write anything, but that any cause or idea may be argued by somebody. So long as dissent is not suppressed, there will always be some who will query the ideas ruling their contemporaries and put new ideas to the test of argument and propaganda. This inter-action of individuals, possessing different knowledge and different*

views, is what constitutes the life of thought. The growth of reason
is a social process based on the existence of such differences.[9]

Freedom of expression is endorsed in Article 18 of the Universal Declaration of Human Rights. Today, however, freedom of speech in the West is under threat from radical Islam and even from mainstream Muslim authorities. The Organization of Islamic Cooperation has already succeeded in pushing resolutions through the UN Human Rights Council in Geneva that undermine the very notion of free speech. Meanwhile, many liberals in the West, from government officials to academics and journalists, have failed to stand up for our fundamental liberties—as guaranteed in the U.S. Constitution—but instead have engaged in appeasement and self-censorship. The shameful abandonment of principle by many intellectuals in response to the fatwa on Salman Rushdie was a foreshadowing of things to come.

WESTERN APPEASEMENT: THE RUSHDIE AFFAIR

When Salman Rushdie's novel *The Satanic Verses* first appeared in Britain in September 1988, the reaction by Muslims who considered it blasphemous was swift and violent. Within a few months, the book was banned in several countries. A number of bookshops were firebombed in Great Britain, including Collets and Dillons in central London. Soon after the book was published in the United States, in February 1989, firebombs were thrown into Cody's Books and a branch of Waldenbooks in Berkeley, California. Many other American bookstores were threatened, and many withdrew the book from their shelves.

Meanwhile, the Ayatollah Khomeini delivered a fatwa on Salman Rushdie, in effect calling for his murder, and Iranian officials offered a bounty on his head. Rushdie went into hiding for nine years. The

Japanese translator of *The Satanic Verses* was stabbed to death, and the Italian translator was also stabbed. The Norwegian publisher of the book was gravely wounded by gunshots. In supposedly secular Turkey, thirty-seven people were killed when an Islamist mob set fire to a hotel where Aziz Nesin, a translator of *The Satanic Verses,* was staying.

One might have expected Western intellectuals and statesmen to take a clear stand in defense of free speech, a fundamental liberal value. Instead, there was much equivocation and worse. While Jimmy Carter condemned the death sentence and affirmed Rushdie's right to freedom of speech, he also asserted that the author "must have anticipated a horrified reaction throughout the Islamic world." Carter criticized the book as "a direct insult to those millions of Moslems whose sacred beliefs have been violated and are suffering in restrained silence the added embarrassment of the Ayatollah's irresponsibility."[10] In effect, Carter was suggesting self-censorship to protect the tender sensibilities of Muslims.

Some Western intellectuals blamed Rushdie for bringing the barbarous sentence upon himself. Roald Dahl labeled Rushdie "a dangerous opportunist," claiming that he "must have been totally aware of the deep and violent feelings his book would stir up among devout Muslims. In other words, he knew exactly what he was doing and cannot plead otherwise." Dahl contended that Rushdie's "sensationalism" was "a cheap way" of getting his book high on the bestseller list, and that Rushdie had put "a severe strain" on the idea that "the writer has an absolute right to say what he likes." He went on to advocate self-censorship explicitly: "In a civilized world we all have a moral obligation to apply a modicum of censorship to our own work in order to reinforce this principle of free speech."[11] This, of course, is Orwellian doublespeak: *Censorship is Freedom of Speech.*

Along similar lines, John le Carré said in an interview, "I don't think it is given to any of us to be impertinent to great religions with impunity," adding that he himself would choose to withdraw the book.[12] Germaine Greer described Rushdie as "a megalomaniac, an Englishman with dark skin." Reportedly she also said, "Jail is a good place for writers."[13] Most astonishingly, the eminent historian Hugh Trevor-Roper (Lord Dacre) seemed to suggest that violence against Rushdie might be excusable:

> *I wonder how Salman Rushdie is faring these days under the benevolent protection of British law and British police, about whom he has been so rude. Not too comfortably I hope. . . . I would not shed a tear if some British Muslims, deploring his manners, should waylay him in a dark street and seek to improve them. If that should cause him thereafter to control his pen, society would benefit and literature would not suffer.[14]*

Many intellectuals and politicians did speak out in support of Rushdie and his right to free speech, among them Fay Weldon, Christopher Hitchens, Harold Pinter, Susan Sontag, Norman Mailer, and Stephen Spender. I wrote my first book, *Why I Am Not a Muslim*, to add my name to this distinguished group, and as a response to the pusillanimity of so many Western intellectuals who seemed incapable of seeing the implications of the Rushdie affair for the survival of Western freedoms.

Speaking at the Massachusetts Institute of Technology in November 1993, Rushdie said that the attempted assassination of his Norwegian publisher in October had fortified his determination to "make sure that this is the last such atrocity." He asked for the help of his audience, since his only weapon was public opinion. "If this form of terrorism seems to be working, it will be repeated," he explained; and conversely, "The only defense against terrorism is to refuse to be terrorized." At the same event, his friend Susan Sontag remarked that the "worst kind of censorship is self-censorship" and called Rushdie's troubles "a great test of where we stand on the issue of freedom and solidarity and the future of our culture."[15]

Following his visit to MIT, Rushdie met with President Clinton, who, according to the *New York Times,* wanted to "convey America's abhorrence of Iran's refusal to lift the death threat against the novelist."[16] Twenty years later, however, the West seems unable to stand unequivocally for freedom of speech. It seems reluctant to defend its own core values, which are increasingly under attack from militant Islam—as the murder of Theo van Gogh on a street in Amsterdam in 2004 made dramatically evident. Instead, some Western intellectuals and politicians are inclined to respond to such events, or just the threat of violence, with appeasement and self-censorship.

PICTURING MUHAMMAD

While *The Satanic Verses* presented a deliberately irreverent treatment of Islamic doctrines, the hammers of censorship have also come down on neutral or even positive depictions of the prophet Muhammad. We have already seen how Muslim ambassadors in the 1950s demanded that a statue honoring Muhammad as one of the world's major lawgivers be removed from the Manhattan Appellate Courthouse. Even though they were living in the United States only temporarily, and despite the small number of Muslims in the country at the time, the ambassadors had the temerity to dictate their values to a non-Islamic nation, and they succeeded with a minimum of lobbying effort. A repetition of this scenario began taking shape in 1997 when the Council on American-Islamic Relations (CAIR) objected to the inclusion of Muhammad, holding a Koran and a sword, in one of the friezes representing historic lawmakers in the courtroom of the United States Supreme Court (built in the 1930s). When CAIR requested its removal, Chief Justice Rehnquist informed the group that it was unlawful to remove or injure any architectural feature of the Supreme Court; but an explanatory note was added to the tourist literature in an effort to placate Muslim sensitivities.[17]

Several years later, the climate of fear surrounding Muslim taboos was such that a Danish author had difficulty finding anyone willing to illustrate a children's book on the life of Muhammad. This and several other instances of self-censorship around the same time prompted Flemming Rose, the culture editor of the Danish newspaper *Jyllands-Posten,* to take a stand on principle. He invited Danish cartoonists "to draw Muhammad as you see him" and then published the twelve resulting cartoons on September 30, 2005. Alongside them was an eloquent defense of free speech:

> *Artists, writers, illustrators, translators and theatre directors avoid the most important cultural encounter of our time, the one between Islam and the secular Western societies that grew out of the Christian world. The modern, secular society is rejected by some Muslims. They demand a special position, insisting on special consideration of their own religious feelings. This is incompatible with contemporary democracy and freedom of speech, where one must be ready to put up with insults, mockery and ridicule.*

Rose went on to note the similarity with totalitarian societies, where people are jailed for "telling jokes or depicting dictators in a critical way."[18]

Several Muslim ambassadors complained about the cartoons to Denmark's prime minister, Anders Fogh Rasmussen, who replied that he could not interfere with press freedom in his country. But as protests spread around the world and became violent, other Western political leaders began apologizing to the fanatics for having hurt their tender sensibilities. For example, during a tour of Qatar, the former president Bill Clinton decried "these totally outrageous cartoons against Islam," which he cited as an example of "stereotypes about people of different races, different ethnic groups, and different religions." At the U.S. State Department, Kurtis Cooper employed the classic "but clause" to have it both ways, saying, "We all fully recognize and respect freedom of the press and expression but it must be coupled with press responsibility. Inciting religious or ethnic hatreds in this manner is not acceptable." The British foreign secretary, Jack Straw, pronounced the republication of the cartoons not only "unnecessary" but also "insensitive" and "disrespectful" and, furthermore, "wrong."

News organizations that rely on freedom of the press were mostly unwilling to defend it against Muslim rage. The *New York Times* tried to cover its own cowardice under the guise of reasonableness in explaining why, like "much of the rest of the nation's media," it had not displayed the cartoons in its reporting on the controversy. "That seems a reasonable choice for news organizations that usually refrain from gratuitous assaults on religious symbols, especially since the cartoons are so easy to describe in words," the *Times* opined.[19]

There were courageous people who defiantly expressed their support for the Danish cartoonists and for freedom of speech. A minister in the Italian government, Roberto Calderoli, appeared on television in February 2006 wearing a T-shirt displaying a cartoon that *France Soir* had published along with the Danish twelve. The prime minister, Silvio Berlusconi, demanded his resignation. Before complying, Calderoli quite rightly declared that Western civilization itself was at stake. By March, twenty-eight American periodicals had published some or all of the cartoons; ten of these were university newspapers. *Free Inquiry* magazine, true to its name, published four of the cartoons, but some bookshops refused to stock the issue. Two years later, three men were arrested in Denmark on suspicion of planning to assassinate the cartoonist Kurt Westergaard, who had submitted the drawing that became the most iconic image of the controversy. Seventeen Danish newspapers reprinted his famous "Turban Bomb Muhammad" in solidarity.

In other cases, bold statements were followed up with apologies and appeasement. *Studi Cattolici,* in March 2006, published a cartoon satirizing Italian politicians who gave in to Muslim pressure.

WHY THE WEST IS BEST

Even though Muhammad was not portrayed, Italian Muslims were outraged, and the Catholic organization Opus Dei—one of whose members publishes *Studi Cattolici*—promptly issued an apology. Later that year, Pope Benedict XVI won praise for his boldness in some quarters when, in a lecture at Regensburg University on reason versus violence, he quoted a comment by the fourteenth-century Byzantine emperor Manuel II Paleologus: "Show me just what Muhammad brought that was new, and there you will find things only evil and inhuman, such as his command to spread by the sword the faith he preached." But after a massive outcry from Muslims around the world, he issued two apologies on successive days.

One institution after another buckled in the face of Islamic demands or threats. In 2002 and again in 2006, Italian police were able to foil a plot by fundamentalist Muslims to bomb the Cathedral of Bologna, which houses a fifteenth-century fresco depicting Muhammad in hell.[20] The section that portrays Muhammad has since been closed to the public, which is a victory for the Islamists. Also in 2006, the Deutsche Oper in Berlin cancelled a production of *Idomeneo* out of concerns about its representation of Muhammad. The Whitechapel Art Gallery in London censored an upcoming exhibit by removing its life-size nude dolls, most likely to avoid offending Muslims in the area.[21] Publishers have taken to submitting their manuscripts to Muslims for vetting. The litany of capitulation is long and growing.

Adding irony to cowardice, Yale University Press in 2009 published a book titled *The Cartoons That Shook the World,* by Jytte Klausen, from which it omitted the cartoons at issue. Perhaps the most disgraceful surrender of principle, however, was by the Index on Censorship, which touts itself as "Britain's leading organisation promoting freedom of expression." Its website boasts that it "provides up-to-the-minute news and information on free expression from around the world. Our events and projects put our causes into action." If only they would live up to their aspirations. In rationalizing its decision not to republish the Danish cartoons, the Index on Censorship said that doing so would have put the lives of the staff in danger, and that it was "unnecessary" and "gratuitous." A dissenting board member, Kenan Malik, remarked:

> *I cannot see what could be less unnecessary or gratuitous than using cartoons to illustrate an interview with the author of a book that was censored by a refusal to publish those very cartoons. Almost every case of pre-emptive censorship, including that of Yale University Press, has been rationalized on the grounds that the censored material was not necessary anyway. Once we accept that it is legitimate to censor that which is "unnecessary" or "gratuitous," then we have effectively lost the argument for free speech.*[22]

Even the most benign images of Muhammad have raised protests on the grounds that Islam forbids visual representations of the prophet, yet the historical record tells a different story. There are numerous miniatures from across the centuries depicting Muhammad in the holdings of museums throughout Europe and the United States. The Smithsonian has four such images, including a gold-touched illumination in a book that is "familiar to all students of Persian miniatures," reported the *Washington Post* in February 2006. "For reasons that include 'cultural sensitivity,' and today's bloody news, none of these old paintings is currently on view."[23] In January 2010, the Metropolitan Museum of Art in New York removed images of Muhammad from its Islamic exhibit and said they were "under review."[24] While major institutions cave, several websites are now devoted to displaying images of Muhammad from both Islamic and Western sources.[25] In 2009, Dr. Gary Hull founded Voltaire Press at Duke University and published *Muhammad: The Banned Images* under its imprint. The book presents all the images that Yale University Press censored from *The Cartoons That Shook the World,* including the twelve original Muhammad cartoons along with fine reproductions of Persian and Mughal miniatures, and depictions by Western artists such as William Blake.[26]

COMEDY AND IRREVERENCE

The Danish cartoon episode illustrates the essential link between comedy and freedom of speech. Cartoons begin with caricature, adding a sort of wry commentary on political and social issues. As Isabel Johnson observed, "The cartoon prospers in an atmosphere of political freedom."[27] Cartoonists and comedians function in part as social critics, highlighting the absurdities of the prevailing order or of those in power. It could even be said that cartoons have brought down governments. In the nineteenth century, Charles Philipon and Honoré Daumier portrayed King Louis Philippe as a pear, or as Bluebeard preparing to murder his new wife, named "Constitution," and also satirized various members of his cabinet. The cartoonists "literally laughed the *roi citoyen* off his throne" in 1848.[28] It is no wonder that autocratic rulers and totalitarian regimes fear cartoonists.

A long and distinguished Western tradition leads up to Kurt Westergaard, for example, and to Trey Parker and Matt Stone, creators of the satirical animated sitcom *South Park*. They have been equally fearless in criticizing the Catholic Church or Buddhists or even Scientologists, a group that has succeeded in silencing many a critic with intimidating and costly lawsuits. No institution, it seemed, was safe from their crude and often scatological brand of satire; but the fear of Islamic extremists was enough to send the Comedy Central network scurrying for cover. *South Park* had depicted Muhammad in 2001 without incident, but in 2006 the network censored a depiction of the prophet from an episode about the Danish cartoon controversy.

Parker and Stone boldly revisited the issue of Islamic censorship in April 2010, satirizing the fear that surrounds any discussion of

Islam by representing Muhammad as masquerading in a bear costume. A group calling itself Revolution Muslim claimed on its website that the episode had insulted the prophet and all Muslims, and suggested that Parker and Stone would "probably wind up like Theo van Gogh." Perhaps as legal cover, the statement went on to say, "This is not a threat but a warning of the reality of what will likely happen to them."

In the following week's episode of *South Park,* the character in the bear suit is revealed to be Santa Claus. Muhammad was supposed to make an appearance as well, but he was kept hidden behind a black "censored" box. Comedy Central also bleeped out every mention of Muhammad and even a whole speech about intimidation that didn't include the prophet at all.[29]

Some journalists and pundits have commented that the episode was not really offensive, or even more fatuously that it was not funny. But that is beside the point. The issue is freedom of expression. Whether the cartoons were offensive or unfunny or lacking in artistic merit, we should still defend the right of the artists to carry on with their indispensable vocation. At the height of the Rushdie affair, some fellow writers had the courage to hold public readings of *The Satanic Verses.* In a similar spirit, a cartoonist from Seattle responded to the censored *South Park* episode of April 2010 by announcing "Everybody Draw Mohammed Day." Far from being frivolous, as some people suggested, this initiative was a magnificent and courageous act of solidarity.

At the height of the Danish cartoon rage, a small town in France paid homage to an earlier champion of free speech no matter how irreverent. Voltaire spent nineteen years of his life in Ferney, now called Ferney-Voltaire, in eastern France. Three miles away is the little town of Saint-Genis Pouilly, which in December 2005 staged a public reading of Voltaire's *Le fanatisme, ou Mahomet le Prophète.* (Another reading took place in Geneva.) Local Muslims had complained that the play was an insult to the entire Muslim community and demanded that the event be cancelled in order to preserve peace. The town's mayor, Hubert Bertrand, instead called in police reinforcements and upheld the principle of free speech guaranteed by the French constitution. Bertrand was justly proud that his town did not cave in to intimidation. "For a long time we have not confirmed our convictions, so lots of people think they can contest them," he said. The theater director who produced the readings, Hervé Loichemol, had proposed staging the Voltaire play in 1994 but authorities nixed the idea. He realized that there would be angry reactions this time around. His motive was not to provoke Muslims, however, but to stand against the imposition of blasphemy taboos on public performances. Banning blasphemy, he said, "admits private beliefs into public space. This is how catastrophe starts."[39]

Too many in the media and the arts, in academia and politics have failed in their moral duty to display solidarity with those who are threatened for practicing their right of free expression. One result, in effect, is that blasphemy laws are being enforced in Western societies. In Europe, where there is no equivalent to the First Amendment of the U.S. Constitution, courts have acted as enforcers of blasphemy laws under the guise of curbing hate speech. The best known of these cases is the trial of the Dutch politician Geert Wilders.

ꙮ

TRUTH ON TRIAL

When Geert Wilders released his brief film titled *Fitna* in March 2008, attempts had already been made to prosecute him on charges of hate speech in the Netherlands, and he had been living under police protection since 2004, when a plot to assassinate him was exposed shortly after the murder of Theo van Gogh. *Fitna* centers on some of the most barbaric verses of the Koran (including Surahs III.118, VIII.39, IX.73, IX.34, V.63–64), which call for hatred against

Jews, Christians, and non-Muslims generally. The film illustrates how Islamic preachers draw on those verses, and then presents images of violent acts that reflect the incitement. For this and for prior public statements, Wilders was criminally charged with inciting hatred and discrimination; the trial began in January 2010.

Wilders did not invent a single quotation from the Koran, but rather gave a truthful account of what it teaches. He did what every figure in Western public life has a responsibility to do: help the public understand the threats to its safety. Authorities in the Netherlands seemed to prefer suppressing that knowledge. Wilders was denied a fair trial when he was not allowed to call the witnesses that he had planned. More to the point, he should never have been put on trial in the first place for exercising his right to criticize Islam and to speak the truth. He should be applauded, feted, lionized as a hero for his fearless defense of Western values.

John Stuart Mill once wrote, "A man who has nothing for which he is willing to fight; nothing he cares about more than his own personal safety; is a miserable creature who has no chance of being free, unless made and kept so by exertions of better men than himself."[31] Geert Wilders is a far better man than those who put him on trial, who seemed collectively determined to commit civilizational suicide in exchange for immediate personal safety. Wilders has put his own safety at serious risk in his fight for the future of Western civilization. He explained his reasons in the *Wall Street Journal* while the trial was proceeding:

> *When I stand before my judges I do so in defense of free speech and human liberty. Freedom is the source of human creativity and development. People and nations wither away without the freedom to question what is presented to them as the truth. There is reason for concern if the erosion of our freedom of speech is the price we must pay to accommodate Islam. There is reason for concern if those who deny that Islam is a problem do not grant us the right to*

debate the issue. I want to be able to make my case without needing to fear criminal prosecution. It is already bad enough that I have been living under permanent police protection for more than six years because jihadists want to murder me.

My trial is a political trial. It is tragic that after the fall of the Soviet Union in 1989, political trials in Europe were not cast onto the ash heap of history. Former Soviet dissident Vladimir Bukovsky has previously referred to the European Union as the "EUSSR." One of his arguments is that in the EU, as in the former USSR, there is no freedom of speech.[32]

Wilders' acquittal in June 2011—at the request of the public prosecutor as well as the defense—was a surprise to many who had watched the spectacle, and it was a victory of no small consequence for the West.

♔
TAKING A STAND

The threat on Geert Wilders' life in 2004 also targeted Ayaan Hirsi Ali, who wrote the script for Theo van Gogh's film *Submission*, drawing from her experience living under Islam in Somalia. Subsequently she has continued her intrepid campaign for freedom. "I absolutely wish that Theo had not been killed," she said in 2007. "But I don't regret that I made it. In fact, I'm proud of that film. To feel otherwise would be to deny everything I stand for."[33]

Many liberals in the West say that Islam needs a reformation, yet at the same time they would restrict the speech of those who call attention to what needs to be reformed. They would censor people like Ayaan Hirsi Ali, Geert Wilders, and Wafa Sultan, the Syrian-born psychiatrist who wants Muslims to have freedom to ask questions, hear different viewpoints, even choose their own religion. How can Islam be reformed if its doctrines and its holy book are closed off to any critical examination? Moreover, a "reformation" of Islam implies only adjustments and modifications to what would still result in a theologically ordered society. What we need is an Enlightenment in the Islamic world, a profound change of the Muslim mindset to allow freedom of conscience. This cannot happen when speaking candidly about Islam is taboo.

In its reluctance to pass judgments on other cultures, the West is far too ready to take the most shrill and publicity-savvy Muslims as legitimate spokesmen for the worldwide Muslim community on matters of Islamic doctrine. Some fringe group threatens Comedy Central, and the latter accepts uncritically the group's claim that human representation is forbidden in Islam. As we have seen, that particular principle is far from certain. But even if human representation were clearly forbidden in Islam, we should still defend our own right to freedom of speech and expression without equivocation.

It is commendable and understandable to wish to protect the innocent—for instance, to shield the personnel of a publishing house from any violence that might follow the publication of material that Muslims regard as blasphemous. But such violence cannot be considered the responsibility of the publisher, either legally or morally. Writers, cartoonists, comedians, and filmmakers must be permitted to exercise their constitutional rights. Publishers must stand by their writers, newspapers by their cartoonists, television networks by their creative producers, intellectuals and artists with their peers. Where was Hollywood when Theo van Gogh, a fellow filmmaker, was brutally murdered? Unless we show more solidarity—massive, public, noisy solidarity—and demonstrate that we care for our freedoms, we risk losing them to Islamist thuggery.

The cowardly censorship of Comedy Central, or Yale University Press, or the Metropolitan Museum of Art should be held up to public scorn. The United States government should stand up unequivocally for freedom of speech, reassuring artists, filmmakers, novelists, and so on that the liberties of American citizens guaranteed in the

U.S. Constitution will not be curtailed. Unfortunately, the U.S. government, particularly under Barack Obama, has exhibited an aversion to candor about Islam.

Even journalists normally sympathetic to President Obama have noticed a trend in vocabulary that amounts to self-censorship. The administration has tried to eliminate certain words and phrases from American policy documents and statements concerning Islam, so that analysts and advisors cannot speak of "radical Islam," "Islamic extremists," "Islamists," or "Islamic terrorists." While it is true that avoidance of terms like "Islamic terrorism" began in the Bush administration, and in Britain under Tony Blair, the restrictions then applied to public statements. Now they also cover internal government documents. This kind of censorship can only compromise our understanding of events and actors in various hot spots of the world, as Barry Rubin explained:

> *Suppose I'm an intelligence analyst in the State Department, Defense Department, armed forces, or CIA, and I'm writing about one of these groups or this ideology. How can one possibly analyze the power and appeal of this ideology, the way that ideas set its strategy and tactics, why it is such a huge menace if any reference to the Islamic religion and its texts or doctrines isn't permitted?*[34]

President Obama is determined to appease Muslims at all costs, to the extent of denying the role of Islam, even qualified as "radical Islam" or "political Islam," in current threats to the United States. In his Cairo speech in 2009 he said, "I consider it part of my responsibility as President of the United States to fight against negative stereotypes of Islam whenever they appear." Nina Shea has reported that the Obama administration is not only collaborating with the Organization of Islamic Cooperation in its global campaign against "Islamophobia," but is actually "taking the lead in an international effort to 'implement' a U.N. resolution against religious 'stereotyping,' specifically as applied to Islam." The result would be to outlaw freedom of expression worldwide if such expression is displeasing to Muslims.[35]

Self-censorship and appeasement will not solve problems in the Middle East. Surrendering the liberties guaranteed to us in the Bill of Rights will not bring peace to the world. We have a right to expect that our government will defend our constitutional rights instead of kowtowing to those who emphatically reject our values.

Artists, writers, and intellectuals who are threatened by Islamists should demand a public statement from political leaders and law enforcement agencies, such as the FBI, pledging every necessary protection. Legal action should be taken against those making such threats, even if they are based abroad. Daniel Pipes has established the Legal Project in order to protect researchers and analysts working on the subjects of radical Islam, terrorism and terrorist funding from predatory legal action designed to silence them. Ideally, such a task should be taken on by the government, not just private citizens. The U.S. government could also sponsor a major conference on freedom of speech that would feature readings of Voltaire's *Le fanatisme, ou Mahomet le Prophète,* Geert Wilders' *Fitna,* images of Muhammad taken from Gary Hull's *Muhammad: The "Banned" Images,* and talks defending freedom of expression by some of its courageous champions, such as Salman Rushdie, Ayaan Hirsi Ali, Trey Parker and Matt Stone. A free-speech conference would send a clear message to all Islamic—yes, Islamic—terrorists, and all easily offended Muslims, that we are proud of our values, we will defend them at all costs, and we will not be terrorized.

಄

CHAPTER SEVEN

HOW TO DEFEND
WESTERN CIVILIZATION

In 1964, James Burnham published *Suicide of the West: An Essay on the Meaning and Destiny of Liberalism,* arguing that the contradictions inherent in liberalism could lead to the West's self-destruction.[1] There are central principles of Western civilization—rationalism, universalism, self-criticism—that can yield undesirable results if pushed to an extreme. Rationalism can lead to scientism, with its adulation of science and technology at the expense of human values, and to the undermining of a nation's foundational myths. Universalism can lead to cosmopolitanism, which tends to diminish any sense of loyalty or belonging to a particular culture or nation. Cultural self-criticism, in itself a useful tool for improvement, can turn into hatred of one's own culture, as witnessed in the buffooneries of Michael Moore, the exaggerations of Robert Fisk, or the fanaticism of Noam Chomsky.

Burnham described how a sense of guilt that runs through Western liberalism can produce a corrosive self-hatred: "When the Western liberal's feeling of guilt and his associated feeling of moral vulnerability before the sorrows and demands of the wretched become obsessive, he often develops a generalized hatred of Western civilization and of his own country as part of the West." A liberal, as Robert Frost famously put it, is one who won't even take his own side in a quarrel.[2]

In 1933, Winston Churchill wrote about the dangers of excessive cultural self-criticism from "a peculiar type of brainy people." In Churchill's view,

> The worst difficulties from which we suffer do not come from without. They come from within. . . . Our difficulties come from the mood of unwarrantable self-abasement into which we have been cast by a powerful section of our own intellectuals. They come from the acceptance of defeatist doctrines by a large proportion of our politicians. . . . Nothing can save England if she will not save herself. If we lose faith in ourselves, in our capacity to guide and govern, if we lose our will to live, then indeed our story is told.[3]

Today, multiculturalism and moral relativism have left Western intellectuals unprepared or unwilling to defend the West when its values are attacked. Marianne Talbot, a lecturer in philosophy at the University of Oxford, noted the debilitating effects of relativism on the young:

> [M]any of the young have been taught to think their opinion is no better than anyone else's, that there is no truth, only truth-for-me. . . . The young have been taught, or so it seems, that they

should never think of the views of others as false, but only as dif-
ferent. They have been taught that to suggest someone else is wrong
is at best rude and at worst immoral: the truth that one should
always be alive to the possibility that one is wrong has become the
falsehood that one should never be so arrogant as to believe that
one is right.[4]

In order to preserve our culture, we need to be certain of what our values are, and be confident in asserting their superiority.

Anyone who has lived elsewhere knows that life in the West offers more freedoms than any other civilization, even if they are ideologically reluctant to admit so. Those who value the life of the mind cannot but appreciate the vast gulf that divides the West from totalitarian societies and dictatorships, with their thought police and censors, their stultifying conformity. The peoples of such societies are indeed leading impoverished lives in every way. It is only the sentimental nonsense of "sophisticated" Western intellectuals to pretend otherwise. Many of these sophisticates prefer to see spirituality where there is only squalor and superstition, or to eulogize the "family values" that permit child abuse, forced marriages, marital rape, and utter subservience of all women and girls.

There are some who do candidly acknowledge what the West has given to the world. Here is one assessment:

My attitude towards Western civilization is an attitude based on
obvious facts and great accomplishments; here is a reality full of
wonderful and amazing things. [Recognizing] this doesn't mean
that I am blindly fascinated. This is the very opposite of the atti-
tude of those who deny and ignore the bright lights of Western civi-
lization. Just look around . . . and you will notice that everything
beautiful in our life has been produced by Western civilization:
even the pen that you are holding in your hand, the recording
instrument in front of you, the light in this room, and the journal

in which you work, and many innumerable amenities, which are like miracles for the ancient civilizations. . . . If it were not for the accomplishments of the West, our lives would have been barren. I only look objectively and value justly what I see and express it honestly. Whoever does not admire great beauty is a person who lacks sensitivity, taste, and observation. Western civilization has reached the summit of science and technology. It has achieved knowledge, skills, and new discoveries, as no previous civilization before it. The accomplishments of Western civilization cover all areas of life: methods of organization, politics, ethics, economics, and human rights. It is our obligation to acknowledge its amazing excellence. Indeed, this is a civilization that deserves admiration.

This hearty encomium does not come from a Westerner, but from Ibrahim al-Buleihi, a member of the Saudi Shura Council.[5] He added that "The horrible backwardness in which some nations live is the inevitable result of their refusal to accept" the abundance of Western ideas and visions; it stems from "denial and arrogance." It is extraordinary that al-Buleihi was able to express himself so freely. The force of his remarks comes mainly from his perspective as an outsider. A Westerner might be embarrassed to speak in such terms, but what al-Buleihi said is true.

In the West, freedom of thought and intellectual curiosity produced the theories of Kepler and Tycho Brahe, Copernicus and Galileo, Newton and Einstein, Darwin and Crick. Rationalism gave us the wonderful edifice of modern science, a deeper comprehension of the universe, a fuller understanding of our own origins. Darwin once said about his theory of origins: "There is grandeur in this view of life, with its several powers, having been originally breathed by the Creator into a few forms or into one; and that, whilst this planet has gone cycling on according to the fixed law of gravity, from so simple a beginning endless forms most beautiful and most wonderful have been, and are being evolved."[6] This comment illustrates Karl Popper's suggestion that the West's scientific achievements might be seen as the result of spiritual activities.

Western civilization strives for objective truth and explanations, and also for meaning—not just the meaning imposed by some medieval text, but something richer and deeper. Freedom of expression allowed leaps of imagination to bear magnificent spiritual fruits, the literary, artistic, musical, and philosophical creations of astonishing diversity, power, beauty, profundity, and truth: the words of Chaucer and Dante, Shakespeare and Racine, Goethe and Samuel Johnson; the paintings of Giotto and Cimabue, Raphael and Michelangelo; the architecture of Alberti and Palladio, Wren and Hawksmoor; the music of Bach and Palestrina, Haydn and Mozart, Wagner and Verdi.

This artistic treasure, in various ways, reflects the Western sense of man as an individual, a rational being with moral responsibility and intentionality. The Western idea of personhood underlies its tradition of law as a human construction, though influenced by the Judea-Christian understanding of God's commandments. Law in the West is a "human attempt to resolve our own conflicts by treating each party to them as a responsible individual, acting freely for himself," as Roger Scruton observes. "The common law consists of freedoms won by the citizen from the state, which the state must then uphold."[7]

In Islam, there is the concept of an individual with legal obligations, but not of the moral person who may freely choose his own path in life. There is no sense of the individual who can make rational decisions and accept moral responsibility for his actions. Ethics is reduced to obeying orders. Under Islam, the limits to the possible contents of your life are set by Allah and his law, while the collective will of the Muslim people is emphasized over any sense of individual rights.

Hayek wrote that "individual freedom cannot be reconciled with the supremacy of one single purpose to which the whole society must be entirely and permanently subordinated."[8] In the West, individuals have rights that no mystical collective goal can justifiably deny. Liberal democracy extends the sphere of individual freedom and elevates the value of each person. It enables citizens to criticize their government, offer alternatives, and find ways to improve their lot. Thomas Jefferson said, "A bill of rights is what the people are entitled to against every government on earth, general or particular, and what no just government should refuse, or rest on inferences."9 The Bill of Rights to the U.S. Constitution (or its equivalents elsewhere) safeguards the civil and political rights of the individual against the government.

✆
PERILS OF MULTICULTURALISM

The astonishing vitality and creativity of Paris, London, Rome, and New York are largely a result of freedom and respect for the individual. So too are the West's scientific achievements. Our freedoms should be cherished, and the cultural riches they have produced ought to be celebrated. But many academics, intellectuals, artists, writers, and philosophers are busy denouncing any such celebration as racist or shamefully Eurocentric. Do they not realize that their own freedoms are in danger? The political correctness that inhibits cultural comparisons may be as great a danger as secret police in the long run, effectively silencing any defense of the West. Multiculturalism and relativism constitute an ongoing assault on Western civilization from the inside.

David Cameron, Nicolas Sarkozy, and Angela Merkel have all recently acknowledged that the multiculturalist agenda imposed on Europe over the past three decades has failed. Multiculturalism does not sustain the values of liberty and equality.10 Moreover, it is based on fundamental misconceptions about cultural and ethnic groups. Multiculturalists tend to treat ethnic groups as if they were "internally homogenous, clearly bounded, mutually exclusive," with "specific determinate interests."[11] They also may harbor a sentimental belief that all cultures have the same values deep down; or that the different values they hold are all equally worthy of respect. Multiculturalism, being a child of relativism, does not permit cross-cultural judgments or criticism.

Thus, multiculturalism often ends up providing cover for the most reactionary beliefs and practices of other cultures, rather than encouraging the more liberal strands to develop.[12] An attentive ear is given mostly to the community elders and traditionalists, who often are the least educated and most determined to preserve their power in the status quo. Thus we essentially defend the most oppressive beliefs and practices of a minority culture, ignoring the denial of rights to its women and children. In Britain the rate of suicide among Asian (i.e. Muslim) women is higher than the national average because these women and girls are denied autonomy; the vaunted tight-knit families and communities are in fact suffocating them [13]

Whereas the antiracism struggles of the 1960s were a campaign for equality, multiculturalism demands separate rights, exemptions, and provisions for various groups.[14] It is a politics of difference that undermines universal principles of justice and human rights.[15] After thirty years of multiculturalism in certain Western European cities, the result is "segregation, ghettoization, resentment, alienation, communal stress" instead of a cohesive and tolerant society.[16] Multiculturalism pushes individuals back into a cultural ghetto that earlier generations tried to escape. It forces an identity onto individuals that they may not welcome. It offers the promise of group equality at the price of bondage for individuals.

The failures of multiculturalism should be answered with a universalism of fundamental values, supported by national traditions. The Western heritage—Greece, Rome, Judeo-Christianity, the Renaissance and the Enlightenment—gave us the Universal Declaration of Human Rights. But a structure is needed to ensure these rights. Only the nation-state is large and generous enough to sustain diversity yet cohesive enough to guarantee rights to its citizens.[17] The nation-state achieves stability through a shared loyalty and the common benefits of citizenship. It asks that we put aside any primary allegiance to family, tribe, or faith, and commit our loyalty to a country defined by territory, history, culture, and law.[18]

A nation-state must rise above the promiscuous pluralism that ends in moral relativism, and come to some agreement on core values. In the United States, those central values have been set forth in the founding documents, the Declaration of Independence and the Constitution, in which all individuals are proclaimed to be endowed with the same rights. As Gary Nash points out, the United States' nonethnic ideological tradition has fueled "virtually every social and political struggle carried out by women, religious minorities, labor, and people of color."[19] But too often, these victories have been viewed in terms of the particular rights of a specific group. We must reaffirm that these are the rights of all, equally, under the U.S. Constitution. We need to safeguard that precious ideal of equality before the law when it is challenged by the siren song of multiculturalism. Equality before the law accords with the individualism that promises liberation from oppressive cultural ghettos, allowing us to choose our own affiliations.

As long ago as 1993, I wrote about the implications of giving in to demands for special accommodations by Muslims living in the West. It is now even more evident that many of them have no intention of assimilating into the host society. Instead, they insist that the host society must change in line with their beliefs, or grant them separate rights and privileges. While European societies are threatened with fragmentation into religious and cultural ghettos, each with its own laws, it is imperative that we exercise more vigilance lest our precious freedoms be squandered in an orgy of multicultural appeasement and surrender.

In February 2008, the Archbishop of Canterbury, Dr. Rowan Williams, said that "the application of Sharia in certain circumstances" in the United Kingdom was "unavoidable," and he was not troubled by that prospect. In subsequent interviews, he asserted that a belief in "one law for all" was dangerous—one of the cornerstones of Western civilization, equality under the law, a danger! In July 2008, the Lord Chief Justice of England and Wales, Lord Phillips, also opined that sharia principles could be the basis for mediation, and that national courts should recognize these decisions.

There are already eighty-five sharia courts operating in Great Britain, many working out of mosques, applying Islamic law to resolve domestic, marital, and business disputes. These courts are intrinsically divisive, placing some Muslims above the law that the rest of the community has to obey, while denying certain rights to other Muslims, particularly women. The very existence of sharia courts threatens the system of laws passed by elected representatives in Parliament. Insouciant government officials assure us that these courts may not contradict the law of the land. But some decisions of the Islamic tribunals are already considered legally binding and could be enforced in civil courts in England and Wales. A report by Civitas, a leading think tank in London, revealed that the rulings handed down by sharia tribunals have included some that went against the human rights standards applied in British courts.[20]

The situation in Germany is equally worrying. Chancellor Angela Merkel said that Islamic law had no place in Germany, but a little research shows that in fact it has been applied there for years. *Der Spiegel* reported in 2010 that elements of sharia are most often used in cases involving family and inheritance disputes.

Jordanian couples, for example, are married (and divorced) in Germany according to Jordanian law, which is partially based on Shariah. Furthermore, multiple wives in a polygamous marriage, provided the marriages were legal in their home country, have legal rights to alimony, social security benefits stemming from their husband's occupation and a portion of the inheritance should he

*die. . . . A federal court in Kassel, for example, cited Islamic law in
a ruling several years ago in which the court found that a widow
had to share her husband's pension with his second wife. Another
case saw a court in Koblenz granting residency to the second wife
of a man from Iraq. A Cologne court forced an Iranian man to
pay his ex-wife 600 gold coins in "bride price" (money paid by the
groom or groom's family to the bride or bride's family) upon divorce
and cited the Shariah system applied in Iran. A court in Düsseldorf
arrived at a similar verdict, forcing a Turkish man to pay 30,000 in
bride price to his former daughter-in-law.[21]*

Hilmar Krüger, a law professor at the University of Cologne,
called this all "a good thing." Mathias Rohe, a lawyer and Islam
expert in Erlangen, said it was merely a product of "globalization."[22]
They seem to be unaware of the implications of accepting sharia
into the Western mainstream. Laws passed by democratically elected
representatives are now being superseded by barbaric laws from
seventh-century Saudi Arabia, putatively decreed by God. The principles of justice enshrined in Western constitutions and the rights
achieved through centuries of struggle are to be given no precedence
over a system derived from a very different worldview, one in which
women are the property of men and where freedom of conscience is
nonexistent.

Sharia is totally incompatible with Western liberal democracy
and with human rights in general, because it is a totalitarian construct designed to control every aspect of the life of Muslims and
even non-Muslims. It discriminates against women in many ways:
their testimony in court is worth half of a man's testimony (Surah
II.282); they inherit half what men do (IV.11); they may be beaten by
men (IV.34); they may not marry non-Muslims (II.221). Sharia prescribes amputation of hands for theft (V.38), crucifixion for spreading
disorder (V.33), stoning to death for adultery (*Reliance of the Traveller,* p. 610), execution of homosexuals and apostates (XXVI.165–66;

Reliance, pp. 109 and 665).[23] In other words, Muslims want to reintroduce practices that we in the West long ago deemed barbaric.

Moreover, Islamic law is considered infallible and immutable. In contrast to the fixed edicts of sharia, Western law is bound up with the realities of human life and conflict. It allows the flexibility of making new law to accommodate changing circumstances, within a framework of fundamental principles. The Western constitutions and systems of law are magnificent creations; are we really prepared to jettison them in the name of multiculturalism and globalization?

Most troubling are the efforts to enforce Islamic laws against "blasphemy" throughout the world. The Organization of Islamic Cooperation is taking steps toward outlawing "defamation of religion" (i.e. Islam) worldwide, and these efforts have, in effect, been abetted by Western governments under the guise of suppressing "hate speech." As Islamic countries consolidate their hold on the UN Human Rights Council and demand national laws to suppress criticism of Islam, how long will it be before Western legislation forbids research into the origins of the Koran or early Islamic history?

A STRATEGY FOR DEFENDING THE WEST

At conferences where the topics of reforming Islam and combating radical Islam are discussed, I am often asked what we should do. I reply that first we should defend our values without hesitation or apology. In doing so, we would give encouragement to the liberals in the Islamic world, who look on with dismay each time we sacrifice our principles to self-doubt and cultural masochism. Radical Muslims would have more to think about if we resisted their demands rather than caving to them. We are certainly not going to change their thinking by folding like some third-rate poker player who throws in the cards at the first aggressive bluff when he is in fact holding the winning hand. Appeasing fundamentalists only reinforces their cruel certainties. Specious arguments about "engagement and mutual respect" will not bring about a reformation or an enlightenment in the Islamic world. By standing firm on our principles, we clearly present an alternative set of values that may perhaps give pause for reflection.

Besides making an unambiguous commitment to the values we are defending, we must stand up to the enemies of the West, even militarily if necessary. It wasn't just Jimmy Carter and Bill Clinton but even Ronald Reagan who failed to do anything decisive when U.S. interests, personnel, and forces were attacked in Iran, Lebanon, and the Gulf of Aden.

We need to recapture the moral clarity of that moment in 1948 when Eleanor Roosevelt shepherded us through to the signing of the Universal Declaration of Human Rights. We must defend these rights without compromise, without fear of hurting the feelings of putatively friendly Islamic regimes. Let us change their way of thinking. We can establish centers for teaching human rights in Iraq, in Afghanistan, in Pakistan. We must demand the rewriting of Saudi textbooks that preach hatred of non-Muslims. We need to push for a restructuring of the UN Human Rights Council so that it will no longer be controlled by the Islamic states. We certainly should be more assertive in taking Muslim leaders to task, and be ready to complain or take mullahs to court when they issue fatwas that violate international law and norms.

The rights of women in Islamic lands have been shamefully neglected by Western feminists, with a few noble exceptions such as Phyllis Chesler. In the West, we must say no to segregation of Muslim girls in school activities, no to arranged marriages against the wishes of the girl, no to polygamy. We must say no to sharia, *tout court*. We must insist on equality before the law.

Since Islamic countries have systematically suppressed knowledge of their pre-Islamic past, we can help fund museum exhibits both in the West and in the Islamic world to celebrate the ancient civilizations of Iran, Iraq, Pakistan, and North Africa. We need to recognize and support the non-Islamic and non-Arab peoples who live under Islamic rule—such as Berbers, Kurds, Armenians, Assyrians, Jews, and Zoroastrians.

At the same time, we should not be diffident about promoting and exporting the best achievements of our own culture. We do not need to apologize for the many inventions and initiatives that have made the world a better place: from computers to penicillin, from the Red Cross to Doctors Without Borders. We should exhibit works of Western art in Islamic countries. More easily, we could host concerts of classical music, which is surely one of the greatest gifts of Western civilization to the world, one which alone would justify its existence. We could sponsor debates on politics, art, and philosophy on Islamic soil. Book fairs and readings are also ways of showing the vitality of Western culture and how it expresses the manifold possibilities of life, revealing different and perhaps richer ways of living. To this end, we need translations into the vernaculars of the Islamic world, and funds to support such a project.

∽
A NEW COLD WAR TRANSLATION PROJECT

In *Foreign Affairs,* David C. Engerman wrote that "militant Islam represents not just an army but an idea," much like the Soviet Union. He went on to lament that "the U.S. government does not seem to have absorbed the useful lessons from the creation of Soviet studies programs in its efforts to study this new threat." Sovietology was a serious intellectual field that contributed much to top-secret government discussions as well as public debate. Looking at the methods and successes of Sovietology is indispensable to "shaping how the U.S. government defines and studies the threat of Islamic fundamentalism," argues Engerman, making a number of useful suggestions for the study of cultures at the Pentagon.[24] But he does not refer to the main obstacle in the way of creating a discipline of Islamology that would be equivalent to Cold War Sovietology: from President Obama and his administration, to top officials at the Pentagon, to scholars and public intellectuals and the media, there is a great reluctance and even a refusal to look critically at Islam. Translating a few remarks by various leaders of al-Qaeda will not give us a complete understanding of the threat.

At the moment, however, there is surely a greater need for translations *into* Arabic, as well as Farsi, Urdu, Bengali, Bahasa Malaysia, and Indonesian. The Arab Human Development Report of 2003, published by the United Nations Development Programme, found that "the total number of books translated into Arabic in the last 1,000 years is fewer than those translated in Spain in one year. Greece, with a population of fewer than 11 million, translates five times as many books from abroad into Greek annually as the 22 Arab countries combined, with a total population of more than 300 million, translated into Arabic."[25] The Arab world and the larger realm of Islam need an initiative similar to the Central and East European Publishing Project, which was launched by Western European scholars in 1986 to help independent Eastern European writers and publishers both at home and in exile. The goals were to ensure publication in the original languages and to encourage more translations, thus fostering a "common market of the mind" throughout Europe.[26] Before the project ended in 1994, it produced a list of the one hundred books that had been most influential in the West since 1945.[27] We can draw up our own lists of the most influential works in the West from across the centuries. Above all, we need to provide the Islamic world with accessible works that discuss the Koran and hadith, sharia, Islamic theology and history in an open and scholarly way, without a stultifying concern about Islamic "sensitivities."

I cannot repeat too often that an enlightenment in the Islamic world will never be achieved without introducing critical thinking about the Islamic religion and culture. Most Americans, including many in conservative think tanks, have been held back from such an effort by a general respect for religion and a reluctance to attack the belief system of a large part of the world. Another reason is fear. I asked one eminent Western scholar of Islam why we did not initiate a project to help Muslims examine their own culture and beliefs, and he replied that it was "much too dangerous. It's up to the Muslims themselves to do that."

In the last twenty years, a number of books have been published in Arabic, by Muslims, that are critical of the Koran and hadith. These books should be translated into other languages of the Islamic world. There are many works in classical Arabic displaying rationalism and critical thinking that are inaccessible to the man in the Arab street as well as those Muslims, the majority, who are not Arabic speakers. The skepticism of al-Maarri and Omar Khayyam, the rationalism of Avicenna and Averroës should be made available to all Muslims.

In 2003, I drew up a list of books critical of Islam, which could serve as a point of departure for a long-term translation project.[28] Such an effort would need financial commitments from, for example, the Pentagon, or a think tank or a university. An "Arabo-Islamic Publishing Project" could run at a cost of around $5 million a year, a tiny fraction of the sums that the Pentagon has been spending in Iraq or Afghanistan.[29]

☯

ANTI-AMERICANISM AND ANTI-WESTERNISM

Defending the West is made more difficult by the fact that so many Europeans harbor an extreme anti-Americanism. Many do not accept that the United States is a part of the same Western civilization, and that it stands or falls together with Europe in the face of a new totalitarian threat. For Islamists, however, American culture is the prime manifestation of the Western civilization they despise.

Understanding the roots of anti-Americanism worldwide can help us explain the more general phenomenon of anti-Westernism. One explanation is the sole superpower status of the United States and the global success of its popular culture. Another is the human need for scapegoats. Paul Hollander has argued that an aversion to modernity, or at least an ambiguity about it, is also a source of anti-Americanism, which may often be an angry response to the loss of traditional beliefs that gave people their sense of meaning and identity.[30] At the same time, our own schools and universities are reinforcing anti-Americanism and anti-Westernism.

A few years ago, one senior editor for the *New York Times Book Review* apologized to me for not reviewing my critique of Edward Said's anti-Westernism (2007), saying that all concerned at the *Times* felt that Said was no longer much of an influence on the culture.[31] Alas, such is not the case. When I was invited to give a talk on the book at the Barnes & Noble bookstore at Columbia University, I was confronted with two enormous piles of Said's *Orientalism,* perhaps a hundred copies in all, on the front table. There were no copies of my own book in the front of the store and only five copies available at the back, where I gave my poorly attended lecture, which apparently was also poorly advertised. In 2010, a student at New York University told me that Said's *Orientalism* and his *Culture and Imperialism* are compulsory reading in some courses, along with collections of his essays.

Then there is the scandal of the "whiteness studies" programs that have been created at dozens of educational institutions, among them Princeton and UCLA. The apparent goal of these courses, as Hollander explains, is "to immerse (white) students in feelings of collective guilt about their conscious or unconscious racism and their 'white privilege,' and to persuade them that the pervasive and profound racism of American society is virtually ineradicable." Hollander cites a critic of these programs who points out that "Black studies celebrates blackness, Chicano studies celebrates Chicanos, women's studies celebrates women, and white studies attacks white people as evil." The claim that "incorrigible and ubiquitous racism" pervades American society is central to an attempt at moral delegitimation.[32]

It is urgently necessary to teach real history to our schoolchildren and college students, including the facts about the worldwide phenomena of slavery, racism, and imperialism, and about the West's unique initiatives to confront and eradicate these evils. Western diplomats should know enough about history that they do not cringe and grovel whenever slavery or racism or imperialism is brought up in international forums. They must be properly educated in the history and achievements of Western civilization. Is it too much to ask of them to learn the rudiments of Western culture before they purport to represent that culture abroad? Let us revive the "great books" programs that were developed at a time when we were far more confident of our civilization.

Something must also be done about the United Nations. Besides being inefficient and corrupt, it has become the foul center of anti-American and anti-Western hatred. It is truly grotesque that time is accorded to Third World dictators to denounce the West as the source of all evil, when they themselves are responsible for the torture, incarceration, rape, and murder of thousands of their own citizens. It is obscene that they are welcomed to the West, to New York, where they ask for reparations from Western countries for slavery and imperialism, when they themselves have stolen many billions of dollars intended for their people from Western donors—much more than the West ever made from the slave trade or colonialism.

Let us teach Islamic and African nations to take responsibility for their own plight. Some four billion of the world's people still have a quality of life that is poor in every way imaginable. Around half of the adults in twenty-three countries are illiterate; in thirty-five countries, at least half the women are illiterate. Life expectancy is below sixty years in forty-five countries; more than one in ten children die before the age of five in over thirty countries. Democratic institutions are weak in Africa and the Islamic countries and in Asia generally. At the end of the twentieth century, Lawrence Harrison found the world to be "far poorer, far more unjust, and far more authoritarian than most people at mid-century expected it would be."[33] It is true that poverty, unemployment, and illiteracy also exist in the West. But Western societies have addressed these problems far better than any others.

As I argued earlier, the West did not get rich because of slavery or imperialism or because of a neocolonialism that supposedly siphons off the riches of Third World countries. It is successful because of its culture, rooted in the Greco-Roman and Judeo-Christian heritage, because of the distinctive institutions that developed over centuries, because of the freedom granted to individuals. The West is prosperous thanks to a state of mind that is open and able to learn from others, willing to apply self-criticism, to subject even the most cherished beliefs to rational scrutiny. The West has succeeded because of an insatiable curiosity that has fueled countless experiments and innovations. That is surely something to be proud of.

NOTES

Preface

1. Nirad C. Chaudhuri, *Thy Hand, Great Anarch! India 1921–1952* (New York: Addison-Wesley, 1987), p. 28.

2. G. B. Singh, *Gandhi: Behind the Mask of Divinity* (Amherst, N.Y.: Prometheus Books, 2004), pp. 102–3.

3. Alison Granito, "80% of Indians live on less than $2 a day: WB," *LiveMint.com* and *Wall Street Journal*, October 16, 2007.

4. "India has highest number of underweight children," *Indian Express*, April 14, 2009.

5. Somini Sengupta, "As Indian Growth Soars, Child Hunger Persists," *New York Times,* March 13, 2009.

6. India has an estimated 70 million drug addicts and the number is rising as the problem spreads to semi-urban and backward areas, according to official figures. A source from the Ministry of Social Justice and Empowerment said, "Drug and alcohol abuse is becoming an area of concern as this is increasing while traditional moorings, social taboos, emphasis on self-restraint and pervasive control and discipline of the joint family and community are eroding." See "Over 70M drug addicts in India," *SiliconIndia,* May 4, 2006.

7. Geoffrey Moorhouse, *India Britannica* (London: Paladin, 1986), pp. 19, 196–97.

8. Robert V. Remini, *Andrew Jackson* (New York: Harper Perennial, 1999), p. 217.

Prologue: The Superiority of Western Values in Eight Minutes

1. Bruce Thornton, "Golden Threads: Former Muslim Ibn Warraq Stands Up for the West," *City Journal,* August 17, 2007.

2. Roger Scruton, "The glory of the West is that life is an open book," *Sunday Times* (UK), May 27, 2007.

3. Alan Charles Kors, "Can there be an 'after socialism'?" *Social Philosophy and Policy,* vol. 20, no. 1 (2003), pp. 1–17.

4. Bertrand Russell, *The Problems of Philosophy* (London: Williams & Norgate, 1912), ch. 15.

5. Roger Scruton, "The Defence of the West," lecture at the Columbia Political Union, New York, April 14, 2005.

6. Caroline Cox and John Marks, *The 'West', Islam and Islamism: Is Ideological Islam Compatible with Liberal Democracy?* (London: Civitas, 2003), pp. 12–13.

7. Arthur M. Schlesinger, Jr., *The Disuniting of America: Reflections on a Multicultural Society* (New York: Norton, 1992), p. 128.

8. Ibid., p. 129.

Chapter One: New York, New York

1. Henry James, *The American Scene* (New York: Harper & Bros., 1907), p. 72.

2. P. G. Wodehouse, "Extricating Young Gussie," *Saturday Evening Post,* 1915, reprinted in *Enter Jeeves: 15 Early Stories,* ed. David A. Jasen (Mineola, N.Y.: Dover, 1997), p. 6.

3. Steve Cohen, "New York City: Sustainable City?" Treehugger, http://www.treehugger.com/files/2006/10/new_york_city_waste.php.

4. David Owen, "Green Manhattan: Everywhere should be more like New York," *New Yorker,* October 18, 2004.

5. Howard Pollack, *George Gershwin: His Life and Work* (Berkeley and Los Angeles: University of California Press, 2006), p. 6.

6. David A. Jasen, *Tin Pan Alley: The Composers, the Songs, the Performers and Their Times* (New York: Donald I. Fine, 1988), p. xxii.

7. Quoted in Philip Furia, *The Poets of Tin Pan Alley: A History of America's Great Lyricists* (1990; New York: Oxford University Press, 1992), p. 17.

8. Laurence Bergreen, *As Thousands Cheer: The Life of Irving Berlin* (New York: Viking, 1990), p. 128.

9. Quoted in ibid., p. 580.

10. Quoted in ibid., p. 222.

11. Ibid., p. 17.

12. Ibid., p. 277.

13. Ibid., p. 309.

14. Ibid., p. 322.

15. Ibid., p. 506.

16. Ibid., p. 339.

17. Pollack, *George Gershwin: His Life and Work,* p. 41.

18. Quoted in ibid., p. 42.

19. Ibid., p. 42.

20. Quoted in ibid., p. 297.

21. Ibid., p. 391.

22. Ibid., pp. 299–300.

23. Quoted in ibid., p. 306.

24. Quoted in ibid., p. 309.

25. Ibid., p. 234.

26. Stephen Banfield, *Jerome Kern* (New Haven: Yale University Press, 2006), p. 71.

27. Ibid., p. 75.

28. Pollack, *George Gershwin: His Life and Work,* p. 269.

29. Ibid., p. 279.

30. Ibid., p. 499.

31. Ibid., p. 504.

32. Benjamin DeCasseres, quoted in ibid., p. 511.

33. Ibid., p. 511.

34. Ibid., p. 513.

35. Ibid., p. 591.

36. Ibid., p. 606.

37. Ibid., p. 617.

38. Furia, *The Poets of Tin Pan Alley,* pp. 101, 132.

39. Ibid., p. 132.

40. Mark Steyn, *Mark Steyn's American Songbook* (Woodsville, N.H.: Stockade Books, 2008), pp. 3–11.

41. Roger Scruton, "The Decline of Laughter," *American Spectator,* July, 23, 2007. I am much indebted to Scruton for his insights on humor.

42. Ibid.

43. Leon Kass, *The Hungry Soul: Eating and the Perfecting of Our Nature* (Chicago: University of Chicago Press, 1999), pp. 125–27.

44. Roger Scruton, *I Drink Therefore I Am: A Philosopher's Guide to Wine* (London and New York: Continuum, 2009); also, Roger Scruton, "Islam and the West: Lines of Demarcation," *Azure,* no. 35 (Winter 5769 / 2009), pp. 46–47.

45. Scruton, "Islam and the West: Lines of Demarcation."

46. Hanif Kureishi, *My Beautiful Laundrette and The Rainbow Sign* (London: Faber & Faber, 1986), p. 16.

47. Charles Glass, in *Times Literary Supplement,* April 22, 1994.

48. Norval White and Elliot Willensky, *AIA Guide to New York City* (New York: Crown, 2000), pp. xiii, 19–20.

49. Christopher Gray, *New York Streetscapes: Tales of Manhattan's Significant Buildings and Landmarks* (New York: Abrams, 2003), p. III.

50. The story of the Muhammad statue is based on several articles: Ira Henry Freeman, "Mohammed Quits Pedestal Here On Moslem Plea After 50 Years," *New York Times,* April 9, 1955; John Kifner, "Images of Muhammad, Gone for Good," *New York Times,* February 12, 2006; Daniel Pipes, "Destroying Sculptures of Muhammad," *Jerusalem Post,* February 28, 2008; Andrew Bostom, "NYC's Insane Capitulation to Islam, Circa 1955—Past as Prologue?" (reproducing the aforementioned articles by Freeman and Kifner), http://www.andrewbostom.org/blog, August 5, 2010.

51. Gray, *New York Streetscapes,* pp. 92–94.

52. White and Willensky, *AIA Guide to New York City,* p. 129.

53. His name has been changed to protect him and his family.

54. F. A. Hayek, *The Road to Serfdom* (1944; Chicago: University of Chicago Press, 1976), p. 162. See p. 172 above.

55. I am following Hayek's distinction between "liberal" democracy and "social" or totalitarian democracy. Cf. F. A. Hayek, "Freedom, Reason, and Tradition," *Ethics: An International Journal of Social, Political, and Legal Philosophy,* vol. 68, no. 4 (July 1958), p. 229.

56. Titus: "Come, and take choice of all my library, And so beguile thy sorrow." William Shakespeare, *Titus Andronicus,* Act IV, Scene I.

57. Phyllis Dain, *The New York Public Library: A Universe of Knowledge* (New York: The New York Public Library, 2000), p. 13.

58. Ibid., p. 15.

59. Ibid., p. 19.

60. Austin Dacey, personal communication.

61. V. I. Lenin, quoted in Dain, *The New York Public Library: A Universe of Knowledge,* p. 29.

62. Evgeny Kuzmin, "Russian Libraries in the Context of Social, Economic and Political Reforms," Proceedings, 60th IFLA (International Federation of Library Associations and Institutions) General Conference, August 21–27, 1994, http://archive.ifla.org/IV/ifla60/60-kuze.htm.

63. Dain, *The New York Public Library: A Universe of Knowledge,* p. 32.

64. Ibid., p. 32.

65. Ibid., p. 33.

66. Ibid., p. 67.

67. Henry Hope Reed, *The New York Public Library: Its Architecture and Decoration* (New York: W. W. Norton, 1986), pp. 15–16.

68. F. Schiller, *On the Aesthetic Education of Man,* Letter Nine, quoted by Thomas Carlyle, *The Life of Friedrich Schiller* (New York: P. F. Collier & Son, 1901), p. 202. I think the translation is Carlyle's. An alternative translation is: "Mankind has lost its dignity, but Art has recovered it in significant stones."

69. Reed, *The New York Public Library: Its Architecture and Decoration,* p. 24.

70. Ibid., p. 10.

71. Roger Scruton, *The Aesthetics of Architecture* (Princeton, N.J.: Princeton University Press, 1980).

72. E. B. White, *Here Is New York* (1949; New York: The Little Bookroom, 1999), p. 34.

73. White and Willensky, *AIA Guide to New York City,* p. 214.

74. Gersh Kuntzman, "What was in store for forgotten Prez," *New York Post,* September 16, 2002. According to Kuntzman, Arthur was found sobbing in his room (presumably from fear rather than sorrow at Garfield's death).

75. Richard Brookhiser, "City of Many Worlds," *National Review,* March 8, 2010, p. 55. This wonderful article is what first alerted me to the address.

76. Walt Whitman, "Human and Heroic New York," *Specimen Days,* in *The Portable Walt Whitman,* ed. Mark Van Doren (New York: Penguin, 1977), pp. 531–32.

Chapter Two: Why Did the West Become Successful?

1. Dierdre N. McCloskey, *Bourgeois Dignity: Why Economics Can't Explain the Modern World* (Chicago: University of Chicago Press, 2010), p. 182.

2. Lawrence E. Harrison, "Why Culture Matters," introduction to *Culture Matters: How Values Shape Human Progress,* ed. Harrison and Samuel P. Huntington (New York: Basic Books, 2000), p. xxviii.

3. Ibld.

4. McCloskey, *Bourgeois Dignity,* p. 182.

5. Ibid., pp. 184–85.

6. David S. Landes, *The Wealth and Poverty of Nations: Why Some Are So Rich and Some Are So Poor* (New York: W. W. Norton, 1999), p. 516.

7. Walter Burkert, *The Orientalizing Revolution: Near Eastern Influence on Greek Culture in the Early Archaic Age* (Cambridge, Mass.: Harvard University Press, 1992); Burkert, *Babylon, Memphis, Persepolis: Eastern Contexts of Greek Culture* (Cambridge, Mass.: Harvard University Press, 2004); *Selected Lectures of Rudolf Wittkower: The Impact of Non-European Civilizations on the Art of the West,* ed. Donald Martin Reynolds (Cambridge, UK: Cambridge University Press, 1989); Rudolf Wittkower, *Allegory and the Migration of Symbols* (Boulder, Col.: Westview Press, 1977).

8. This is the conclusion of Max Müller, a German scholar who is a pioneer in the study of Sanskrit scriptures including the *Rig Veda.*

9. Philippe Nemo, *What Is the West?* (Pittsburgh: Duquesne University Press, 2006), p. 5. I have leaned heavily on Nemo's lucid defense of the West in this chapter.

10. Ibid., p. 8ff.

11. Roger Scruton, *The West and the Rest: Globalization and the Terrorist Threat* (Wilmington, Del.: ISI Books, 2002), pp. 2–3.

12. See Sophocles, *Antigone,* lines 450–460; and G. W. F. Hegel, *Aesthetics: Lectures on Fine Art,* trans. T. M. Knox (Oxford, UK: Clarendon Press, 1988), vol. 1, p. 464.

13. Sophocles, *Antigone,* trans. Robert Fagles (New York: Penguin, 1984), p. 37.

14. Ibid., p. 77.

15. Alcmaeon of Croton is quoted in Bruce Thornton, *Greek Ways: How the Greeks Created Western Civilization* (San Francisco: Encounter Books, 2000), p. 144.

16. Anaxagoras is quoted in ibid., p. 145.

17. Aristotle, *Metaphysics*, 980a, book I, part 1, trans. W. D. Ross, in *Complete Works,* ed. Jonathan Barnes (Princeton, N.J.: Princeton University Press, 1985), vol. 2, p. 1552.

18. E. R. Dodds, *The Greeks and the Irrational* (Berkeley and Los Angeles: University of California Press, 1962), p. 136.

19. Nemo, *What Is the West?* pp. 7–16.

20. Ibid., pp. 23–24.

21. Ibid., p. 27.

22. Landes, *The Wealth and Poverty of Nations*, pp. 34–35.

23. Ibid., p. 34.

24. Ibid., pp. 58–59.

25. Nemo, *What Is the West?* p. 29.

26. Ibid., p. 32.

27. Ibid., pp. 43–54.

28. Ibid., p. 51.

29. Ibid., p. 72.

30. See Milton V. Anastos, "Constantinople and Rome," in *Aspects of the Mind of Byzantium: Political Theory, Theology, and Ecclesiastical Relations with the See of Rome,* ed. Speros Vryonis, Jr., and Nicholas Goodhue, Variorum Collected Studies Series (Aldershot, UK: Ashgate, 2001), chap. 7, pp. 484–519. The section on "the doctrine of the two powers" is available at http://www.myriobiblos.gr/texts/english/milton1_7.html#b.

31. Scruton, *The West and the Rest,* p. 4 (see n. 11 above).

32. Nemo, *What Is the West?* pp. 40–43.

33. Toby Huff, *The Rise of Early Modern Science: Islam, China, and the West* (Cambridge, UK: Cambridge University Press, 1993), p. 128.

34. Nemo, *What Is the West?* pp. 40–43.

35. Huff, *The Rise of Early Modern Science,* pp. 134–35.

36. Ibid., p. 137.

37. Ibid., p. 120.

38. Hastings Rashdall, quoted in ibid., p. 64, n. 59.

39. Ibid., p. 137.

40. Ibid., p. 161.

41. Ibid., p. 161.

42. A. C. Crombie, *Medieval and Early Modern Science* (1952; New York: Doubleday Anchor, 1959), p. xii.

43. Charles Freeman, *The Closing of the Western Mind* (New York: Vintage, 2005), p. 317.

44. "Carolingian Schools," in *The Oxford Dictionary of the Christian Church*, 3rd ed. (New York: Oxford University Press, 1997), pp. 290–91.

45. "Alcuin of York," The MacTutor History of Mathematics, School of Mathematics and Statistics, University of St. Andrews, http://www-history.mcs.st-andrews.ac.uk/Mathematicians/Alcuin.html.

46. "Theodulf," in *The Oxford Dictionary of the Christian Church*, 3rd ed., p. 1603.

47. Henri Pirenne, *Mohammed and Charlemagne* (1939; New York: Barnes & Noble Books, 1961), p. 164.

48. R. W. Southern, *Western Views of Islam in the Middle Ages* (Cambridge, Mass.: Harvard University Press, 1978), p. 7.

49. Crombie, *Medieval and Early Modern Science,* p. 35.

50. Ibid., p. 35.

51. A. I. Sabra, quoted in Huff, *The Rise of Early Modern Science,* p. 86.

52. Huff, *The Rise of Early Modern Science,* p. 144 (see n. 33 above).

53. Al-Ghazali, *Deliverance from Error,* trans. and ed. R. J. McCarthy (Louisville, Ky.: Fons Vitae, 2004), pp. 62–63.

54. Tina Stiefel, *The Intellectual Revolution in Twelfth-Century Europe* (New York: St. Martin's Press, 1985), pp. 35–46.

55. Ibid., p. 36.

56. Ibid., p. 36.

57. Ibid., p. 16.

58. Ibid., p. 41.

59. Ibid., p. 41.

60. Ibid., p. 45.

61. Ibid., p. 53.

62. Ibid., p. 55.

63. Ibid., p. 78.

64. Ibid., p. 78.

65. Ibid., p. 79.

66. Ibid., p. 38.

67. Perhaps more correctly, *syneidesis. Synderesis* or *synteresis* was not used by Paul, as it was not a Greek word at the time; it became current in Scholastic philosophy after Saint Jerome derived it from what is now thought to have been a transcription error. See "Synteresis," in *The Oxford Dictionary of the Christian Church,* 3rd ed., p. 1570.

68. Stiefel, *The Intellectual Revolution in Twelfth-Century Europe,* pp. 82–83.

69. Herbert Butterfield, *The Origins of Modern Science, 1300–1800,* rev. ed. (New York: Free Press, 1957), pp. 7–8, quoted in Toby Huff, *Intellectual Curiosity and the Scientific Revolution: A Global Perspective* (Cambridge, UK: Cambridge University Press, 2011), pp. 15–16.

70. Landes, *The Wealth and Poverty of Nations,* pp. 200–5.

71. Lawrence Stone, "The Educational Revolution in England, 1560–1640," *Past and Present,* vol. 68, no. 28 (1964), quoted by Huff, *Intellectual Curiosity,* p. 303.

72. Sascha O. Becker and Ludger Woessmann, "Was Weber Wrong? A Human Capital Theory of Protestant Economic History," *Quarterly Journal of Economics,* vol. 124, no. 2 (May 2009), pp. 531–96, quoted by Huff, *Intellectual Curiosity,* p. 309.

73. Huff, *Intellectual Curiosity,* p. 307.

74. Nemo, *What Is the West?* pp. 67, 71.

75. Scruton, *The West and the Rest,* p. 6.

76. Lewis Vaughn and Austin Dacey, *The Case for Humanism: An Introduction* (Lanham, Md.: Rowman & Littlefield, 2003). My discussion of church-state separation is indebted to this work.

77. Leonard Busher, *Religion's Peace: or, a Plea for Liberty of Conscience* (1614), cited in H. Leon McBeth, *A Sourcebook for Baptist Heritage* (Nashville: Broadman Press, 1990), p. 72; and in Vaughn and Dacey, *The Case for Humanism.*

78. John Locke, *A Letter Concerning Toleration* (Amherst, N.Y.: Prometheus Books, 1990), p. 20.

79. Thomas Paine, *The Age of Reason* (Secaucus, N.J.: Carol Publishing Group, 1974), p. 52.

80. Thomas Nagel, "Moral Conflict and Political Legitimacy," *Philosophy and Public Affairs,* vol. 16 (1987), pp. 230–31, quoted in Vaughn and Dacey, *The Case for Humanism,* p. 211.

81. Scruton, *The West and the Rest,* p. 6.

82. Ibid., p. 7.

83. Jonathan I. Israel, *Radical Enlightenment: Philosophy and the Making of Modernity 1650–1750* (New York: Oxford University Press, 2001), p. vi.

84. Ibid., p. 202.

85. Ibid., p. 296.

86. Ibid., p. vi.

87. Quoted by Jonathan Israel, *A Revolution of the Mind: Radical Enlightenment and the Intellectual Origins of Modern Democracy* (Princeton, N.J.: Princeton University Press, 2010), p. 46ff.

88. Nemo, *What Is the West?* p. 76.

89. Ibid., pp. 61–84.

90. Lawrence E. Harrison, "Why Culture Matters," p. xx (see n. 2 above).

91. Jared Diamond, *Guns, Germs, and Steel: The Fates of Human Societies* (1997; New York: W. W. Norton, 1999), p. 16.

92. See pp. 97–98 above.

93. Harrison, "Why Culture Matters," p. xx.

94. David Richardson, "Slave Trade," in *The Oxford Encyclopedia of Economic History,* ed. Joel Mokyr, quoted by McCloskey, *Bourgeois Dignity,* p. 229 (see n. 1 above).

95. Stanley Engerman, "The Slave Trade and British Capital Formation in the Eighteenth Century: A Comment on the Williams Thesis," *Business History Review,* vol. 46 (1972), pp. 430–43; Patrick K. O'Brien, "European Economic Development: The Contribution of the Periphery," *Economic History Review,* vol. 35, no. 2 (1982), pp. 1–18.

96. Robert Paul Thomas and Richard N. Bean, "Fishers of Men: The Profits of the Slave Trade," *Journal of Economic History,* vol. 34 (1974), pp. 885–914.

97. David Eltis and Stanley L. Engerman, "The Importance of Slavery and the Slave Trade to Industrializing Britain," *Journal of Economic History,* vol. 60, no. 1 (March 2000), p. 129.

98. Ibid., p. 123.

99. Ibid., p. 129.

100. McCloskey, *Bourgeois Dignity*, p. 231.

101. Ibid., p. 232. Robert Clive, for example, made a fortune in India, but "his stock of capital was under a million pounds, and was below 1 percent of the annual £115 million flow of U.K. national income."

102. Ibid., p. 240.

103. Ibid., p. 241.

104. Ibid., p. 233.

105. Om Prakash, "India: Colonial Period," in *The Oxford Encyclopedia of Economic History*, ed. Joel Mokyr, quoted by McCloskey, *Bourgeois Dignity*, p. 234.

106. Quoted in David S. Landes, "Culture Makes All the Difference," in *Culture Matters*, ed. Harrison and Huntington, p. 6 (see n. 2 above). After giving Brazil its first strong currency in years, Cardoso was elected president.

107. McCloskey, *Bourgeois Dignity*, p. 242.

108. Diamond, *Guns, Germs, and Steel*, p. 410.

109. James Michael Blaut, "Environmentalism and Eurocentrism: A Review Essay," *Geographical Review*, July 1, 1999.

110. McCloskey, *Bourgeois Dignity*, pp. xi–xii.

111. Ibid.

112. Huff, *Intellectual Curiosity*, p. 15 (see n. 69 above).

113. Joel Mokyr, "Eurocentricity Triumphant," review of *The Wealth and Poverty of Nations* by David S. Landes, *American Historical Review*, vol. 104, no. 4 (October 1999).

114. Ibid.

115. Philippe Nemo lists some of these in *What Is the West?* pp. 61–62.

Chapter Three: Drugs, Sex, and Rock 'n' Roll

1. Dinesh D'Souza, *The Enemy at Home: The Cultural Left and Its Responsibility for 9/11* (New York: Doubleday, 2007), p. 2.

2. Quoted by Tom Stoppard, *Rock 'n' Roll* (New York: Grove Press, 2007), p. xv.

3. Quoted in ibid., p. xvii.

4. Ibid., p. xvii.

5. Ibid., p. xviii.

6. Roger Scruton, "Islam and the West: Lines of Demarcation," *Azure,* no. 35 (Winter 5769 / 2009), p. 48.

7. Robert Spencer, "The D'Souza Follies," *FrontPage Magazine,* January 30, 2007.

8. "Qatar: Record Divorce Rate, 50% of Marriages Fall Apart," ANSAmed, April 20, 2011, http://www.ansamed.info/en/top/ME. XAM48296.html.

9. For example, Abdelwahab Bouhdiba, *Sexuality in Islam* (London: Routledge, 2007).

10. Tawfik Hamid, *The Roots of Jihad* (n.p.: Top Executive Media, 2005), p. 25.

11. Howard Bloom, *The Lucifer Principle: A Scientific Expedition into the Forces of History* (New York: Atlantic Monthly Press, 1997), pp. 239–40.

12. Sharabi was quoted by Halim Barakat, "The Arab Family and the Challenge of Social Transformation," *Women and Family in the Middle East: New Voices of Change,* ed. Elizabeth Warnock Fernea (Austin: University of Texas Press, 1985), in turn quoted by Bloom, *The Lucifer Principle,* p. 241.

13. Bloom, *The Lucifer Principle,* p. 239.

14. Ibid., p. 243.

15. "Drug addiction blights Pakistan," Al Jazeera, January 12, 2010.

16. "Iran has 130,000 new drug addicts each year," Reuters, November 15, 2009.

17. Declan Walsh, "Alcoholism blooms in 'dry' Pakistan," *Guardian,* December 27, 2010.

18. "Child Prostitution: The Commercial Sexual Exploitation of Children: Islamic Republic of Pakistan," http://gvnet.com/child-prostitution/Pakistan.htm.

19. Ibid.

20. Ibid.

21. The following is a translation of the Persian document on *muta*:

> *Bismillah ar-Rahman ar-Rahim*
>
> Temporary Marriage (Marriage is among the traditions of the Prophet Mohammad)
>
> In order to elevate the spiritual atmosphere, create proper psychological conditions and tranquility of mind, the Province of the Quds'eh-Razavi of Khorassan has created centers for temporary marriage (just next door to the shrine) for those brothers who are on pilgrimage to the shrine of our eighth Imam, Imam Reza, and who are far away from their spouses.
>
> To that end, we call on all our sisters who are virgins, who are between the ages of 12 and 35 to cooperate with us. Each of our sisters who signs up will be bound by a two-year contract with the province of the Quds'eh-Razavi of Khorassan and will be required to spend at least 25 days of each month temporarily married to those brothers who are on pilgrimage. The period of the contract will be considered as a part of the employment experience of the applicant. The period of each temporary marriage can be anywhere between five hours and ten days. The prices are as follows:
>
> * Five-hour temporary marriage—50,000 Tomans ($50 US)
> * One-day temporary marriage— 75,000 Tomans ($75 US)
> * Two-day temporary marriage—100,000 Tomans ($100 US)
> * Three-day temporary marriage—150,000 Tomans ($150 US)
> * Between four- and ten-day temporary marriage—300,000 Tomans ($300 US)

Our sisters who are virgins will receive a bonus of 100,000 Tomans ($100 US) for the removal of their hymen.

After the expiration of the two-year contract, should our sisters still be under 35 years of age and should they be so inclined, they can be added to the waiting list of those who are seeking long-term temporary marriage. The employed sisters are obligated to donate 5 percent of their earnings to the Shrine of Imam Reza. We ask all the sisters who are interested in applying, to furnish two full-length photographs (fully hijabed and properly veiled), their academic diplomas, proof of their virginity and a certificate of good physical and psychological health which they can obtain through the health and human services of the township of their residence. Please forward all compiled material and send to the below address by the 31st of the month of Ordibehesht, 1389 (May 21, 2010).

Attention: For sisters who are below 14 years of age, a written consent from their fathers or male guardian is required.

Address: Mash'had, Shrine of Imam Reza, Shaheed Navab-Safavi, Kossar passage, Bureau of Temporary Marriages or call Haji Mahmood Momtaz: 98/511/222-5790. For further information, please refer to the Quds'eh-Razavi website.

22. "Drug addiction worries Pakistan," BBC News, June 26, 2000.

23. "Drug addiction blights Pakistan," Al Jazeera, January 12, 2010.

24. Sarah Alam, "The rising toll of drug addicts," Youth Concern, http://users.otenet.gr/~tzelepisk/yc/24.htm.

25. ANI, "Ban of alcohol in Pakistan is giving rise to drug addiction," Pakistan Defence, February 9, 2007.

26. Declan Walsh, "Alcoholism booms in 'dry' Pakistan," *Guardian,* December 27, 2010.

27. Karl Vick, "Opiates of the Iranian People: Despair Drives World's Highest Addiction Rate," *Washington Post,* September 23, 2005, p. A1.

28. "Iran tops world drug addiction-rate list," *Iran Focus,* September 24, 2005.

29. Golnaz Esfandiari, "Iran: New Ways Considered for Tackling Growing Drug Use among Young People," Radio Free Europe / Radio Liberty, December 3, 2003, http://www.rferl.org/content/article/1105201.html.

30. Golnaz Esfandiari, "Iran: Prize-Winning Documentary Exposes Hidden Side of Iranian Society," Radio Free Europe / Radio Liberty, March 25, 2005, http://www.rferl.org/content/article/1058130.html.

31. "Official Laws against Women in Iran," Women's Forum Against Fundamentalism in Iran, http://www.wfafi.org/laws.pdf.

32. Ibid.

33. The first week of January 2006 brought the following:

January 1 Iran's notorious Islamic court in the city of Rasht, northern Iran, sentenced Delara Darabi to death by hanging. She was charged with murder when she was seventeen years old. Darabi has denied the charges, but Iran's Supreme Court upheld her sentence.

January 2—Ahmadinejad ordered the closure of a daily newspaper and banned a proposed women's publication.

January 4—Iran's paramilitary forces, the Basijis and Ansar-e-Hezbollah, launched an "acid attack" on female university students in the town of Shahroud, northeastern Iran. Vigilantes on a motorbike threw acid on the faces of two female students because they were not observing the strict Islamic dress code. Ahmadinejad regularly addresses meetings of Islamic vigilantes, praising their efforts "to purify the Islamic Republic of the vestiges of corrupt Western culture" and urging them to step up the campaign against the "mal-veiling" of women and girls.

January 7—Iran's Islamic court sentenced an eighteen-year-old female rape victim to death by hanging after she confessed that she had unintentionally killed a man who had tried to rape both her and her niece, according to the state-run daily *Etemaad*. Nazanin and her niece Somayeh (who were seventeen and sixteen at the time) were attacked by three men, and Nazanin killed one of them in self-defense.

January 7—Ahmadinejad started a plan to segregate Iran's pedestrian walkways on a gender basis. As part of a government initiative called "Increase the hejab (veil) culture and female chastity," the Ministry of Housing and Urban Development received orders to construct separate pedestrian walkways for men and women.

See: "Ahmadinejad Begins 2006 with Escalated Violence against Women and New Gender Apartheid Policies in Iran," Women's Forum Against Fundamentalism in Iran, http://www.wfafi.org/wfafistatement23.htm.

34. "Official Laws against Women in Iran," Women's Forum Against Fundamentalism in Iran, http://www.wfafi.org/laws.pdf.

35. Ibid.

36. Ibid.

37. "Child Protection," UNICEF Pakistan Media Centre, 2005, http://www.unicef.org/pakistan/ media_1775.htm.

38. Geoffrey K. Pullum, *The Great Eskimo Vocabulary Hoax and Other Irreverent Essays on the Study of Language* (Chicago: University of Chicago Press, 1991), pp. 159–71.

39. Jared Diamond, *Guns, Germs, and Steel: The Fates of Human Societies* (1997; New York: W. W. Norton, 1999), p. 19.

40. Ibid., p. 19.

41. Ibid., p. 20.

42. Ibid., p. 19.

43. Shepard Krech, *The Ecological Indian: Myth and History* (New York: W. W. Norton, 1999).

44. Nathaniel Philbrick, *Sea of Glory: America's Voyage of Discovery, the U.S. Exploring Expedition, 1838–1842* (New York: Penguin, 2004), p. 143.

45. Dale Riepe, *The Naturalistic Tradition in Indian Thought* (Seattle: University of Washington Press, 1961), p. 247.

46. R. A. Nicholson, *The Mystics of Islam* (1914; London: Routledge & Kegan Paul, 1975), pp. 10–27.

47. See Evelyn Underhill, *Mysticism: A Study in the Nature and Development of Man's Spiritual Consciousness* (1911; New York: Dutton, 1961); and William James, *The Varieties of Religious Experience* (1902; New York: Modern Library, 1999), lectures 16 and 17, Mysticism.

48. Luc Barbulesco and Philippe Cardinal, *L'Islam en questions: Vingt-quatre écrivains arabes répondent* (Paris: Grasset, 1986), pp. 203–14.

49. *The Chambers Dictionary* (Edinburgh: Chambers, 2003), s.v. spiritual, p. 1461.

50. Javed Majeed, *Ungoverned Imaginings: James Mill's "The History of British India and Orientalism"* (Oxford, UK: Clarendon Press, 1992).

51. Bernard Williams, *Morality: An Introduction to Ethics* (New York: Harper & Row, 1972), pp. 24–25.

52. Richard A. Shweder, "Moral Maps, 'First World' Conceits, and the New Evangelists," in *Culture Matters: How Values Shape Human Progress,* ed. Lawrence E. Harrison and Samuel P. Huntington (New York: Basic Books, 2000), pp. 158–76.

53. Danielle Etounga-Manguelle, "Does Africa Need a Cultural Adjustment Program?" in *Culture Matters,* pp. 65–78.

54. Quoted by Samuel P. Huntington, "Culture Counts," foreword to *Culture Matters,* p. xiv.

55. Janadas Devan, "Singapore Way," *New York Review of Books,* June 6, 1996:

"Crucially, the claim of differential cultural identities also enables Asian establishments to reject the democratic ethos already present in modern Asian history—from the May Fourth movement in China to the nationalist, anti-colonial struggles in India, Indonesia, and elsewhere—as an aberrant foreign importation. Such erasures of recent Asian history are especially useful in Singapore because the state there is itself the agent of a democratizing process—involving social and economic enfranchisement as well as the ballot box—that it also wishes to contain. The very success of Singapore's modernity has led the state to formulate a sanitized cultural inheritance to restrain its citizens from demanding rights and responsibilities beyond those already granted to achieve modernity. By misrepresenting, thus, political possibilities within Asian modernity as a choice between Eastern and Western cultural identities, the state can contain the threats to its power that its own success has generated."

Devan concludes, "Is it too much to claim, really, that Asian nationals have agency? that when they seek a more democratic future for themselves it is because democracy is as much a part of their modernity as it is of the West's?"

56. The charter is available at the Asian Human Rights Commission website, http://material.ahrchk.net/charter/mainfile.php/eng_charter.

57. David Gilmour, *The Long Recessional: The Imperial Life of Rudyard Kipling* (New York: Farrar, Straus & Giroux, 2002), p. 69.

58. Quoted by Denis Judd, *Empire: The British Imperial Experience from 1765 to the Present* (London: Fontana Press, 1997), p. 16.

59. A translation of Asoka's edicts is available at the Human Rights Solidarity website, http://www.hrsolidarity.net/mainfile.php/2001vol11no067/148/. See also *The Oxford History of India*, ed. Vincent A. Smith and Percival Spear (1911; New Delhi: Oxford University Press, 1981), pp. 129–32.

Rock Edict 12: "Beloved-of-the-Gods, King Piyadasi [Asoka], honours both ascetics and the house-holders of all religions, and he honours them with gifts and honours of various kinds. But Beloved-of-the-Gods, King Piyadasi, does not value gifts and honours as much as he values this: there should be growth in the essentials of all religions. Growth in essentials can be done in different ways, but all of them have as their root restraint in speech, that is, not praising one's own religion or condemning the religion of others without good cause. And if there is cause for criticism, it should be done in a mild way. But it is better to honour other religions for this reason. By so doing, one's own religion benefits and so do other religions while doing otherwise harms one's own religion and the religions of others. Whoever praises his own religion due to excessive devotion and condemns others with the thought "Let me glorify my own religion" only harms his own religion. Therefore, contact [between religions] is good. One should listen to and respect the doctrines professed by others. Beloved-of-the-Gods, King Piyadasi, desires that all should be well-learned in the good doctrines of other religions. Those who are content with their own religion should be told this: Beloved-of-the-Gods, King Piyadasi, does not value gifts and honours as much as he values that there should be growth in the essentials of all religions. And to this end many are working—Dhamma Mahamatras, Mahamatras in charge of the women's quarters, officers in charge of outlying areas and other such officers. And the fruit of this is that one's own religion grows, and the Dhamma is illuminated also."

60. Hirad Abtahi, "Reflections on the Ambiguous Universality of Human Rights: Cyrus the Great's Proclamation as a Challenge to the Athenian Democracy's Perceived Monopoly on Human Rights," in *The Dynamics of International Criminal Justice,* ed. Hirad Abtahi and Gideon Boas (Leiden: Brill, 2006), p. 12.

61. Plato, *Laws,* III, 694a, 694b, quoted by Abtahi, "Reflections on the Ambiguous Universality of Human Rights," p. 30.

62. For instance, the Abdorrahman Boroumand Foundation for the Promotion of Human Rights and Democracy in Iran (ABF) "is a non-governmental non-profit organization dedicated to the promotion of human rights and democracy in Iran. The Foundation is an independent organization with no political affiliation. It is named in memory of Dr. Abdorrahman Boroumand, an Iranian lawyer and

pro-democracy activist who was assassinated allegedly by the agents of the Islamic Republic of Iran in Paris on April 18, 1991." ABF website, http://www.abfiran.org/english/foundation.php. The Iranian Action Committee, a nonprofit nongovernmental organization, has tried to bring the Islamic Republic of Iran in front of international human rights tribunals for crimes against humanity; see http://www.rozanehmagazine.com/MayJune05/acrimnal.html. Other organizations include Regime Change Iran (http://www.regimechangeiran.com) and the Alliance of Iranian Women (http://allianceofiranianwomen.org), which advocates "a free, democratic, secular, and nationalistic government in Iran."

63. William Empson, *Argufying: Essays on Literature and Culture,* ed. John Haffenden (London: Hogarth Press, 1988), p. 578.

64. Amy Chua, *Battle Hymn of the Tiger Mother* (New York: Penguin, 2011), p. 208.

65. Quoted by Steve Sailer in his review of "Together," a film by Chen Kaige, in *The American Conservative,* July 14, 2003, available at http://www.isteve.com/Film_Together.htm.

66. Ibid.

Chapter Four: Slavery, Racism, and Imperialism

1. William Gervase Clarence-Smith, "The Economics of the Indian Ocean and Red Sea Slave Trades in the 19th Century: An Overview," in *Slavery and Abolition,* vol. 9, no. 3 (December 1988), pp. 11–12.

2. Sheldon M. Stern, "It's Time to Face the Whole Truth About the Atlantic Slave Trade," History News Network, August 13, 2007.

3. Quoted in ibid.

4. Ibid. Stern cites Charles Johnson, Patricia Smith, and the WGBH Series Research Team, *Africans in America: America's Journey through Slavery* (New York: Harcourt Brace, 1998), pp. 2–3; and Howard W. French, "On Slavery, Africans Say the Guilt Is Theirs, Too," *New York Times,* December 27, 1994, p. A4.

5. "Benin Officials Apologize for Role in U.S. Slave Trade," *Chicago Tribune*, May 1, 2000.

6. Stern, "It's Time to Face the Whole Truth About the Atlantic Slave Trade."

7. Ibid.

8. Robert Paul Thomas and Richard N. Bean, "Fishers of Men: The Profits of the Slave Trade," *Journal of Economic History*, vol. 34 (1974), pp. 885–914.

9. John Thornton, *Africa and Africans in the Making of the Atlantic World, 1400–1680* (Cambridge, UK: Cambridge University Press, 1992), p. 7.

10. Ibid., p. 7.

11. Ibid., p. 74.

12. Ibid., p. 97.

13. Stern, "It's Time to Face the Whole Truth About the Atlantic Slave Trade."

14. All the quotations in this paragraph are from Bernard Lewis, *Race and Slavery in the Middle East: An Historical Enquiry* (New York: Oxford University Press, 1990), pp. 50–53.

15. Tidiane N'Diaye, *Le génocide voilé: Enquête historique* (Paris: Gallimard, Continents noirs, 2008).

16. Ibid., pp. 10–11.

17. Olivier Pétré-Grenouilleau, *Les traites négrières: Essai d'histoire globale* (Paris: Gallimard, 2004), pp. 147–48.

18. Clarence-Smith, "The Economics of the Indian Ocean and Red Sea Slave Trades in the 19th Century," p. 1.

19. Ibid., p. 4.

20. Ibid., p. 5.

21. Jan Hogendorn, "The Hideous Trade: Economic Aspects of the 'Manufacture' and Sale of Eunuchs," *Paideuma*, vol. 45 (1999), p. 137.

22. Ibid., p. 146.

23. Clarence-Smith, "The Economics of the Indian Ocean and Red Sea Slave Trades in the 19th Century."

24. Robert C. Davis, *Christian Slaves, Muslim Masters: White Slavery in the Mediterranean, the Barbary Coast, and Italy, 1500–1800* (New York: Palgrave Macmillan, 2003), p. 23.

25. Quoted in Giles Milton, *White Gold: The Extraordinary Story of Thomas Pellow and North Africa's One Million European Slaves* (London: Hodder & Stoughton, 2004), p. 68.

26. Ibid., p. 67.

27. Ibid., p. 97.

28. Ibid., p. 78.

29. Ibid., p. 107.

30. Ibid., p. 106.

31. Quoted in ibid., p. 105.

32. Bernard Lewis, *Cultures in Conflict: Christians, Muslims, and Jews in the Age of Discovery* (Oxford, UK: Oxford University Press, 1995), p. 72.

33. See, for example, the pathbreaking comparative study by Olivier Pétré-Grenouilleau, *Les traites négrières: Essai d'histoire globale* (see n. 17 above).

34. Hugh Thomas, *The Slave Trade: The Story of the Atlantic Slave Trade: 1440–1870* (New York: Touchstone, 1997), p. 556.

35. Ibid., p. 695.

36. Clarence-Smith, "The Economics of the Indian Ocean and Red Sea Slave Trades in the 19th Century," pp. 11–12.

37. Ehud R. Toledano, *The Ottoman Slave Trade and Its Suppression, 1840–1890* (Princeton, N.J.: Princeton University Press, 1982), pp. 91, 272, 273, quoted in Pétré-Grenouilleau, *Les traites négrières,* pp. 289–90.

38. Y. H. Erdem, *Slavery in the Ottoman Empire and Its Demise, 1800–1909* (New York: St. Martin's Press, 1996), p. xix, quoted in Pétré-Grenouilleau, *Les traites négrières,* p. 290.

39. John Alembillah Azumah, *Islam and Slavery* (London: Centre for Islamic Studies, London Bible College, 1999), p. 5, quoted in Caroline Cox and John Marks, *The 'West', Islam and Islamism: Is*

Ideological Islam Compatible with Liberal Democracy? (London: Civitas, 2003), p. 40. See also John Alembillah Azumah, *The Legacy of Arab-Islam in Africa* (Oxford, UK: One World, 2001).

40. Note presented by the secretary general to the fiftieth session of the United Nations General Assembly, October 16, 1995, quoted in Cox and Marks, *The 'West', Islam and Islamism,* p. 40.

41. John Eibner, "Eradicating Slavery in Sudan," *Boston Globe,* February 22, 2006.

42. P. Lovejoy and J. Hogendorn, eds., *Slow Death for Slavery: The Course of Abolition in Northern Nigeria, 1897–1936* (Cambridge, UK: Cambridge University Press, 1993), p. 30, quoted in Cox and Marks, *The 'West', Islam and Islamism,* p. 40.

43. Fatma Abdallah Mahmoud, "Accursed Forever and Ever," translated by MEMRI (Middle East Media Research Institute), Special Dispatch no. 375, May 3, 2002.

44. Speech by Prime Minister Mahathir Mohamad of Malaysia to the Tenth Islamic Summit Conference, Putrajaya, Malaysia, October 16, 2003, available at http://www.adl.org/anti_semitism/Malaysia.asp.

45. Amartya Sen, *Identity and Violence: The Illusion of Destiny* (New York: W. W. Norton, 2006), p. 66, and also p. 16: "distinguished Jewish philosopher fled an intolerant Europe."

46. Fouad Ajami, "Enemies, a Love Story: A Nobel Laureate Argues That Civilizations Are Not Clashing," *Washington Post,* April 2, 2006.

47. Moses Maimonides, *Epistle to Yemen: The Arabic Original and the Three Hebrew Versions,* ed. Abraham S. Halkin, trans. Boaz Cohen (New York: American Academy for Jewish Research, 1952).

48. Ibid., p. ii.

49. Ibid.

50. Ibid., p. iv. On "the Madman" see Norman Stillman, *The Jews of Arab Lands: A History and Source Book* (Philadelphia: Jewish Publication Society of America, 1979), p. 236.

51. Maimonides, *Epistle to Yemen,* p. viii.

52. Ibid., p. xviii.

53. Ibid., p. xviii.

54. A. Guillaume, *The Life of Muhammad: A Translation of Ibn Ishaq's Sirat Rasul Allah* (1955; Oxford, UK: Oxford University Press, 1987), p. 369.

55. Other victims named in A. Guillaume, *The Life of Muhammad,* include Ka'b b. al-Ashraf (pp. 364–69), Sallam ibn Abu'l-Huqayq (pp. 482–83), and al-Yusayr (pp. 665–66).

56. Ibn Sa'd, *Kitâb al-Tabaqât al-Kabirs,* trans. S. M. Haq (New Delhi: Kitab Bhavan, n.d.), vol. 1, p. 32.

57. A. Guillaume, *The Life of Muhammad,* pp. 461–69.

58. Ibid., pp. 437–45.

59. Ibid., p. 368.

60. "Therefore man was created alone, (1) to teach you that whoever destroys a single Israelite soul is deemed by Scripture as if he had destroyed a whole world." Fourth Division: The Order of Damages, Sanhedrin 4:5, in *The Mishnah: A New Translation* by Jacob Neusner (New Haven: Yale University Press, 1988), p. 591.

61. Robert Wistrich, *Antisemitism: The Longest Hatred* (New York: Schocken Books, 1991), p. 196.

62. Jeffery Herf, *Nazi Propaganda for the Arab World* (New Haven: Yale University Press, 2009), p. x.

63. Martin Jacques, "The Middle Kingdom Mentality," *Guardian,* April 16, 2005.

64. Frank Dikötter, introduction to *The Construction of Racial Identities in China and Japan: Historical and Contemporary Perspectives,* ed. Dikötter (Honolulu: University of Hawai'i Press, 1997), p. 2.

65. Ibid., p. 6.

66. Ibid., p. 7.

67. Ibid., p. 9.

68. Ibid., p. 10.

69. Ibid., p. 11.

70. Chris Hogg, "Japan racism 'deep and profound,'" BBC News, July 11, 2005.

71. Joe Wood, "The Yellow Negro," *Transition,* no. 73 (1997), pp. 40–66.

72. Aparna Pallavi, "Racism in North India," Boloji.com, October 6, 2006, http://www.boloji.com/wfs5/wfs677.htm.

73. National Campaign on Dalit Human Rights website, http://www.dalits.org.

74. "Delhi Declaration of National Summit on Reservation in Private Sector," NCDHR website, August 9, 2005, http://dalits.org/delhideclaration.htm.

75. "The Shame of Haryana," *Outlook India,* September 5, 2005, http://www.outlookindia.com/article.aspx?228490; and the reports collected at *Valmikans in News,* http://www.bhagwanvalmiki.com/gohana.htm.

76. Gautaman Bhaskaran, "Battles with racism in India's own backyard," *Japan Times,* July 7, 2009.

77. Mike Marqusee, "India in denial," Comment Is Free, *Guardian,* January 8, 2008.

78. Chun-shu Chang, *The Rise of the Chinese Empire,* vol. 1, *Nation, State, and Imperialism in Early China, ca. 1600 B.C.–A.D. 8* (Ann Arbor: University of Michigan Press, 2007), p. 161.

79. David Chandler, *A History of Cambodia* (Boulder, Col.: Westview Press, 2008); G. E. Harvey, *History of Burma from the Earliest Times to 10 March 1824* (London: Frank Cass & Co., 1925).

80. Bruce Gordon, *To Rule the Earth,* http://my.raex.com/~obsidian/earthrul.html. I have drawn much of my information on Japan from Yuki Tanaka, *Hidden Horrors: Japanese War Crimes in World War II* (Boulder, Col.: Westview Press, 1996), as well as general reference works.

81. Chalmers Johnson, "The Looting of Asia," *London Review of Books,* vol. 25, no. 22 (November 20, 2003), pp. 3–6.

82. Rudolph J. Rummel, *Statistics of Democide: Genocide and Mass Murder since 1900* (Charlottesville: Center for National Security Law, School of Law, University of Virginia, 1997).

83. Iris Chang gives an estimate of 300,000 Chinese killed during the Rape of Nanking; her figure is not universally accepted though it may well be true, hence my circumlocution, "at least 200,000." The Tokyo War Crimes Tribunal estimated "about 200,000 Chinese killed, and 20,000 women raped." See Tanaka, *Hidden Horrors,* p. 219, n. 17; also Rummel, *Statisics of Democide.*

84. Hua-ling Hu, *American Goddess at the Rape of Nanking: The Courage of Minnie Vautrin* (Carbondale: Southern Illinois University Press, 2000), p. 97.

85. Zhang Kaiyuan, *Eyewitness to Massacre: American Missionaries Bear Witness to Japanese Atrocities in Nanjing* (Armonk, N.Y.: M. E. Sharpe, 2001).

86. M. J. Thurman and Christine A. Sherman, *War Crimes: Japan's World War II Atrocities* (Paducah, Ky.: Turner Publishing Co., 2001).

87. Tanaka, *Hidden Horrors,* p. 8.

88. Gavan Daws, *Prisoners of the Japanese: POWs of World War II in the Pacific* (New York: William Morrow, 1994).

89. I cannot bear to relate the details here; interested readers can find ample accounts on the Internet, many with references to academic studies. For example, http://www.skycitygallery.com/japan/japan.html. See also Steven Butler, "A half century of denial: the hidden truth about Japan's unit 731," *US News and World Report,* July 31, 1995; Peter Williams and David Wallace, *Unit 731: Japan's Secret Biological Warfare in World War II* (New York: Free Press, 1989); Tanaka, *Hidden Horrors,* pp. 135–66.

90. Daniel Barenblatt, *A Plague upon Humanity: The Secret Genocide of Axis Japan's Germ Warfare Operation* (New York: Harper Collins, 2004), pp. xii, 17; Christopher Hudson, "Doctors of Depravity," *Daily Mail* (London), March 2, 2007.

91. Yuki Tanaka, "Poison Gas: The Story Japan Would Like to Forget," *Bulletin of the Atomic Scientists,* October 1988, pp. 16–17.

92. "Japan tested chemical weapon on Aussie POW: new evidence," *Japan Times,* July 27, 2004.

93. Tanaka, *Hidden Horrors,* p. 127. Tanaka devotes an entire chapter to Japanese cannibalism.

94. Lord Russell of Liverpool (Edward Russell), *The Knights of Bushido: A Short History of Japanese War Crimes* (Barnsley, UK: Greenhill Books, 2002), p. 121.

95. Zhifen Ju, "Japan's Atrocities of Conscripting and Abusing North China Draftees after the Outbreak of the Pacific War," paper delivered to Joint Study of the Sino-Japanese War conference, "Wartime China: Regional Regimes and Conditions, 1937–45," Harvard University, June 28, 2002, Session 6, summary at http://www.fas.harvard.edu/~asiactr/sino-japanese/session6.htm.

96. Library of Congress, Country Studies, "Indonesia: World War II and the Struggle for Independence, 1942–50: The Japanese Occupation, 1942–45," November 1992.

97. Lionel Wigmore, *The Japanese Thrust: Australia in the War of 1939–1945* (Canberra: Australian War Memorial, 1957), p. 588.

98. Yoshiaki Yoshimi, *Comfort Women: Sexual Slavery in the Japanese Military during World War II* (New York: Columbia University Press, 2000).

99. Hugh Kennedy, *The Great Arab Conquests: How the Spread of Islam Changed the World We Live In* (London: Weidenfeld & Nicolson, 2007).

100. Speros Vryonis, Jr., *The Decline of Medieval Hellenism in Asia Minor and the Process of Islamization from the Eleventh through the Fifteenth Century* (Berkeley and Los Angeles: University of California Press, 1986).

101. Quoted in ibid., p. 164.

102. Quoted in ibid., p. 286.

103. Ibid., p. 402.

104. Ibid., p. 500.

105. Michael Cook and Patricia Crone, *Hagarism: The Making of the Muslim World* (Cambridge, UK: Cambridge University Press, 1977), p. viii.

106. V. S. Naipaul, *Among the Believers: An Islamic Journey* (New York: Knopf, 1981), pp. 141–42.

107. Ibid., p. 142.

108. K. S. Lal, *Growth of Muslim Population in Medieval India, A.D. 1000–1800* (Delhi: Research Publications in Social Sciences, 1973), pp. 77–85, 433–61, 631–53.

109. Sir Jadunath Sarkar, *History of Aurangzib,* 5 vols. (Calcutta: Sarkar & Sons, 1912–1924).

110. Vincent A. Smith *The Oxford History of India,* 4th ed., ed. Percival Spear (New York: Oxford University Press, 1981), p. 350.

111. Ibid., p. 297.

112. Quoted in David Kopf, *British Orientalism and the Bengal Renaissance: The Dynamics of Indian Modernization, 1773–1835* (Berkeley and Los Angeles: University of California Press, 1969), p. 1.

113. R. C. Majumdar, ed., *The History and Culture of the Indian People,* vol. 6, *The Delhi Sultanate* (London: G. Allen & Unwin, 1952), p. 623.

114. Smith, *The Oxford History of India,* 4th ed., pp. 235–36.

115. J. C. Harle, *The Art and Architecture of the Indian Subcontinent* (London: Penguin, 1986), p. 199.

116. Sita Ram Goel, *Hindu Temples: What Happened to Them,* vol. 2, *The Islamic Evidence* (New Delhi: Voice of India, 1993), sec. 3, chap. 8.

117. David Gilmour, *Curzon* (New York: Farrar, Straus & Giroux, 2003), p. 178.

118. Quoted in ibid., p. 179.

119. Ibid., pp. 179–81.

120. Edward W. Said, *Orientalism* (New York: Pantheon, 1978), pp. 33, 57.

121. C. A. Bayly, "The Second British Empire," in *The Oxford History of the British Empire: Historiography,* ed. Robin W. Winks (Oxford, UK: Oxford University Press, 1999), p. 70.

122. Christopher Hitchens, Letter to the editor, *Atlantic Monthly,* November 2003.

123. Susan Bayly, "Colonial Cultures: Asia," in *The Oxford History of the British Empire: The Nineteenth Century,* ed. Andrew Porter (Oxford, UK: Oxford University Press, 1999), p. 469.

124. Iris Chang, *The Rape of Nanking: The Forgotten Holocaust* (New York: Basic Books, 1997).

125. Jung Chang and Jon Halliday, *Mao: The Unknown Story* (New York: Knopf, 2005).

126. Ben Kiernan, *The Pol Pot Regime: Race, Power, and Genocide in Cambodia under the Khmer Rouge, 1975–79,* 2nd ed. (New Haven: Yale University Press, 2002).

127. S. K. Bhattacharyya, *Genocide in East Pakistan / Bangladesh: A Horror Story* (Houston: A. Ghosh, 1988); also Anthony Mascarenhas, *The Rape of Bangladesh* (Delhi: Vikas, 1971).

128. James Barter, *Idi Amin* (Chicago: Lucent, 2004).

129. Human Rights Watch has many articles on the situation in Sudan at http://www.hrw.org/. For the period up to 1993, see Millard Burr, *A Working Document: Quantifying Genocide in the Southern Sudan, 1983–1993* (Washington, D.C.: U.S. Committee for Refugees, 1993); and U.S. Committee for Refugees World Refugee Survey 2002: Sudan, http://www.unhcr.org/refworld/publisher,USCRI,,,3d04c15528,0.html.

130. Nicholas Thompson, "Adopt a Peacekeeper," *Boston Globe,* March 6, 2005; also Marc Lacey, "Tallying Darfur Terror: Guesswork with a Cause," *International Herald Tribune,* May 11, 2005.

131. V. N. Dadrian, *The History of the Armenian Genocide: Ethnic Conflict from the Balkans to Anatolia to the Caucasus* (Oxford, UK: Berghahn Books, 1995); Ara Sarafian, ed., *United States Official Documents on the Armenian Genocide,* 4 vols. (Watertown, Mass.: Armenian Review, 1995).

132. Kanan Makiya, *The Republic of Fear* (Berkeley and Los Angeles: University of California Press, 1998).

133. The Syrian Human Rights Committee, http://www.shrc.org/default.aspx.

134. Ibid.; see also Marius Deeb, *Syria's Terrorist War on Lebanon and the Peace Process* (New York: Palgrave Macmillan, 2003).

135. This figure does not include the number of Iranians killed in the Iran/Iraq war. See especially the website Human Rights and Democracy for Iran, a project of the Abdorrahman Boroumand Foundation, www.abfiran.org, which has just begun the grim task of documenting all the assassinations, executions, and murders of Iranian civilians; and also Amnesty International, *Iran Violations of Human Rights: Documents Sent by Amnesty International to the Government of the Islamic Republic of Iran* (London: Amnesty International Publications, 1987).

136. Arthur M. Schlesinger, Jr., *The Disuniting of America: Reflections on a Multicultural Society* (New York: W. W. Norton, 1992).

Chapter Five: Irony, Self-Criticism, and Objectivity

1. Stuart Hampshire, *Freedom of Mind and Other Essays* (Oxford, UK: Clarendon Press, 1972), p. 227.

2. E. H. Gombrich, "Eastern Inventions and Western Response" *Daedalus,* vol. 127 (Winter 1998), pp. 193–205.

3. Bultmann summarized this view in a 1941 lecture, "New Testament and Mythology: The Problem of Demythologizing the New Testament Message."

4. *The Oxford Classical Dictionary,* s.v. εἰρωνεία [eirōneía].

5. Norman D. Knox, "Irony," *Dictionary of the History of Ideas,* ed. Philip P. Wiener (1968; New York: Charles Scribner's Sons, 1973), vol. 2, pp. 627–34; also available at the Autodidact Project, http://www.autodidactproject.org/other/ironydhi.html.

6. The Ironic Catholic, http://www.ironiccatholic.com/

7. Knox, "Irony."

8. Jeff Keller, "Irony," at University of Chicago: Theories of Media: Keywords Glossary, http://csmt.uchicago.edu/glossary2004/irony.htm.

9. Knox, "Irony."

10. "The poet describes fourteenth-century English society in terms of its failure to represent an ideal society living in accord with Christian principles; hence the satirical poetry for which Langland is noted. Society's failure, of course, is attributable in part to the corruption of the church and ecclesiastics, and whenever he considers clerical corruption, he pours out savagely indignant satire. But he is equally angry with the failure of the wealthy laity—untaught by the church to practice charity—to alleviate the sufferings of the poor." Introduction to *Piers Plowman* in *The Norton Anthology of English Literature,* vol. 1, *The Middle Ages,* 7th ed., ed. David Alfred and Stephen Greenblatt (New York: W. W. Norton, 2000), p 317.

11. Matthew Arnold, *Culture and Anarchy: An Essay in Political and Social Criticism* (London, 1869), preface.

12. Arthur M. Schlesinger, Jr., *The Disuniting of America: Reflections on a Multicultural Society* (New York: W. W. Norton, 1992), p. 124.

13. Roy Porter, *Enlightenment: Britain and the Creation of the Modern World* (London: Penguin, 2001), p. 360.

14. Quoted in *Unchained Voices,* ed. Vincent Carretta (Lexington: University Press of Kentucky, 1996), p. 6, and in Porter, *Enlightenment,* p. 360.

15. Quoted in Porter, *Enlightenment,* p. 360.

16. Quoted in ibid.

17. Laurence Sterne, "Reply to Sancho, July 27, 1766," in *The Norton Anthology of English Literature,* vol. 2, *The Restoration and the Eighteenth Century,* 7th ed., ed. David Alfred and Stephen Greenblatt (New York: W. W. Norton, 2000), p. 2808.

18. Samuel Johnson, *The Idler* no. 11, June 24, 1758.

19. Samuel Johnson, *The Idler* no. 87, December 15, 1759.

20. James Boswell, *The Life of Johnson,* ed. R. W. Chapman (1904; Oxford, UK: Oxford University Press, 1983), pp. 876–78.

21. Arthur Herman, *How the Scots Invented the Modern World* (New York: Three Rivers Press, 2001), pp. 104–5.

22. Richard Brinsley Sheridan, "On the Abolition of Slavery: House of Commons, 17th March 1807," in *The Speeches of the Right Honourable Richard Brinsley Sheridan, with a Sketch of His Life,* edited by a Constitutional Friend (London, 1842).

23. Frederick Douglass, *My Bondage and My Freedom* (Auburn, N.Y.: Miller, Orton & Co., 1857; and Ann Arbor: University of Michigan Library, 2005), ch. XI, p. 158. Also quoted in *The Columbian Orator,* ed. Caleb Bingham, rev. Val J. Halamandaris (1979; Washington, D.C.: Caring Publications, 1997), p. ix. It is sometimes assumed that Douglass read Sheridan's celebrated antislavery speech of 1807 in *The Columbian Orator,* but the anthology was published in 1797, and a close reading of Douglass's words points to a different speech.

24. Douglass, *My Bondage and My Freedom,* ch. XXV, pp. 397–98; also quoted in Lewis Vaughn and Austin Dacey, *The Case for Humanism: An Introduction* (Lanham, Md.: Rowman & Littlefield, 2003), p. 193.

25. Keith Windschuttle, "Liberalism and Imperialism," in *The Betrayal of Liberalism,* ed. Hilton Kramer and Roger Kimball (Chicago: Ivan R. Dee, 1999), pp. 73–74.

26. Jonathan Swift, *Gulliver's Travels* (1726; Harmondsworth, UK: Penguin, 1985), p. 243.

27. George Birkbeck Hill, *Boswell's Life of Johnson* (Oxford, UK: Clarendon Press, 1934–50), vol. 1, p. 308; Jeremy Bentham, "Emancipate Your Colonies," in *The Works of Jeremy Bentham,* ed. John Bowring (1843; Bristol: Thoemmes Press, 1995), vol. 4, p. 407; quoted in Porter, *Enlightenment,* p. 355.

28. Adam Smith, *An Inquiry into the Nature and Causes of the Wealth of Nations,* ed. Edwin Cannan, 5th ed. (London: Methuen,

1904), bk. 4, chap. 7, "Of Colonies," paragraph 152 (quoted by Windschuttle, "Liberalism and Imperialism," p. 71):

"To propose that Great Britain should voluntarily give up all authority over her colonies, and leave them to elect their own magistrates, to enact their own laws, and to make peace and war as they might think proper, would be to propose such a measure as never was, and never will be adopted, by any nation in the world. . . . If it was adopted, however, Great Britain would not only be immediately freed from the whole annual expense of the peace establishment of the colonies, but might settle with them such a treaty of commerce as could effectually secure to her a free trade, more advantageous to the great body of the people, though less so to the merchants, than the monopoly which she at present enjoys. . . . [I]nstead of turbulent and factious subjects, [they would] become our most faithful, affectionate, and generous allies; and the same sort of parental affection on the one side, and filial respect on the other, might revive between Great Britain and her colonies, which used to subsist between those of ancient Greece and the mother city from which they descended."

29. John Malcolm Ludlow, *British India, Its Races, and Its History, Considered with Reference to the Mutinies of 1857*, A Series of Lectures Addressed to the Students of the Workingmen's College (Cambridge, UK: Macmillan, 1858), vol. 1, p. 172.

30. Ibid., p. 198.

31. David Pryce-Jones, *The Closed Circle: An Interpretation of the Arabs* (London: Paladin Grafton, 1990), pp. 34–35.

32. Personal communication with the author, 1998.

33. Daniel Pipes, *The Hidden Hand: The Middle East Fears of Conspiracy* (New York: St. Martin's Griffin, 1998), p. 26.

34. Czeslaw Milosz, *The Captive Mind* (New York: Vintage, 1959), pp. 54 55.

35. I owe this reference to Professor Fred Siegel of the Cooper Union for Science and Art in New York.

36. Barry Rubin, *The Long War for Freedom: The Arab Struggle for Democracy in the Middle East* (Hoboken, N.J.: Wiley, 2006), p. 16.

37. Ibid., p. 17.

38. Ibid., pp. 80–81. Rubin quotes from the following works of al-Afif al-Akhdar: "How Our Narcissistic Wound and Religious Narcissism Combine to Destroy Our Future"; "Why Religious Narcissism Is the Golden Collar [Obstructing] Our Assimilation into the Modern Age"; "Irrational Religious Education Is the Obstacle to the [Arabs'] Joining the Modern Age" (June 15, 16, and 23, 2003), as translated by MEMRI (Middle East Media Research Institute), "Tunisian Intellectual Al-Afif Al-Akhdar on the Arab Identity Crisis and Education," Special Dispatch no. 576 (September 21, 2003), http://www.memri.org/report/en/0/0/0/0/0/137/955.htm.

39. Tarek Heggy, "Comments on the Required Change in Egypt," *Watani,* December 22 and 29, 2002, quoted in Rubin, *The Long War for Freedom,* pp. 85. (*Watani* is a weekly newspaper published in Cairo.)

40. Rubin, *The Long War for Freedom,* p. 26.

41. Ibid., pp. 41–42.

42. Democritus, quoted in Bruce Thornton, *Greek Ways: How the Greeks Created Western Civilization* (San Francisco: Encounter Books, 2000), p. 145.

43. Aristotle, *Parts of Animals,* quoted in Thornton, *Greek Ways,* p. 145.

44. Aristotle, Fragments, in *Complete Works,* vol. 2, p. 2408. See also Aristotle, *Invitation to Philosophy,* ed. and trans. D. S. Hutchinson and Monte Ransome Johnson (2002), p. 82, at http://www.kennydominican.joyeurs.com/GreekClassics/AristotleProtrepticusE.pdf

45. Marcus Tullius Cicero, *De Officiis/On Duties,* trans. Harry G. Edinger (Indianapolis: Bobbs-Merrill, 1974), bk. 1, sec. 13, p. 9.

46. John Henry Cardinal Newman, *The Idea of a University* (San Francisco: Rinehart Press, 1960), pp. 77–79.

47.   Arnold, *Culture and Anarchy,* chap. 1, p. 7 (see n. 11 above). Also, Matthew Arnold, "The Function of Criticism at the Present Time," in *Essays in Criticism* (London: Macmillan, 1865).

48.   Bernard Lewis, *The Muslim Discovery of Europe* (London: Phoenix, 1994).

49.   Ibid., p. 75.

50.   Ibid., p. 73.

51.   Ibid., p. 73.

52.   Ibid., p. 137.

53.   Remi Brague, *Eccentric Culture: A Theory of Western Civilization* (South Bend, Ind.: St. Augustine's Press, 2002).

54.   Lewis, *The Muslim Discovery of Europe,* p. 151.

55.   Sir John Chardin, *Travels in Persia, 1673–1677* (New York: Dover, 1988), pp. 143–44.

56.   Ibid., pp. 193–95.

57.   Michael Field, *Inside the Arab World* (Cambridge, Mass.. Harvard University Press, 1994), p. 165, quoted in Pipes, *The Hidden Hand,* pp. 235–36 (see n. 33 above).

58.   Ibn Khaldun, *The Muqaddimah,* trans. Franz Rosenthal, 2nd ed. (1967; Princeton, N.J.: Princeton University Press, 1980), vol. 2, p. 438.

59.   Muhammad Talbi, *Interreligious Dialogue for Convergence* [*Dialogue interreligieux ou conflireligieux pour Dialogue de Témoignage, d'Emulation et de Convergence*], http://www.unesco.org/webworld/ peace_library/tunisia/andalous/french1.htm, originally published in *Revue d'études andalouses,* Tunisia. Talbi cites Maryam Jameelah, "Review of Seyyed Hossein Nasr, A Young Muslim's Guide to the Modern World," *Muslim World Book Review,* vol. 14, no. 4 (1994).

60.   F. R. Rosenthal, *The Classical Heritage of Islam* (London: Routledge, 1975), pp. 13–14.

61.   Ernest Renan, *L'Islamisme et la science,* lecture at the Sorbonne, March 29, 1883.

62. G. E. von Grunebaum, *Islam: Essays in the Nature and Growth of a Cultural Tradition* (London: Routledge & Kegan Paul, 1955), p. 114.

63. Ibid., p. 15.

64. T. J. De Boer, *The History of Philosophy in Islam* (1933; New York: Dover, 1967), p. 153.

65. See Steven Weinberg, "A Deadly Certitude," *Times Literary Supplement*, January 17, 2007.

66. Von Grunebaum, *Islam*, p. 114.

67. George Sarton, *Introduction to the History of Science*, quoted in von Grunebaum, *Islam*, p. 123.

68. F. A. Hayek, *The Road to Serfdom* (1944; Chicago: University of Chicago Press, 1976), p. 162.

69. Ibid.

70. Charles Habib Malik, *A Christian Critique of the University* (1982; Waterloo, Ontario: North Waterloo Academic Press, 1990), at http://www.wardconsultation.org/Readings/Charles_Malik.pdf.

71. Ibid.

72. For instance, Denis MacEoin was booted from a Saudi-funded position at Newcastle University because he taught courses on Shi'ism and Sufism as well as Sunnism and the central texts of Islam. See his biography at the Middle East Forum, http://www.meforum.org/staff/Denis+MacEoin. He has written under the pen name Daniel Easterman; see e.g. *New Jerusalems* (London: Grafton, 1992), pp. 92–93.

73. The Carter Center, founded by the former president Jimmy Carter, is also funded in part by Prince Alwaleed.

74. Stephen Pollard, "Libya and the LSE: Large Arab gifts to universities lead to 'hostile' teaching," *Telegraph*, March 3, 2011.

75. Robin Simcox, *A Degree of Influence: The Funding of Strategically Important Subjects in UK Universities* (London: Centre for Social Cohesion, 2009), available at http://www.socialcohesion.co.uk/files/1238334247_1.pdf.

76. "LSE funding row: more donations from dictators to British universities," press release, Centre for Social Cohesion, March 4, 2011, available http://www.militantislammonitor.org/article/id/4828.

77. Pollard, "Libya and the LSE."

78. Simcox, *A Degree of Influence*, pp. 11–12.

Chapter Six: Two Freedoms

1. Brian Moynahan, *The Faith: A History of Christianity* (New York: Random House, 2003), p. 728.

2. Interested readers will find an abundance of source material for this topic cited at http://en.wikipedia.org/wiki/Persecution_of_Christians.

3. David F. Miller, "Christian Community of Iraq Halved in Seven Years," posted at *Daily News Egypt*, September 17, 2010.

4. Raymond Ibrahim, "Is the Media 'Fair and Balanced' on Christian Persecution?" Pajamas Media, January 23, 2011, http://www.raymondibrahim.com/8655/is-the-media-fair-and-balanced-on-christian.

5. Ibid.

6. Owen Chadwick, *The Secularization of the European Mind in the Nineteenth Century* (Cambridge, UK: Cambridge University Press, 1975), p. 21.

7. Ibid., p. 23.

8. John Stuart Mill, *On Liberty,* 2nd ed. (London: John Parker & Son, 1859), pp. 33, 41.

9. F. A. Hayek, *The Road to Serfdom* (1944; Chicago: University of Chicago Press, 1976), p. 122.

10. Jimmy Carter, "Rushdie's Book Is an Insult," op-ed, *New York Times,* March 5, 1989, quoted by Rachel Donadio, "Fighting Words on Sir Salman," *New York Times,* July 15, 2007.

11. Roald Dahl, letter to *The Times* of London, quoted in Donadio, "Fighting Words on Sir Salman."

12. Le Carré, quoted in ibid.

13. Quoted in Paul Lewis, "'You sanctimonious philistine'—Rushie v Greer, the sequel," *Guardian,* July 29, 2006.

14. Quoted in Mark Humphrys, "Salman Rushdie," http://markhumphrys.com/rushdie.html.

15. Daniel C. Stevenson, "Rushdie Stuns Audience 26-100," *The Tech,* online edition, November 30, 1993, http://tech.mit.edu/V113/N61/rushdie.61n.html.

16. Douglas Jehl, "Clinton and Aides Meet Rushdie at White House in Rebuke to Iran," *New York Times,* November 25, 1993.

17. Gary Hull, ed., *Muhammad: The "Banned" Images* (Voltaire Press, 2009), p. 42. I am heavily indebted to Dr. Hull's book, and to the time line at http://muhammadimages.com/

18. Hull, *Muhammad: The "Banned" Images,* pp. 44–45; Flemming Rose, "Why I Published Those Cartoons," *Washington Post,* February 19, 2006.

19. "Those Danish Cartoons," editorial, *New York Times,* February 7, 2006.

20. Hull, *Muhammad: The "Banned" Images,* p. 20.

21. Kenan Malik, "Shadow of the Fatwa," Index on Censorship, http://www.indexoncensorship.org/tag/kenan-malik/

22. Kenan Malik, comment, Index on Censorship, December 18, 2009, http://www.indexoncensorship.org/2009/12/kenan-malik/

23. Paul Richard, "In Art Museums, Portraits Illuminate a Religious Taboo," *Washington Post,* February 14, 2006.

24. Isabel Vincent, "'Jihad' jitters at the Met," *New York Post,* January 10, 2010.

25. Mohammed Image Archive: Depictions of Mohammed Throughout History, http://www.zombietime.com/mohammed_image_archive/

26. Hull, *Muhammad: The "Banned" Images.*

27. Isabel Simeral Johnson, "Cartoons," *Public Opinion Quarterly,* vol. 1, no. 3 (July, 1937), p. 21.

28. Ibid., p. 31.

29. Joshua Rett Miller, "'South Park' Creators Could Face Retribution for Depicting Muhammad, Website Warns," FOX News, April 20, 2010; "South Park creators warned over Muhammad depiction," BBC News, April 22, 2010; Alexandra Silver, "*South Park* and Muhammad," Top 10 Controversial Cartoons, *Time* Special, April 27, 2010.

30. Andrew Higgins, "Blame It on Voltaire: Muslims Ask French to Cancel 1741 Play," *Wall Street Journal,* March 6, 2006; see also Hull, *Muhammad: The "Banned" Images,* p. 36.

31. John Stuart Mill, "The Contest in America," *Fraser's Magazine,* February 1862, later published in *Dissertations and Discussions* (1868), vol. 1, p. 26; see also http://www.columbia.edu/cu/tat/core/mill.htm.

32. Geert Wilders, "European Free Speech Under Attack," *Wall Street Journal,* February, 22, 2011.

33. Quoted in David Cohen, "Violence Is Inherent in Islam," *Evening Standard,* February 7, 2007.

34. Barry Rubin, "Is the U.S. Diplomatic and Intelligence Community Being Brainwashed in Dealing with Islamism?" *The Rubin Report,* April 27, 2010, http://rubinreports.blogspot.com/2010/04/is-us-diplomatic-and-intelligence.html.

35. Nina Shea, "The Administration Takes On 'Islamophobia': The White House is giving free-speech opponents a megaphone," *National Review Online,* September 1, 2011.

Chapter Seven: How to Defend Western Civilization

1. James Burnham, *Suicide of the West: An Essay on the Meaning and Destiny of Liberalism* (1964; New York: Regnery, 1985).

2. Ibid., p. 201. See also Arthur Farnsworth quoting a conversation with Robert Frost, October 22, 1977, in Eugene C. Gerhart, *Quote It Completely! World Reference Guide to More Than 5,500 Memo-*

rable Quotations from Law and Literature (Buffalo, N.Y.: William S. Hein & Co., 1998), p. 658.

3. Winston Churchill, speech at the Royal Society of St. George, April 24, 1933, quoted in Richard M. Langworth, "Immortal Words: 'Our Qualities and Deeds Must Burn and Glow': Churchill's Wisdom Calls to Us Across the Years," *Finest Hour,* Journal of the Churchill Center & Societies, no. 112 (Autumn 2001), pp. 8–10, http://www.winstonchurchill.org/images/finesthour/Vol.01%20 No.112.pdf.

4. Marianne Talbot, "Relativism," *Sunday Times* (London), July 24, 1994, quoted in Douglas Murray, *Neoconservatism: Why We Need It* (New York: Encounter Books, 2006), pp. 102–3. See also Marianne Talbot, "Against Relativism," in *Education in Morality,* ed. J. M. Halstead and T. McLaughlin (London: Routledge, 1998).

5. These remarks were made during an interview in 2009 in the Saudi daily *'Okaz,* translated by MEMRI (Middle East Media Research Institute), "Saudi Intellectual: Western Civilization Has Liberated Mankind," Special Dispatch no. 2332 (April 29, 2009), http://www.memri.org/report/en/0/0/0/0/0/0/3264.htm.

6. Charles Darwin, *The Origin of Species* (London, 1859).

7. Roger Scruton, "The Defence of the West," lecture at the Columbia Political Union, New York, April 14, 2005.

8. F. A. Hayek, *The Road to Serfdom* (1944; Chicago: University of Chicago Press, 1976), pp. 152–53.

9. "Thomas Jefferson to James Madison, 1787," *The Writings of Thomas Jefferson,* ed. Andrew Adgate Lipscomb and Albert E. Bergh (Washington, D.C.: Thomas Jefferson Memorial Association, 1903–1904), vol. 6, p. 388; and *The Papers of Thomas Jefferson,* ed. Julian P. Boyd (Princeton, N.J.: Princeton University Press, 1950), vol. 12, p. 440.

10. Brian Barry, *Culture and Equality: An Egalitarian Critique of Multiculturalism* (Cambridge, Mass.: Harvard University Press, 2001), p. 12.

11. Alison M. Jagger, "Multicultural Democracy," *Journal of Philosophy*, vol. 7 (1999), p. 314, quoted by Barry, *Culture and Equality*, p. 11.

12. Rumy Hasan, *Multiculturalism: Some Inconvenient Truths* (London: Politico's, 2010), p. 14.

13. Ibid., p. 26.

14. Ibid., p. 14.

15. Ibid., p. 20.

16. Ibid., p. 21.

17. David A. Hollinger, *Postethnic America: Beyond Multiculturalism* (New York: Basic Books, 2000), p. 143.

18. Ironically, this notion was well expressed by British-educated Muhammad Ali Jinnah, considered the founder of Pakistan, during his 1947 address to the Constitutional Assembly of Pakistan:

"You are free; you are free to go to your temples, you are free to go to your mosques or to any other place or worship in this State of Pakistan. You may belong to any religion or caste or creed that has nothing to do with the business of the State. As you know, history shows that in England, conditions, some time ago, were much worse than those prevailing in India today. The Roman Catholics and the Protestants persecuted each other. Even now there are some States in existence where there are discriminations made and bars imposed against a particular class. Thank God, we are not starting in those days. We are starting in the days where there is no discrimination, no distinction between one community and another, no discrimination between one caste or creed and another. We are starting with this fundamental principle that we are all citizens and equal citizens of one State. The people of England in course of time had to face the realities of the situation and had to discharge the responsibilities and burdens placed upon them by the government of their country and they went through that fire step by step. Today, you might say with justice that Roman Catholics and Protestants do not exist; what exists now is that every man is a citizen, an equal citizen of Great Britain and they are all members of the Nation.

"Now I think we should keep that in front of us as our ideal and you will find that in course of time Hindus would cease to be Hindus and Muslims would cease to be Muslims, not in the religious sense, because that is the personal faith of each individual, but in the political sense as citizens of the State."

19. Gary B. Nash, "American History Reconsidered: Asking New Questions About the Past," in *Learning from the Past*, ed. Diane Ravitch and Maris A. Vinovskis (Baltimore: The Johns Hopkins Press, 1995), p. 160.

20. Denis MacEoin, Civitas report, cited by Steve Doughty, "Britain has 85 sharia courts: The astonishing spread of the Islamic justice behind closed doors," *Daily Mail,* June 29, 2009.

21. "Crossing Borders with Shariah: The Role of Islamic Law in German Courts," *Spiegel Online,* October 11, 2010.

22. Ibid.

23. Ahmad ibn Naqib al-Misri, *'Umdat al-Salik: Reliance of the Traveller—The Classic Manual of Islamic Sacred Law,* with translation and commentary by Nuh Ha Mim Keller (Beltsville, Md.: Amana Publications, 1991).

24. David C. Engerman, "How the Creation of Sovietology Should Guide the Study of Today's Threats," *Foreign Affairs,* December 8, 2009.

25. *Arab Human Development Report 2003: Building a Knowledge Society* (New York: United Nations Development Programme, Regional Bureau for Arab States, 2003), p. 82.

26. "The Hundred Most Influential Books Since the War," *Times Literary Supplement,* October 6, 1995.

27. *Freedom for Publishing, Publishing for Freedom: The Central and East European Publishing Project,* ed. Timothy Garton Ash (New York: Oxford University Press, 1995).

28.   Ibn Warraq, *Leaving Islam: Apostates Speak Out* (Amherst, N.Y.: Prometheus Books, 2003), Appendix E, p. 467.

29.   According to the economists Linda Bilmes and Joseph Stiglitz, these costs "are now running at $12 billion a month—$16 billion if you include Afghanistan. By the time you add in the costs hidden in the defense budget, the money we'll have to spend to help future veterans, and money to refurbish a military whose equipment and materiel have been greatly depleted, the total tab to the federal government will almost surely exceed $1.5 trillion." Linda J. Bilmes and Joseph E. Stiglitz, "The Iraq War Will Cost Us $3 Trillion, and Much More," *Washington Post,* March 9, 2008.

30.   Paul Hollander, "Introduction: The New Virulence and Popularity," in *Understanding Anti-Americanism: Its Origins and Impact at Home and Abroad,* ed. Hollander (Chicago: Ivan R. Dee, 2004), pp. 12–13.

31.   See Ibn Warraq, *Defending the West: A Critique of Edward Said's "Orientalism"* (Amherst, N.Y.: Prometheus Books, 2007).

32.   Darryl Fears, "Hue and Cry on 'Whiteness Studies,'" *Washington Post,* June 20, 2002, quoted by Hollander, "Introduction: The New Virulence and Popularity," pp. 27–28.

33.   Lawrence E. Harrison, "Why Culture Matters," Introduction to *Culture Matters: How Values Shape Human Progress,* ed. Harrison and Samuel P. Huntington (New York: Basic Books, 2000), pp. xvii–xviii.

INDEX